THE ZERO-MILE DIET

A Year-Round Guide To Growing Organic Food

THE ZERO-MILE DIET

A Year-Round Guide To Growing Organic Food

Carolyn Herriot

Harbour Publishing

Harbour Publishing Co. Ltd.
P.O. Box 219, Madeira Park, BC, V0N 2H0
www.harbourpublishing.com

Cover: Carolyn Herriot at The Garden Path.
All photos courtesy Carolyn Herriot except where noted. Photo page 1 (right), Kristin Ross. Photos pages 66, 170, 179 (right) and 249, iStockphoto.
Edited by Carol Pope, Cliff Rowlands.
Index by Erin Schopfer.
Text design by Roger Handling.
Cover design by Anna Comfort.
Illustrations page 13 and 220 by Teresa Karbashewski. Diagram on page 13 based on information courtesy Soil Foodweb, Inc. and Dr. Elaine Ingham.
"Trouble in the Fields," page 9, is reprinted with the permission of Nanci Griffith, by arrangement of Gold Mountain Entertainment. "The Ode to the Dandelion," page 42, is reprinted with the permission of Rosie Emery.

Printed and bound in China on FSC-certified paper containing a combination of fibres from well-managed forests and post-consumer recycled content or other controlled forest friendly sources.

Harbour Publishing acknowledges financial support from the Government of Canada through the Book Publishing Industry Development Program and the Canada Council for the Arts, and from the Province of British Columbia through the BC Arts Council and the Book Publishing Tax Credit.

Library and Archives Canada Cataloguing in Publication

Herriot, Carolyn
 The zero-mile diet : a year-round guide to growing organic food / Carolyn Herriot.

ISBN 978-1-55017-481-6

 1. Organic gardening—Canada. I. Title.

SB453.5.H466 2010   635'.04840971   C2010-900054-4

We believe deeply in the oneness of all life including the human body, the soil, the earth and the universe, and in the inherent divinity in all life. When we all look back to our minds and recover the balance, then peace and harmony will be restored to Earth.

We do not have to do anything special to accomplish this. Working, eating, sharing with people, living with a partner or family, raising children—we can look into our own minds honestly through ordinary daily life. We will get to know the power that always leads us in the direction of harmony and live in consonance with it. Daily activities that raise our spirits will bring harmony and peace to the world.

A Konohana Family

Contents

INTRODUCTION

IT ALL BEGAN IN THE "SUMMER HOUSE"...

I suppose it was inevitable that I would become a passionate food gardener—after all, according to my mother, the first two words I learned to say were "more food!" This passion was cultivated at an early age while spending many summer holidays up north at my Auntie Loo's home in Lancashire, England. Lucy was a satisfied spinster and a wonderful cook who supported herself taking in lodgers and feeding them three times a day—often from the kitchen garden behind her home. Many of her lodgers never left!

Life was thrilling and carefree in those times. My sister, Julie, and I slept in the "Summer House" in the garden, where we giggled madly before bed every night while checking the sheets for earwigs. A glass greenhouse overflowing with ripe tomatoes and long English cucumbers led into Lucy's luscious kitchen garden, full of fruit trees and vegetables. I have never forgotten the happy summer hours spent picking scarlet runner beans for dinner, or making plum jam with my Auntie Loo.

For the past 20 years I have made a good living selling food plants from The Garden Path Nursery. I learned about growing herbs, shrubs, flowers, roses, fruits and vegetables from seed, and I figured out how to propagate from division and by cuttings. When The Garden Path became certified organic I picked up a lot about the products and practices that make organic food production safe and successful. Now the fun of the nursery days is behind me, but I continue to grow seeds for my other business, Seeds of Victoria.

I specialize in growing open-pollinated heritage varieties of food plants, because these are the ones we can save seeds from.

'Telegraph' long English cucumber is an heirloom variety offered by few seed savers today.

Where I live on beautiful Vancouver Island, British Columbia:

- The largest crop we grow is hay.
- We grow only five percent of the food we consume.
- In the event of an emergency, we have only three days' worth of food before supermarket shelves will be bare.
- We have lost the infrastructure for food distribution and processing.
- Island farmers are on average 55 years old.
- New farmers have trouble finding affordable land.

Help! We have been depending on a system that provides such an abundance of cheap food that it has become unnecessary to grow it for ourselves. In addition to today's looming food-security concerns, another huge problem is that we have discovered that the nutritional value of industrialized fare is compromised, and "fast food" high in fats and sugars is addictive and disastrous to our health. Heart disease, stroke, type 2 diabetes and cancer——the four leading causes of death in industrialized nations today—are all chronic diseases linked to diet.

It has only taken two generations for the majority of people to forget how to grow their own food. Most city dwellers have become alienated from the source of what sustains them, and have little understanding of the environmental and health impacts of processed and packaged food.

The meat industry produces food from Concentrated Animal Feed Operations (CAFOs), grossly inhumane in practice and which produce massive lagoons of manure that seep into the groundwater. Forced to eat grain, animals that are herbivorous by nature require antibiotics to keep them at a barely acceptable level of health. Now these same antibiotics are infiltrating humans through food, triggering antibiotic resistance.

Meanwhile, agribusiness corporations have been hybridizing and genetically modifying seeds for tolerance to herbicide products, and they are busy patenting seeds. Approval is currently being sought from the Canadian government for a technology that terminates (sterilizes) seeds of food plants, called "Terminator" technology. I believe you will agree with me that with increasing climate change and the potential for global food disruption on the horizon, more centralization and control over how we feed ourselves is absolutely the last thing we need.

TROUBLE IN THE FIELDS

Baby I know that we've got trouble in the fields
When the bankers swarm like locusts and they're
    turning away our yields.
The trains roll by our silos, silver in the rain,
And leave our pockets full of nothing but these dreams
    of the golden grain.

Have you seen folks lined up downtown at the station?
They're all buying their tickets out and talking a
    Great Depression.
Our parents had their hard times 50 years ago,
When they stood out in these empty fields in dust as
    deep as snow.

Now there's a book up on the shelf about the dust bowl
    days,
And there's a little bit of you and a little bit of me in
    the photos on every page.
Now our children live in the city and they rest upon
    our shoulders
They never want this rain to fall or the weather to get
    colder.

And all this trouble in our fields,
If this rain can fall, these wounds can heal,
They'll never take our native soil.
What if we sell that new John Deere
And then we'll work these crops with sweat and tears,
You'll be the mule, I'll be the plough,
Come harvest time we'll work it out,
There's still a lot of love,
Right here in these troubled fields.

Nanci Griffith & Rick West

THE ZERO-MILE DIET

Ten years ago, in order to pacify my concerns about an increasingly uncertain future, I decided to grow as much food as possible. My husband, Guy, and I came to live on the land that would become The Garden Path, and in the process we discovered that it only takes five years to become self-sufficient in fruits and vegetables year round, even when starting with 15 feet of clay fill! So I decided to write this book to inspire others, and thanks to my good friend Dan Jason of Salt Spring Seeds I called it *The Zero-Mile Diet*.

This book follows a year of sustainable homegrown food production, growing healthy organic food, eating seasonal recipes from the garden, saving seeds for future harvests and putting food by for the winter. Growing a "Zero-Mile Diet" is a fun way to increase regional food security while cooling down the planet.

"Making sure your neighbour is fed" is a realistic definition of food security—unless you have the intention of getting a gun! Instead I decided to put everything that I know into this book, so that others can work together toward achieving greater food self-sufficiency without learning the hard way. I hope you enjoy spending a year in the garden at The Garden Path, and that it will change your life for the better.

Above: The small fruit orchard at The Garden Path.

Right: A Thanksgiving harvest from the food garden at The Garden Path.

THE GARDEN OF EATING

The food garden at The Garden Path tends to be quite an ornamental affair. It's laid out as a 50-by-50-ft. square surrounded by herbs on one side and perennial vegetables on the other. Flowering plants that attract beneficials spill out from a border that runs parallel to a 50-ft.-long "Berry Walk" planted with raspberries, loganberries, blackcurrants, gooseberries and strawberries.

My pride and joy is a 50-ft. arbour that screens the vegetable garden from the expansive forecourt. It was built using logs from the half-acre Douglas fir forest that screens us from the road. On the south side of the arbour I planted vines of kiwis and grapes and an assortment of berries—nectar berry, marionberry and thornless blackberry.

My biggest challenge was to establish the small fruit orchard. The wet west coast is not an ideal place to grow fruit. It's very discouraging to have to replant established fruit trees, but half of my saplings had to be replaced due to canker. I recommend buying disease-resistant species from reputable growers. In winter I allow chickens and Muscovy ducks to free range, which cleans up pests in the orchard and fertilizes at the same time!

All winter we have copious pickings of salad greens, kales, chards, spinach, parsley, leeks, beets, radishes, oca and sunchokes...and the list goes on! The freezer bulges with frozen beans, corn, berries and fruit and the pantry with bottled chutneys, sauces, jams and jellies. Dried fruits are great for snacking on during winter hikes, and bottled cherries by the fire a winter luxury. It's the good life in winter!

Above: Overview of the garden in early spring.

Right: The arbour hosts a feast of flowers and fruits.

A FIVE-YEAR VISION FOR GREATER FOOD SECURITY

Vision without action is a daydream.
Action without vision is a nightmare.

Japanese proverb

Imagine where we could be in five years if we had a plan? What would it be like if suddenly "edible landscaping" became *de rigueur*, and everyone started growing plants in their gardens they could eat? What would it feel like if people shared backyards and laneways, established micro-farms with ducks, chickens, geese and rabbits, and grew food in allotment gardens? Imagine food and fruit trees growing on boulevards and in public gardens, and urban farms producing substantial amounts of organic fruits and vegetables. We could create a taste of Tuscany right where we live!

Farmers' markets would thrive as more and more food became available, and young farmers would discover there is good income to be made from growing food after all. "Love your Farmer!" would be the most popular bumper sticker on electric cars. There would be edible gardens in schoolyards, and education on nutrition and growing food in primary and secondary schools, so that children would learn the vital connection between their diet and lifelong health.

Farmers and gardeners would save seeds for future harvests, and community seed banks would spring up to safeguard collective food security. Universities and community colleges would teach sustainable small-scale farming, and institutions and businesses would offer loans and grants to help new farmers get started.

A vision today is the only way to create a new reality in the future. I know from personal experience that growing food leads to a good, healthy and happy life, and that's what I want for all of us. Surely there's no better time to begin than right now?

Carolyn Herriot, January 31, 2010

Davie Village Community Garden, downtown Vancouver.

"Last year's Intergovernmental Panel on Climate Change (IPCC) assessment stated that up to two billion people worldwide will face water shortages, and up to 30 percent of plant and animal species would be put at risk of extinction, if the average rise in temperature stabilizes between 1.5 and 2.5 degrees.

"Ladies and Gentlemen, millions of people throughout the world are deeply concerned about what is happening to our planet, but they feel utterly powerless. So they look to national governments, the European Union and international agencies to act on their behalf, but too often they see nothing but argument, disagreement and prevarication.

"The point is that the solutions do not lie with just the private sector or just the public sector. Climate change presents such a threat that, uniquely in history, it will surely require the effort of every nation and every person to find and implement a solution before it is too late."

HRH The Prince of Wales, 14th February 2008

January

THE SOIL FOOD WEB

If we could travel underground to explore what's going on in the soil, it would be as if we had discovered another planet teeming with alien life forms. Up until recently, gardeners laboured in complete ignorance of this world and how plants derive nourishment from it. It wasn't until we understood more about the intricate web of life in the soil that we learned to see the big picture.

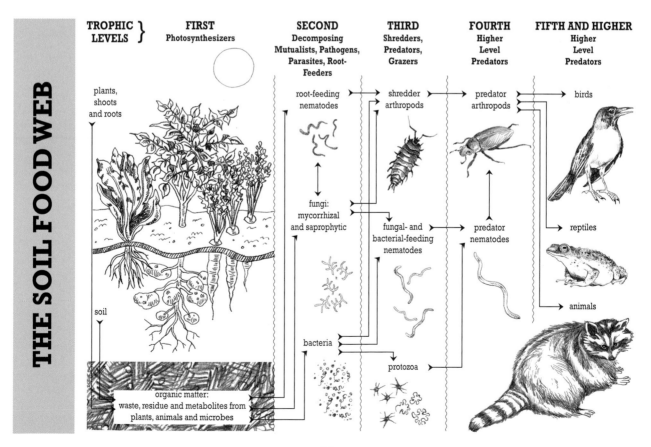

One teaspoonful of healthy soil contains 25,000 species of bacteria, 8,000 species of fungi and myriad other species that interact in complex ways to make nutrients available to plants. This soil food web is comprised of beneficial organisms responsible for healthy growth, strong roots and the plant's ability to fight disease. The soil food web is destroyed by chemical fertilizers and pesticides and over-tillage of the soil. As the complexity of the soil food web diminishes, plant health declines and disease flourishes.

. . . .

Plants depend on amazingly diverse organisms, ranging from bacteria, algae, fungi and protozoa, to more complex nematodes and microarthropods (microscopic bugs) and the more familiar earthworms, insects and small vertebrates.

These combined organisms decompose organic matter, fix nitrogen from the air, store nutrients and make them available to plants, enhance soil tilth, and manage or destroy pests and pollutants. They are critical in creating, regulating and maintaining healthy soils and plant growth.

Soil organisms follow seasonal and daily patterns, being subject to temperature and moisture fluctuations. The greatest activity occurs in spring when temperature and moisture are optimal. When your garden bursts into growth, it is the increasing activity in the soil that triggers this spurt.

Here's a brief introduction to the different levels of life in the soil:

- The primary level consists of plants—lichens, moss and algae—that are photosynthesizers fuelled by the sun's energy to convert the dioxide from carbon dioxide into various life-giving compounds.
- The next level consists of decomposers—bacteria and fungi—that convert complex materials into nutrients and make them available to plants and other soil organisms.
- Then there are the shredders—predators and grazers—represented by earthworms, nematodes and macroarthropods (bugs such as cutworms, millipedes, weevils, beetles, etc.). Their activities enhance soil structure and control root-feeding pests and disease.
- The highest level is represented by mice, birds and above-ground animals and insects—all of which keep the populations of lower-level predators in balance.

All these valuable organisms are most concentrated around roots, in plant litter, and on humus and the surface of soil aggregates. Tillage, insecticides, fungicides and herbicides have an enormous impact on non-target species in this soil level. Disruption of the intricate relationship and balance between the pathogens and beneficial organisms opens the door to problems with pests and diseases.

Organic-gardening practices respect the fragile interdependency of life in the soil. Enriching the soil with organic matter, avoiding synthetic chemical pesticides and fertilizers, and minimizing tillage while maximizing the use of mulch and green manures help to sustain and protect this wonderful underground world on which all plantlife depends.

A one-percent increase of organic matter in the top 12 inches of the soil is equivalent to the capture and storage of 250 tonnes of atmospheric carbon dioxide per square mile of farmland.

DISCOVERING YOUR SOIL TYPE

When you know your soil type, you are in a better position to make gardening decisions. Simply grab a handful of soil, clench it tightly in the palm of your hand and then open your hand:

1. If the ball falls apart, your soil is SANDY.

- Sandy soil is friable when wet and loose and soft when dry.
- Sandy soil has low water-holding capacity.
- Sandy soil needs high levels of organic matter to maintain good levels of fertility.

2. If the ball forms a firm clod that falls apart when provoked, your soil is LOAM.

- Loam is medium-textured soil, friable when wet and slightly hard when dry.
- Loam is ideal because it has good water-holding capacity.
- Loam is easier to cultivate.
- Loam maintains good levels of fertility.

3. If the ball forms a sticky clod that will not fall apart, you have CLAY.

- Clay soils are sticky when wet, hard when dry.
- Clay soils have high water-holding capacity, but less available water in summer than loam soils.
- Clay soils are moderately difficult for maintaining good tilth.
- Compacted clay soil needs to be broken up before organic matter can be incorporated.
- Clay soils need regular amending with organic matter to keep the clay from rising up.

Soil pH

Soil pH refers to the acidity/alkalinity of the soil, measured in a scale ranging from 1 to 14. Most food plants grow best in a pH range between 6.0 and 7.5.
- Above pH 7.0 is alkali
- pH 7.0 is neutral
- Below pH 7.0 is acidic

Elements may be present in the soil but "tied up" and unavailable because pH governs the solubility and availability of plant nutrients.

- Nitrogen (N), phosphorus (P), potassium (K), sulphur, calcium and magnesium are available in a neutral pH range.
- Iron, manganese, boron, copper and zinc are only available below pH 7.0.
- Lime compounds raise pH to reduce acidity.
- Sulphur compounds lower pH to increase acidity.

Taking a Soil Sample

1. Dig a hole from the soil surface to the root zone.

2. Remove a 1-in. (2.5-cm) slice from the smooth side of the hole. Make sure the surface crust is included in the sample.

3. Place in a clean container.

4. Repeat four more times at random around the area being tested. Remove any foreign matter and mix soil thoroughly.

5. Place a 2-cup (475-mL) sample in a zip-lock bag and identify it for laboratory records.

A basic test gives you soil pH and NPK analysis. By paying more you get detailed information on iron, zinc, sulfur, copper, manganese, magnesium, sodium, calcium, organic matter, soluble salts, lime, and the cation exchange capacity (CEC), which indicates the nutrient-holding capacity of the soil. The analysis is normally accompanied by appropriate recommendations, based on the results.

THE FOUR SECRETS OF FEEDING THE SOIL

1. Compost

The quality of compost depends on the residues from which it's made and to what extent decomposition has occurred. Compost needs to reach a temperature of 130°F (54°C) to destroy pathogens and GMOs. Heat-loving thermophilic bacteria break down the organic waste and plant residues. In order to keep them happy you just need mixed materials, good aeration and moisture. Turn the pile when the bin is full—usually one turning is sufficient. What is of key importance is to run the hose over the compost while the pile is being turned.

Compost nice and easy!

2. Leaves

Tree roots penetrate widely through topsoil and deeply into subsoil, taking up valuable nutrients, which are then stored in the leaves. When leaves break down they return these nutrients to the soil.

In fall, heap leaves of big trees, such as maples, oak and chestnut in a corner and forget about them. By spring the pile will have broken down into coarse leaf mulch, which can be used as garden mulch. After a full year, the pile will have broken down into beautiful black leaf mulch that can be used in potting mixes, and is perfect for enriching the garden. Take full advantage in fall by stockpiling leaves. TIP: Run a lawnmower over a pile of leaves on the driveway. This reduces their bulk to a manageable pile of shredded leaves, which can then be spread over beds as mulch without being unsightly.

Stockpile leaves in circular wire cages for year-round use.

3. Seaweed

After winter storms, I head down to the beach and scoop up kelp from the piles washed up. Seaweed contains all the micro-nutrients and trace elements essential for healthy plant growth. It can either be added as mulch directly to the garden, or layered as an ingredient in compost. The secret here is to not be concerned about salt buildup. Usually the proportionately miniscule amount of salt on a 2-in. (5-cm) layer of mulch is diluted by heavy winter rains, and in 25 years of adding seaweed to the garden I've only ever encountered a problem once. Keeping in mind that salt is a preservative, I once made a compost mix with too much seaweed in it, and the salt did prevent if from breaking down!

4. Animal or Green Manure

Try to find a source of animal manure that has not been tainted by growth hormones, antibiotics and genetically modified grains in livestock feed. Animal manures should not be added to food gardens fresh—always compost first. You can also add nitrogen to soil using plant matter rather than animal residues. Grow a winter green-manure crop of fall rye, winter pea, fava beans, winter barley or winter wheat, and plough it under in early spring. In spring/summer you can grow a warm-climate green-manure crop of vetch, clover, buckwheat, alfalfa or phacelia. See "Green Manure" in November.

Rhizobacteria on roots of legumes add nitrogen to soil.

SAVE THE WORMS!

Earthworms

Man's real best friend is the humble earthworm *Lumbricus terrestris*. Earthworms are the true tillers of the garden, as they move through soil, mixing and aerating it. During digestion they humify organic matter, combining it with clay colloids to form nutrient-rich worm castings. The castings aid bacteria, actinomycetes and other micro-organisms that dwell in soil. Earthworms also excrete $CaCO_3$ as they move through soil, which helps maintain a soil pH within the range most plants prefer.

Over half a million earthworms can live in just one hectare of soil. Together they will turn over 40 tons of soil, and eat 10 tons of leaves, stems and roots a year. Excessive tilling, use of pesticides, herbicides, fungicides and chemical fertilizers harm or destroy earthworms. With their populations destroyed, soil loses humus with negative effects on aeration, nutrition, pH and water-holding capacity. What we are doing to these heroes of our ecosystem using current methods is reflected by the fact that agricultural topsoil around the world degrades at the rate of one percent per year.

Vermicomposting

Vermicomposting is a way of turning waste into fertile worm castings. Two pounds of red wigglers (2,000 worms) will consume 1 lb. (454 g) of waste daily. Vermicomposting can be done year round, inside or outside, by apartment dwellers or homeowners. All you need is a worm bin with some bedding such as shredded newspaper. Place the red wigglers (*Eisenia foetida*) and a quantity of fruit and vegetable waste into the bin and get up close and personal with some worms! Worm castings are

Earthworm Lumbricus terrestris.

Compost bin.

excellent for top-dressing houseplants, growing food and blending into soil mixes.

Red wigglers live in waste where they find good food sources, with each worm eating half its weight a day. Red wigglers need moisture because they breathe through their skin. They don't like bright light or high temperatures and will burrow underground to escape. That's why the worms move to cooler edges or crawl out when compost heats up!

A THREE-BIN COMPOSTING SYSTEM

1. One bin for building the pile.

2. One bin for turning the pile into.

3. One bin for holding the finished compost.

It's not necessary to have a structure to make compost—simply piling everything up in a corner eventually results in breakdown. Organizing a system for keeping up with garden waste makes chores lighter, and with the ongoing manufacture of compost there's always some available when it's needed.

When one bin fills up, turn it into another using a pitchfork. When the compost bin is sited in full sun, one turning is sufficient to get finished compost in three months. If shadier it could take up to six months. The secret is to keep a hose running on the compost material as it goes into the new bin. Insufficient moisture is often a factor that prevents breakdown, because when organic matter is dry there's not enough moisture for microbes to survive.

After a pile has been aerated and moistened, it causes thermophilic (heat-loving) bacteria to multiply. Put your hand on top of a pile two days after it has been turned and feel the heat! Hot composting means maintaining the temperature of compost at 130°F (54°C), a temperature at which pathogens and genetically modified organisms (GMOs) are destroyed.

With a three-bin composting system set up, I was soon manufacturing yards of the best "black gold" a gardener could wish for. The best parts are that the ingredients are all free and the organic waste gets recycled and put to use revitalizing the garden. No two batches of compost are created equal; you can just throw garden waste in a pile and hope for the best, or you can make an intentional blend of nutrient-rich organic matter, resulting in compost that really delivers!

How to Build a Three-Bin Composting System

You will need:
- 10 recycled wooden pallets, free from most lumberyards. TIP: Choose those the same size, with no missing or broken rungs
- Assortment of 2-in. (5-cm) and 3-in. (7.5-cm) galvanized nails
- 8 wooden stakes with pointy ends cut (Optional: Use lengths of ¾-in. [2-cm] rebar)
- Twine for tying on the front pallet

Nail two side pallets to a back pallet, and repeat this to make three connected bins. Sledgehammer two wedges into the ground at the front of the pallets, and nail them to the pallets to keep them upright and straight. Tie on the front pallet using twine when the volume of the bins' contents dictate. Each bin holds two yards of organic waste, which breaks down to one cubic yard of finished compost. TIP: During the fall and winter place boards over top of the bins to prevent the heavy rains from leaching out the valuable nutrients.

SUPER-DUPER COMPOST

Experienced gardeners know that the key to successful gardening lies in the soil. Soils high in organic matter and rich in nutrients grow stronger plants that are less vulnerable to insect and disease attack. When you focus on feeding the soil, and allow plants to take up nutrients as needed, you can enjoy gardening without the inconvenience of battling pest problems. When you create natural balance in the garden, it takes care of itself above and below ground.

Over my 20 years of operating a nursery, I made thousands of batches of compost, because being certified organic we grew all our containerized stock in 100-percent-screened compost made using two three-bin composting systems. I soon discovered that by adding comfrey, nettles and seaweed, I created far-superior compost rich in additional micro-nutrients such as boron, iodine, manganese, magnesium,

Three-bin composting system.

molybdenum and zinc. In order to distinguish this from any old run-of-the-mill compost, I call it "Super-Duper" compost—silly, I know, but you'll understand the super-hero properties of this mix once you start using it!

HOW TO MAKE SUPER-DUPER COMPOST
Add what you have available from this list of ingredients:
- Leaves (TIP: store in circular wire cages in fall)
- Weeds (avoid weeds in seed or pernicious weeds)
- Herbaceous prunings
- Green vegetation
- Manure (sheep, goat, horse, llama and rabbit; or chicken and cow where you know your source—see "Know Your Manure!" in January)
- Grass clippings
- Spoiled hay
- Seaweed (in winter)

- Lake algae
- Wood ash (uncontaminated)
- Sawdust and fine woodchips (not cedar and always from untreated wood)
- Chicken litter
- Comfrey (in season)
- Nettles (in season)
- Dried horsetail

Build a pile, ideally 4 by 4 ft (1.2 by 1.2 m) using leaves, weeds (no seeds), herbaceous prunings, manure (can be fresh), grass clippings, spoiled hay, seaweed, lake algae, sawdust and chicken litter in no more than 6-in. (15-cm) layers at a time. Make it "Super-Duper" by adding comfrey, nettles or dried horsetail. These plants contain valuable nutrients that make higher-quality compost. TIP: Leaving food waste out of your compost prevents problems with rodents (see "Rats" in April).

Compost screen.

Putting all your raw materials in one bin simplifies things, and you save time in the process. The resulting high-quality compost is used in multiple ways to feed plants and the garden. When screened it makes a wonderful, rich, crumbly medium for potting mixes and for top-dressing planters and barrels.

GETTING THE RATIO RIGHT

The ideal ratio of compost is 30:1 Carbon:Nitrogen

Carbonaceous (or Brown) Materials
- Leaves
- Herbaceous prunings
- Spoiled hay
- Sawdust and fine woodchips (not cedar and always from untreated wood)
- Chicken litter
- Dried horsetail

TIP: Too much carbon and the pile does not break down; add nitrogen-rich materials to activate the mix.

Nitrogen-rich (or Green) Materials
- Weeds (avoid weeds in seed or pernicious weeds)
- Green vegetation
- Manure (see "Know Your Manure!" in January)
- Grass clippings
- Seaweed
- Lake algae
- Chicken litter
- Comfrey (in season)
- Nettles (in season)
- Fresh horsetail

TIP: Too much nitrogen and the pile smells bad; add carbonaceous materials to balance the mix.

The Dos of Composting

- **Do** mix layers of carbon-rich materials with nitrogen-rich materials. For speedy breakdown the ideal ratio of compost is 30:1 Carbon: Nitrogen.
- **Do** provide aeration by allowing air to flow freely through the pile. (Free pallets from your local lumberyard work perfectly!)
- **Do** make sure the pile is moist for the aerobic bacteria to work. Keep a hose running on the pile as you turn it from one bin to another.
- **Do** avoid compaction by adding no more than a 6-in. (15-cm) layer of material at a time.
- **Do** avoid weeds that have gone to seed, unless you heat compost to reach the high temperature (130°F/54°C) needed to destroy weed seeds.
- **Do** add "activators" to your pile to accelerate decomposition. One of the best you can add is fresh manure, steaming with microbes!
- **Do** empty bins in fall, and apply 2-in. (5-cm) layers of compost to your garden as protective winter mulch. Feeding the soil and smothering weed seeds at the same time is what I call "Organic Weed and Feed."

The Don'ts of Composting

- **Don't** allow your compost piles to become too large—no more than 4 ft. (1.2 m) high and 4 ft. (1.2 m) wide.
- **Don't** compost diseased plant waste, pet litter, toxic chemicals and any pernicious weeds such as couch grass, ivy, mint, goutweed or morning glory.
- **Don't** use cat, dog, pig or human feces in the compost, because it can spread infectious disease or parasites.
- **Don't** use large quantities of seaweed with high salt levels. The salt preserves the compost pile instead of decomposing it.
- **Don't** use meat and fish scraps that attract animals and flies; grease and oil do not break down. To avoid attracting rodents keep kitchen waste in rat-proof composters, or bury in trenches around the garden, covering with 9 in. (23 cm) of soil.

COMPOST AT KEW

The largest compost heap in the UK resides at Kew Gardens. In 1989 Kew suspended the use of peat, a rapidly dwindling natural resource, replacing it with an extensive composting program. Kew now generates 353,000 cu. ft. (9996 cu. m) of waste plant material every year, to which is added 22 tons of horse manure, thanks to some rather distinguished stables at the Royal Horse Artillery and Windsor Great Park! After watering and turning through a cycle of 10 to 12 weeks, Kew produces 70,000 cu. ft. (1982 cu. m) of top-notch compost for use throughout the Gardens.

KNOW YOUR MANURE!

It's important to know the source of what you are adding to soil, especially in the case of a food garden. I avoid cow and chicken manure unless I know the farmer uses organic practices and has not been giving the animals antibiotics and hormone-laced feed containing genetically modified grains. Sheep, goat, rabbit, llama and horse manure are safest, horse being the most commonly available and cheapest. This is because the "pharmaceutical output" from these animals is minimal, reducing the potential for adding unwanted chemicals to soil.

Manure is an excellent soil amendment—a good source of nitrogen, phosphorus, potassium and other nutrients. Manure that is well composted or aged six months is best—a year is even better.

Fresh manure is best added to the compost pile where its dense population of microbes activates decomposition. Fresh manure, less than 90 days old, contains soluble nitrogen compounds and ammonia that can burn plants and interfere with seed germination. There is also a serious risk that pathogens will contaminate edibles. The danger is greatest for root crops such as radishes and carrots, and leafy vegetables such as spinach, where the edible part touches the soil.

To avoid risk of sickness:

- If applying within 120 days of harvest, use only aged or composted manure.
- Never apply fresh manure after the garden has been planted.
- Always thoroughly wash vegetables before eating. Careful washing and/or peeling removes most pathogens, but cooking is the most effective.
- Do not use human, cat, dog or pig manure in gardens or compost piles, because parasites found in these manures may remain infectious for people.
- Turning and heating manure up to temperatures of 130°F (54°C) destroys pathogens and GMOs.

CHICKEN: Chicken manure is high in ammonia, and the "hottest" animal manure. Compost before use, as it can burn plants if used fresh. Beware of manure from birds receiving hormone-laced feed and antibiotics.

COW: Dairy-cow manure is not as hot as other manures, and is more forgiving if applied when fresh. Although it has lower nutrient levels than other manures, it is safer to use in larger quantities. Beware of manure from animals receiving hormone-laced feed and antibiotics.

HORSE: Richer than cow manure, horse is still only half as rich as chicken manure. Watch out for hayseeds in horse manure; they may sprout and be a pain. Ensure the manure has reached a temperature of 130°F (54°C) to kill weed seeds and GMOs. Hog fuel (from untreated wood) is a good mix with horse manure—the nitrogen from the manure and the carbon from the woodchips makes for good humus and speedy decomposition.

LLAMA: I call this the "Rolls Royce of manures" because llamas have five stomachs, a digestive system that destroys weed seeds. Llama manure lacks any significant odour and does not have to be composted before use, plus it comes in tidy piles of 100-percent pellets with no additives of any kind, which can be applied fresh, as they will not burn plants. (Do not harvest food until 120 days have passed if you apply fresh manure.)

MUSHROOM: Mushroom manure is a rich, dark, moist mixture of wheat straw, peat moss, cottonseed meal, gypsum, lime, and chicken litter. This combination of ingredients is used in commercial mushroom farms to grow mushrooms. The material is next composted for many weeks and then placed in a huge room where it is completely sterilized, and the mushroom growing cycle begins. Strangely enough, mushrooms only grow in this mixture for a short time, usually 18 to 20 days, when the compost has to be removed and a brand-new batch will be prepared for the next crop.

I have reservations about using mushroom manure because of the chicken-litter input and the fact that the cottonseed meal is most likely genetically modified. Cotton, corn and soy seed meals are all usually genetically modified nowadays. Certified organic seed meals are the only way to be sure that you are not contaminating your soil with GMO substances.

RABBIT: Rabbit manure can be higher in nitrogen than chicken manure, and contains high levels of phosphorus, important for the formation of flowers and fruit.

SHEEP AND GOAT: Sheep and goat manure is "hot" manure, so compost it before use, or add to garden beds in fall.

Dottie, a silver spangled Hamburg hen.

NPK VALUE OF MANURE
(These figures are approximate, depending on the amount of straw or sawdust in the manure.)

Chicken (fresh)	1.5%N	1.0%P	5%K
Chicken (dry)	4.5%N	3.5%P	2.0%K
Dairy Cow	56%N	23%P	6%K
Horse	.69%N	.24%P	.72%K
Pig (fresh)	.5%N	.32%P	.46%K
Sheep	1.4%N	.48%P	1.2%K
Steer	.7%N	.55%P	.72%K

LIMING THE GARDEN

The majority of plants thrive in soil with near-neutral pH between 6 and 7. A neutral pH supports the reproduction of beneficial bacteria in the soil, which make essential nutrients, locked to organic matter, available to plants. The soils of coastal BC are acidic for two key reasons—the heavy rainfall acidifies the soil, and it's a temperate rainforest with many acidifying plants such as conifers. Forested areas have higher organic content in their soil, which causes it to be acidic. Liming the soil on a regular basis neutralizes pH, and also releases water in clay soils, which improves their texture. I lime vegetable beds every year, except where ericaceous (acid-loving) plants such as potatoes, strawberries and blueberries are going to grow.

Medium- or coarse-grade dolomite lime is inexpensive and easy to apply using a broadcast spreader (or even by hand). A 45-lb. (20-kg) bag covers. 1,000 sq. ft. (93 sq. m) and costs no more than five dollars. Lime is best applied in fall so that it will have broken down by spring, but can be applied any time. TIP: It's best if soil is limed before fertilizing, with two weeks between. If you can, apply lime just before a good rain so that it gets washed in right away.

Dolomite lime is also a good source of calcium and magnesium. Calcium builds and maintains cell walls and helps reduce injury from freezing and heat stress. Magnesium helps plants take up calcium as well as nitrogen and phosphorous, and plays a role in chlorophyll synthesis.

A fruit tree growing in acidic soil benefits significantly from receiving lime annually. Soil acidity is a prime environment for the two fungal diseases—scab and canker—that plague fruit trees. Lime is best applied in fall or in early spring before bud break.

Mycorrhizal fungi are symbiotic with plant roots.

MYCORRHIZAL FUNGI

Mycorrhizal fungi are a specific class of fungi that form a symbiotic relationship with plant roots, whereby both fungi and plant benefit. They are present in most soils, helping host plants access water and nutrients as they feed themselves. Because the surface area of hyphae (feeding structures of mycorrhizae) are several hundred times the surface area of plant roots, the mycorrhizae feed on larger soil masses, and do so more thoroughly. Healthy mycorrhizal populations are key links in the access-to-nutrients chain of host plants. A viable mycorrrhizal colony helps plants become more vigorous, salt and drought tolerant, and less dependent on fertilizers.

Mycorrhizae are relatively plant specific and fragile, thriving in soils of high organic content, but languishing when organic content is low. Rather than digging and disturbing soil, it's better to add mulch. Mycorrhizae are destroyed when soil is ploughed, rototilled, fumigated, sterilized, solarized or drenched with high levels of pesticides—and because mycorrhizae are fungi, fungicides in particular destroy them.

LYNDA'S BLACK MAGIC TEA (N:P:K—7:2:8)

4 Tbsp. (60 mL) liquid fish emulsion

1 Tbsp. (15 mL) seaweed liquid concentrate

1 Tbsp. (15 mL) blackstrap molasses (feeds micro-organisms)

Whisk into 1 gal. (4.5 L) of water. Water in around roots of plants freely!

Russian comfrey.

COMFREY

Comfrey (*Symphytum officinale*) is a perennial herb of the family Boraginaceae with hairy leaves (that may irritate skin) and bell-shaped purple, pink or white flowers. Comfrey is deep-rooted and acts as a dynamic accumulator, mining nutrients from soil and making them available to leaves, which break down into a thick black liquid. The 'Bocking 14' cultivar of Russian comfrey (*Symphytum* x *uplandicum*) is a particularly valuable strain with the added benefit that it produces sterile seeds. It has large leaves that are 74 percent nitrogen, 24 percent phosphorus and 1.19 percent potassium.

Comfrey grows fast in any kind of soil, but prefers damp shade. Watch out for this plant, as it is propagated by root division, and being deep-rooted, it is very difficult to get rid of once it has become established.

Comfrey can be used:

- As a compost activator—add a layer of leaves to compost to add nitrogen and help heat the pile.
- As a liquid fertilizer—add rotting leaves to water to produce "comfrey tea," or stack weighted leaves in a container, with a hole in the base, and allow the "comfrey concentrate" to collect in a pot below; use diluted water:comfrey concentrate 10:1.
- As a mulch—a layer of comfrey leaves placed around plants releases valuable nutrients.

A patch of comfrey growing behind the three-bin composting system makes adding it to compost quick and easy. It's so vigorous that it can be harvested four times a year. The patch never spreads because the plant's energy is used up keeping it coming back! When the flowers first appear, comfrey is at its most potent; cut it back to 2 in. (5 cm) above the ground. Stop harvesting after August to allow the plants to build up reserves in the roots for winter. TIP: Leaves are hairy, so you may want to wear gloves when handling.

For centuries comfrey has been valued for its ability to help set broken bones, and to heal wounds, sprains and burns. It contains two substances—allantoins and choline—that promote healthy growth of red blood cells. Comfrey used to be taken internally as a medicinal or culinary herb, but recent research shows that it contains alkaloids that are carcinogenic so it is no longer recommended for internal use.

COMFREY COMPRESS
Mix fresh grated comfrey root with water and apply to the affected area.

ORGANIC SOIL AMENDMENTS

Coir Coconut Peat

Coir has many similarities to peat:
- It is sterilized.
- It is lightweight.
- It has the capacity to store water.
- It has the ability to release nutrients for extended periods of time.
- It changes the soil texture.
- It is readily available and easy to use.

Peat bogs are a fast-disappearing habitat for rare flowers, insects and birds. Peat is found in damp habitats covered with reeds, rushes, mosses and other bog plants. Over four million cubic yards of peat is mined for horticulture in the UK every year, so that only six percent of its original lowland peat bogs now remain.

Horticulturalists have been searching for an alternative to peat as the primary ingredient in soil-free, sterilized growing mixes. Coir has around neutral pH 6.0 to 7.5, it has the ability to store water and release nutrients for extended periods of time, and its properties make it resistant to bactcrial and fungal growth. Sounds good, eh? I thought so too, so I've been experimenting with using coir—here's what I found:

I blended coco peat (coir) 50:50 with 100-percent screened compost. This was used as a biologically active medium to grow food plants in 4 to 5-gal. (18 to 23 L) containers. I found moisture retention was much improved, which cut down my watering time considerably. All crops (e.g., peppers, tomatoes,

Coir makes a good layer when building a lasagna garden.

Greenhouse in full production. Kristin Ross photo

eggplants, cucumbers, tomatillos, basil and ground cherries) produced optimally under greenhouse conditions. The growing mix responded well to weekly feeds of liquid fertilizer, and fish, seaweed or compost tea later in the season, which helps to extend the harvest.

GRANULAR ORGANIC FERTILIZER RECIPE

(Granular fertilizer takes three to four weeks to break down before roots can access it.)
Blend well:
4 parts seed meal (non-GMO alfalfa, canola or soy) or fish meal (wild, not fish farmed)
1 part dolomite lime
1 part rock phosphate
1 part kelp meal
Combine in soil mixes for planters and containers for boosting food production in confined spaces.
If soil fertility is in question, work lightly into the soil under transplants.
To give plants a boost, sprinkle as a side-dressing alongside existing plants.
Apply around the drip line of fruit trees and berry bushes, working in gently so as not to damage roots.

Q What is the difference between non-organic and organic fertilizer?

A Organic fertilizer comes from natural sources. Granular organic fertilizers are intrinsically slow-release. First they need to be broken down by soil micro-organisms, after which their soluble nutrients are available to plants. This takes anywhere from three to four weeks.

Non-organic fertilizer comes from synthetic sources. Synthetic fertilizers generally provide water-soluble nutrients that can be used immediately by plants.

Q When do you use liquid fertilizers?

A As it takes three to four weeks for soluble nutrients in granular organic fertilizer to be broken down by soil micro-organisms and made available to plants, liquid feeds are the best bet to help newly transplanted plants get established. In addition, young plants need to have roots developed enough to access nutrients before they can benefit from granular fertilizer.

If the plant is all about the foliage (e.g., spinach, lettuce), use fish fertilizer. If it's about the fruits and flowers (e.g., tomatoes, peppers), use liquid seaweed. Liquid fertilizers provide access to soluble organic nutrients fast through both roots and foliage. Applications of compost tea also bridge the nutrient gap for establishing plants.

NATURAL SOURCES OF GRANULAR NPK
Nitrogen (N): alfalfa meal, canola meal, soybean meal
Phosphorus (P): rock phosphate
Potassium (K): kelp meal, greensand, zeolite

Seed meals = nitrogen source (N) for healthy leafy greens
Rock phosphate = phosphorus (P) for fruits and flowers
Kelp meal = potassium (potash) (K) for roots and overall good health

February

PLANTING A POTAGER

Kitchen Gardening for Maximum Food in Minimum Space

The potager originated in twelfth-century France, the word "potager" coming from the French word for soup—*potage*. Potagers were often found in monasteries, tended to by the monks. They were initially designed as a small formal vegetable plot, the objective being to grow the maximum amount of food in the minimum amount of space without losing the esthetic quality of the garden.

The potager was usually based on a square design, divided into beds of differing shapes to accommodate a variety of crops. Attractive obelisks were often used as features, providing support for climbing vegetables such as pole beans. The periphery of the garden was edged with a diversity of plants—mixing flowers, vegetables and herbs together created a sense of abundance and provided esthetic pleasure, in addition to attracting wildlife to the garden for pollination and pest control.

On grander estates the potager would be a larger affair, most likely inside a walled kitchen garden. A crew of gardeners would be employed to grow seasonal fruits and vegetables to supply the domestic needs of the estate. The potager was considered an important part of the household—the grander the

The potager at Hadspen House, UK.

garden the better the family lived, and the more impressed visitors were!

Potagers were filled by crops of early vegetables, followed by later plantings. Spring crops of potatoes, peas and lettuce were followed by summer plantings of kale or cabbage. Onions, chicories and chard happily co-existed alongside teepees of beans, perhaps even intertwined with sweet peas.

After a trip to the United Kingdom visiting different heritage gardens, I returned and redesigned my food garden as a potager, taking into account all the principles outlined above. The raised beds and pathways were levelled and the garden was divided into four equal squares. The soil was amended over the winter with manure, leaves, seaweed and compost, and in spring we began by planting an early crop of peas, along two 20-ft. (6-m) rows of bamboo teepees.

My potager is laid out as a 50-by-50 ft. (15-by-15 m) square, bordered by a bed of perennial vegetables—asparagus, seakale, artichokes and onions. Culinary and medicinal herbs grow in a border along one side of the garden, and flowering plants spill out from a border parallel to a "Berry Walk" of

raspberries, loganberries, blackcurrants, gooseberries and strawberries. I planted a repeat-blooming fragrant-pink *Rosa rugosa* hybrid 'Roseraie de l'Hay' in the middle of my garden, but an obelisk of beans or a birdbath underplanted with herbs would fill the centre nicely as well.

There is access into the garden on all four sides along pathways cribbed with wood and lined with ½-in. (1-cm) screenings that compact down to create a smooth surface that can be raked. Pathways can also be made from bricks and paving stones—or anything,

Top left: This food garden layout works well for crop rotations.

Top right: A patchwork quilt of salad greens.

Above: The food garden, summer 2009.

Right: Lettuce going to seed.

really—just as long as they are wide enough to allow wheelbarrows to manoeuvre easily.

In summer the garden overflows with salad greens, tomatoes, vegetables, herbs, fruits and berries. By sowing crops in straight rows, you can harvest more in less space and keep track of growth better. By varying colours and textures you can create spectacular effects. Like potagers of old, modern-day gardens do not have to lack appeal.

Lettuces can be closely planted and harvested as "cut-and-come-again" greens from spring through summer. Eventually they go to seed and masses of colourful seed heads take over. Lettuces are self-pollinating, so there is little need to worry about isolation distances. I grow an unrelated food plant between rows just to make sure they don't accidentally cross-pollinate.

My belief is that we cannot be food secure without saving food seeds, so being a seed-saving gardener I only grow open-pollinated varieties. I select the healthiest plants which are "true to type" and let them go to seed. In the process I not only save a fortune, but also help protect plant genetic diversity, keeping the food crops our ancestors worked hard to preserve alive for future generations.

GOOD GARDEN DESIGN

The Rule of Thirds

- One-third evergreen
- One-third deciduous
- One-third seasonal colour

Start with the hardscape that provides the bones of the garden—hedges, pathways, patios, etc. Begin with the foundation plantings, striking a good balance between structural and seasonal interest. Create a canopy effect using taller plants as backdrops for shrubs and berries, but do not overshadow them. Use smaller plants and annuals for seasonal interest at the front of the border. Project ahead when planting to avoid having to remove plants later. Set plants free to be themselves or you will forever be a

Sheri's garden, Gabriola Island, BC.

slave to maintaining them as you want them! Create compatible colour themes and combinations. Ask yourself honestly: "Do orange and pink really go together?"

Choose a Style

- English country
- Native; wildlife; naturalistic
- Japanese; zen
- Xeriscape (drought-resistant)
- Wetland, ponds and water gardens
- Contemporary
- Formal

Consider Your Climate

The Pacific Northwest, for example, has wet winters and dry summers. Gardeners in this area should enjoy success with plants that thrive in similar climates:
- Mediterranean
- New Zealand
- Australia
- South Africa
- Central and South America

Create microclimates using windbreaks, smaller trees or shrubs, to protect plants easily damaged by strong winds, salt sprays or early frosts.

MY TOP-10 GARDENING TOOLS

It was 25 years ago that I ventured out as a professional gardener in my first business, Forget-Me-Not Gardening Services. The only tools I had to my name then were a fork, a spade and a wheelbarrow, gifted by friends leaving town. My tool collection has come a long way since then, so just for fun I thought I'd share my top-10 gardening tools now with you (in no particular order).

1. Secateurs

Secateurs should always make clean cuts without crushing the wood. Quality secateurs have replaceable parts and will last forever—if you don't lose them! Secateurs should have red handles, and you should have a holster, as good ones don't come cheap!

2. Fan rake

What a difference a rake makes! Raking beds keeps them free of diseased material, and can instantly makes a mess look like a million dollars. A fan rake makes it quick and easy to pick up piles of gardening debris to transport to the compost.

Willow fences make good windbreaks.

3. Quality hose

If you ask me what the bane of my existence used to be, I'd say garden hoses that kinked. Nothing drove me more nuts! These days I opt for top-quality rubber hose guaranteed "unkinkable," which is always easy to rewind onto the hose reel.

4. Dolly

I still can't believe that it took me 13 years in the nursery business to realize that $35 would save me the expense of trips to the chiropractor! Instead of lugging heavy pots around, alone or with help, I now simply slide a dolly under them and easily move them around the garden with the minimum of exertion.

5. Tarps

There's no easier way of moving large piles of debris than by dragging them on a tarp. I line my trailer with a tarp when I pick up manure. This way I can pull the last of the load out in one action—pulling the back of the tarp forward—and clean the trailer at the same time.

6. Free buckets

Where would we all be without handy buckets? I appreciate recycled food-grade buckets for mixing soil, carrying water, transporting weeds and soaking plants—to name just a few things I have used them for. Go to the back of any restaurant and help yourself before the garbage truck gets there!

7. Dustpans

Believe it or not, one of the fastest ways to clean and mix on a large scale is by using a dustpan. Over many years of gardening professionally, I have found dustpans to be indispensable for many purposes—sweeping up mess, scraping off workbenches, tossing loads of soil together and cleaning out the chicken coop. I find them so handy (and cheap!) that I keep three or four

Above: Wheelbarrows come in handy for all sorts of things!

Left: Hanging tools up helps you keep track of them.

around the place! Staying clean and tidy is imperative for growing healthy plants and having happy hens.

8. Long-handled cultivator

Why bend down when you can do the job efficiently standing up? Choose your favourite cultivator or hoe with a long handle for zipping between plants and along rows to upend pesky weeds in no time flat. See "Hoe a Row in Five" in May.

9. Pitchfork

Farmers know the value of a pitchfork for shifting big loads fast! It's the best tool for turning compost piles, spreading leaves, collecting manure and gathering up blackberry canes and brush. The easy swing of a heritage wood-handled pitchfork always makes the task feel lighter.

10. Wheelbarrow

Preferably lightweight, because wheelbarrows get heavier with each load you lug around the garden. An inner tube that can be re-inflated after tire punctures is an economical way to go, and you can have them put in at your local garage. Replaceable handle grips are wonderful, too, because it's uncomfortable to carry weight when these wear out. I love wheelbarrows because they always make my workload so much lighter!

CARE OF TOOLS

If you want tools to last, keep them cleaned and well maintained during the gardening season. Wipe an oily cloth over blades, and keep edges sharp with several passes of a good oilstone. Once or twice a year preserve wooden-handled tools by wiping them with a rag soaked in a mix of one part linseed oil and one part paint thinner. Allow them to dry in the sun and repeat once more. Tools not only feel great after being oiled, but the handles last longer by not drying out, cracking or breaking.

TIP: Take a 5-gal. (23-L) bucket of clean washed sand and mix it with 2 cups (475 mL) of horticultural oil. After using, plunge tools into the oily sand before hanging them up—this prevents them from getting rusty.

RECYCLING IDEAS FOR THE GARDEN

I always felt proud to say that I built my garden using recycled wood and free lumber, but I always felt bad that so much useful material was being thrown away. In my garden there are always multiple purposes for everything. Here's a sample of what you could do with all those free-wood piles around the city.

Piles of logs make good raised beds. These logs were good for five years before they began to rot; and they are easily replaced. We top-dress the raised beds yearly to replenish the soil. They are perfect for growing garlic, shown here in late winter. Afterwards this made a perennial bed for asparagus, artichokes,

sunchokes, strawberries and horseradish along the edge of the main garden.

Pallets make free composting systems—one, two or three-bin systems, depending on space. We use a three-bin system and turn 2 cu. yd. (1.5 cu. m) of waste into 1 cu. yd. (.75 cu. m) of "Super-Duper" compost in three months after just one turning. You can use wood for a roof to protect compost from winter rains, which wash nutrients away.

This 4-by-6-ft. (1.2-by-1.8-m) propagation box is lined with a heater cable (with thermostat) that keeps the 2-in. (5-cm) layer of sand on top of the cable warm. Providing bottom heat to cuttings means

Above: Logs make good raised beds.

Top right: A three-bin system, using free recycled pallets.

Right: The propagation box.

Far right: 60-ft. (18-m) cold frame made from free wooden pallets.

better rooting success; this table enables me to get a headstart on pepper and basil seedlings that require 75°F (24°C) for germination. It also enables tender plants to overwinter in unheated greenhouses, which saves a lot of energy.

Pallets are free and plentiful around the city, and are useful for lots of projects. We covered this south-facing "cold frame" using a 60-ft. (18-m) roll of vapour barrier, 8½ ft. (2.6 m) wide ($30), which will last two years. A 60-ft. (18-m) cold frame for $15! We attached the 6-mil plastic to long wood poles, by hammering U-hooks through the plastic, which we then rolled up and down as needed. Plants that overwinter in the greenhouse harden off here in spring. Shortly afterwards, they will go outdoors, and tender young seedlings take their place in the cold frame.

Alder poles make great teepees for growing pole beans. Build them in full sun. Plant six bean seeds around the foot of each teepee, and watch the show begin! Kids love hiding inside these living tents!

Long bamboo canes are perfect for making supports for growing peas and beans. I grow a crop of spring peas, followed by a later crop of pole beans. Rhizobia bacteria are then present in the soil for the beans, helping to increase yields.

At The Garden Path we built this 50-ft. (15-m) arbour to support trailing canes of grapes, kiwis, roses, blackberries, tayberries, cascade berries and marionberries.

Top far left: Alder teepees for beans.

Bottom far left: The arbour was built using trees from the forest.

Left: The swing seat under the old-growth Douglas fir at The Garden Path.

Below: Bamboo teepees are great for peas and pole beans.

PERENNIAL FOOD PLANTS

Unlike annual vegetables that rotate around the garden, perennial food plants require a permanent location where they can increase in size and production over time. I plant perennials at the edge of the garden to keep them from interfering with annual crop rotations. I regard many perennial food plants as "ornamental edibles," because they contribute aesthetic pleasure as well as food value.

Artichokes

Artichokes (*Cynara scolymus*) are the biggest showoffs in the garden. They multiply by offsets so it is advisable to separate clumps every three years to keep flower production high. In spring, carefully dig down to remove the outer offsets, and set them out or pot them up. TIP: Don't panic when they wilt like crazy, they do eventually perk up.

Asparagus

Asparagus (*Asparagus officinalis*) takes patience! Growing it from seed takes more patience than I have, so I started by using two-year-old male asparagus roots, choosing a variety called 'Jersey Knight'. By planting these roots I only wait one year to get a decent harvest. Male plants produce fat juicy spears, while females produce long slender spears. TIP: Asparagus roots are heavy feeders, so keep them happy by feeding every fall, so that spring harvests keep getting better.

Oca

Oca or New Zealand yams (*Oxalis tuberosa*) have ornamental leaves that make attractive groundcovers and are very productive in fertile, well-drained sites. Oca is best harvested when the foliage dies down after heavy frost. Store the tubers in a cool dark place for winter, where they remain firm and can be eaten as needed. They are delicious drizzled with olive oil and roasted for 25 minutes, or baked in mixed vegetable casseroles.

Good King Henry

Good King Henry (*Chenopodium bonus-henricus*) can be eaten like spinach and the shoots are also a delicacy. Hilling up soil over the roots in early spring produces blanched shoots that appear two weeks before asparagus. If Good King Henry is well fed it

Left to right: 'Green Globe' artichokes; asparagus 'Jersey Knight'; oca or New Zealand yams; and Good King Henry.

will yield an abundant supply of delicious shoots. The shoots should be peeled, tied up in bunches like asparagus, and boiled in deep water until tender.

Salsify

Salsify or vegetable oyster root (*Tragopogon porrifolius*) has slender, fleshy white taproots with delicate oyster-like flavour. The 3-ft.-tall (90-cm) plants have eye-catching feathery purple flowers. This biennial self-seeds so may be experienced as a perennial. The roots are harvested as required from October through winter and are prepared by boiling until tender. The youngest leaves can also be added to salads.

Sea Kale

Sea kale (*Crambe maritima*) is a wild brassica that thrives in maritime conditions, as the name implies. Not well known today, the Victorians once appreciated it as a winter gourmet treat, forced under terra-cotta pots in January. The delicate shoots taste like hazelnuts crossed with asparagus. The pure-white flowers are highly decorative, as are the light-brown seed pods that follow them. It is easy to propagate this vegetable from root division, as well as from seed sown in fall.

Sprouting Broccoli

'Nine Star' is a cold-hardy, white sprouting broccoli (*Brassica oleracea* var. *botrytis*) that produces copious quantities of snow-white heads in spring, sweet and tender when lightly steamed, and crispy when eaten raw with dips. At the end of harvesting, cut the thick stalks back to make them regrow. TIP: Try this with other brassicas—instead of pulling plants out after harvest, cut stalks back and they may regenerate.

Sunchokes

Sunchokes (*Helianthus tuberosum*) are a good source of carbohydrate that can be harvested all winter as needed. Even when the whole bed of sunchokes is dug up every year to take to Seedy Saturday shows at the end of winter, they come back again in summer like crazy! During chronic food rationing in World War II, people were very grateful for sunchokes and every garden grew some. Sunchokes are sweet and nutty when roasted for 25 minutes, and crunchy pickled or with dips, and they also make a creamy hearty soup (see "Sunchokes, the A to Z of Vegetables" in March, for recipe).

Left to right: Salsify or vegetable oyster root; sea kale; 'Nine Star' sprouting broccoli; red sunchokes.

PRUNING FRUIT TREES

Why Prune?

- To train the plant.
- To maintain plant health.
- To improve the quality of fruit.
- To restrict growth.
- To improve aesthetics.
- To repair damage or remove disease.

Pruning Advice

- Make sure you make clean cuts to avoid injury to the tree—use sharp, disinfected secateurs and loppers.
- When taking branches off, avoid cutting into the branch bark collar where the natural defence system of the tree repairs wounds.
- When pruning a heavy branch, always begin with an under-cut to prevent the branch from splitting, then make the over-cut all the way through.

Pruning Styles

CENTRAL LEADER

The central leader is the tallest, most vertical branch, generally the one that continues with the line of the trunk. The central leader is pruned to half its length, which promotes the growth of horizontal branches referred to as laterals. This style is best for pome fruits—apples and pears.

OPEN VASE

The "open vase" style keeps the inside of the tree open for improved air circulation and penetration of sunlight. Best for stone fruits—peaches, nectarines, cherries, plums and apricots.

ESPALIER AND CORDON-TRAINED

A good site for an espaliered and cordon-trained tree would be a south-facing wall, or against the side of a garden shed. Espaliered trees should be planted 10 ft. (3 m) apart; single cordons 2 ft. (60 cm) apart. Dwarf rootstock (M9) is the most suitable for espalier or cordon-trained trees. Avoid tip-bearers, varieties

that fruit on the end of shoots rather than on spurs. These are unsuitable for training, because there's too much bare wood along the branch before fruit appears. Both systems require a set of supports. The best way is to erect a system of posts (or vine eyes from a wall) between which you can run horizontal wires. Once in place, each horizontal is tightened. Horizontal wires should be spaced 18 in. (46 cm) apart, and plenty of bamboo canes made available for tying to wires. The bottom wire should be 2 ft. (60 cm) above the ground. Branches are tied to the canes, not the wires, using twine. With this framework you can train a tree into a cordon, fan or espalier shape.

CORDON

A maiden tree (a one-year-old tree with no side shoots) is required for this and should be planted at a 45-degree angle. Unlike espaliered trees, all single-stem cordons remain at this angle. There is no need to prune back at planting. All you have to do is

Prune while fruit trees are dormant.

prune side shoots, known as laterals, back to three leaves in summer. This produces a system of fruiting spurs, the basal cluster. The leader must be stopped at the desired height and pruned back every year to that height. Excess growth from the basal cluster is summer-pruned back to three leaves each year.

DOUBLE CORDON

If you want to be really fancy, plant a maiden, cut it back to two buds immediately, train the resultant growth from those two buds horizontally until you decide to bend them up vertically, making a "U" shape on a leg. The tree is then treated in the same way as a normal cordon.

Pruning Tools

Using the proper tool for the job will eliminate twisting or straining. Keep the branch to be cut as deeply in the jaws of the tool as possible and, tempting as it may be, don't ruin the blades by cutting wire with pruning tools.

- Hand secateurs are designed for cutting stems up to ½ in. (12 mm) in diameter. Attempting to cut larger branches will risk making a poor cut or ruining the secateurs.
- When a larger cut is needed, reach for loppers.
- They have long handles operated by both hands and can cut material ½ to 2 in. (1.2 to 5 cm) in diameter, or more if the wood is soft.
- Pruning saws—folding ones, preferably, as they are safer—are useful for branches too large for loppers. These cut on the pull stroke, and are faster and easier than a carpenter's saw. (Bow saws are good only where no obstructions exist for a foot or more around the area to be cut.)
- When the cut required is out of reach, choose extendable pole pruners. These are very effective with a hooked blade above and cutting blade beneath, similar to a large pair of loppers. The cutter is operated by pulling a rope downward. Poles can be fitted with an easy-to-attach saw, which I have found very useful for cutting larger awkward-to-reach branches.
- Hedge shears, manual or electric, are used mainly for shearing hedges and creating formal shapes in the garden. I use electric shears for large-scale jobs and manual for smaller ones.

The Dos for Pruning

- **Do** start by pruning out the 3Ds: dead, diseased and damaged. Avoid cutting too close and injuring the main stem/trunk. Then remove any one of two crossing branches that are rubbing. Removing branches growing into the centre keeps an open habit, beneficial for good air circulation and the penetration of sunlight. TIP: Pruning to an outward facing bud or side shoot encourages outward growth. Cut immediately above a bud or side shoot, making a sloped cut away from the bud.
- **Do** be clear about what you are trying to accomplish. Keeping your objective in mind while pruning will help you achieve it. Don't prune so severely that it stunts the plant's ability to thrive. Don't prune more than 30 percent at one time, which produces water sprouts and an abundance of soft wood. The more you prune the more plants grow, so it's not easy to keep a big plant small!
- **Do** allow a plant to heal itself. Nobody uses tar paste over pruning cuts anymore. Pruning paint has in fact been shown to slow down the healing process.
- **Do** enjoy the new relationship you develop with your garden using proper pruning practices.

The Garden Path orchard.

The Don'ts for Pruning

- **Don't** prune new growth early in the season. Food stored in roots and stems is used up for the development of new growth. This is replenished by the food the foliage returns as a result of photosynthesis. If new foliage is removed too early in the season the plant may become dwarfed.
- **Don't** prune in late summer. This encourages new growth, which may not have time to harden off before winter, resulting in damage or severe winterkill.
- **Don't** buy cheap tools. You will get what you pay for and have to replace them. Buy good quality, which will last a lifetime if cared for.
- **Don't** spread disease among plants; disinfect pruning tools by spraying them with a 10 percent solution of bleach, from a spray bottle, between plants.

Properly pruned trees produce huge yields.

WONDERFUL WEEDS

What is a weed?
A plant whose virtues have not yet been discovered.
Ralph Waldo Emerson

Understanding Weeds

Infestations of weeds point to imbalances in the garden, such as poor drainage, low fertility or nutrient deficiencies, so it helps to know what the weeds are telling you:

- Convolvulus or bindweed thrives in poor, sandy soil—it indicates the addition of some organic matter is required.
- Chickweed, groundsel, chicory and lamb's quarters are shallow-rooted weeds that grow in fertile conditions—they indicate good fertility.
- Clovers, vetches and wild sweet pea indicate nitrogen deficiency—but being legumes that fix nitrogen in soil, they will correct this condition.
- Creeping buttercup thrives in heavy soils—it indicates the drainage needs to be improved.
- Dandelions indicate soil lacks essential minerals and elements—perhaps it's time to get a soil test?
- Daisies are rich in calcium and thrive in soils that lack lime—they add calcium when they decompose.
- Horsetail indicates heavy moist soil—indicating a need for better drainage and improved fertility.

The Benefits of Weeds

- In winter, weeds give soil protection from heavy rain, preventing soil erosion and stabilizing banks.
- Weeds provide food for soil bacteria through winter. Where groundcovers flourish in winter, healthy populations of microbes are already present in early spring.
- Many weeds provide food and shelter for wildlife. (Clover is one of the main nectar sources for honeybees.)
- Broadleaf weeds are perennials with deep roots that penetrate and aerate heavy soils, helping to

improve drainage. Dandelions thrive on heavy clay soils, aerating and breaking up hardpan.

- Deep-rooted weeds have access to deep-seated soil nutrients, which are then stored in roots and leaves. TIP: If weeds are "solarized" in black plastic bags until they dehydrate, they can be returned to soil as compost with no danger of reproducing.
- Nettles and comfrey leaves are rich in nitrogen, potassium and calcium and when steeped in water make good liquid fertilizer for plants.

HORSETAIL FOR RHEUMATISM RELIEF

The folk names for horsetail (*Equisetum*)—scouring rush, bottlebrush and shave grass—allude to this plant's practical use as a fine grade of sandpaper. It has been used to file stone, polish wood and scour cookware. Medicinally *Equisetum* is also a very useful plant. It contains high amounts of the mineral silica, important for healthy hair, skin, nails and connective tissue. Since ancient times, horsetail has been used to heal wounds, treat urinary infections and strengthen bones. *Equisetum* can also help to ease the pain of rheumatism: Add 3.5 oz. (99 g) of fresh or dried horsetail to a hot bath and soak for one hour. Try a hot-water basin soak for hands.

SWEET CLOVER FOR TEAS AND BEES

White clover (*Trifolium repens*) and red clover (*Trifolium pratense*) grow in a great range of soils and climates. Dried flower heads can be steeped in hot water for tasty teas. Farmers with clover pastures are in heavy demand from beekeepers, and both benefit from increased pollination and delicious clover honey.

Weeds That Feed Beneficials

Asclepias (milkweed): butterflies
Cirsium sp. (thistle): butterflies and goldfinches
Chenopodium sp. (lamb's quarters): songbirds
Melilotus sp. (sweet clover): butterflies
Stellaria media (chickweed): songbirds
Taraxacum sp. (dandelion): goldfinches and pine siskins
Trifolium spp. (clover): butterflies
Urtica dioica (nettle): butterflies

Edible Weeds

BITTER CRESS (*Cardamine hirsute*)

Bitter cress (or pepper weed, shot weed or snap weed) is a difficult-to-eradicate annual, forming large mats of lacy rosettes of leaves, with tiny white flowers. Bitter cress is shallow-rooted so can be hoed up easily. While it is reminiscent of watercress in flavour, the fresh taste of the greens in winter is what it's really all about. Watch out! Bitter cress quickly forms explosive seed pods, and has several generations a year.

CHICKWEED (*Stellaria media*)

Chickweed is a common annual that grows as fragile, bright-green cushions of creeping leaves, with tiny white flowers. It's easily harvested in clumps and is delicious lightly steamed. Make sure you rinse greens well in a deep bowl of water to get the grit out before eating.

DANDELION (*Taraxacum officinale*)

Dandelion leaves are best picked before they get tough, which is before the flowers open. Dandelion leaves are high in vitamins A, C and K and are good sources of calcium, potassium, manganese and iron. The flowers can be sautéed as a vegetable dish, or dipped in batter and fried. The flower petals are used to make dandelion wine. The roots when roasted and ground are used as a caffeine-free coffee substitute.

Dandelion Salad

Large bunch of tender young dandelion
  greens (trimmed and soaked in a large
  bowl of water to remove grit)
1 garlic clove, finely minced
3 Tbsp. (45 mL) olive oil
1½ Tbsp. (22 mL) balsamic vinegar
Coarse salt and black pepper, freshly
  cracked
¼ cup (60 mL) red currants
Chives, finely minced

*Add the garlic and vinegar to a stainless-
steel bowl and slowly whisk in the oil until
it becomes emulsified. Toss the dandelion
greens with salt and pepper and add the
vinaigrette and half the red currants. Pile
dandelion greens up on a funky salad plate
and sprinkle minced chives and the remaining
currants all over.*

*If entirely bitter greens are not to your taste
add 50 percent mixed greens.*

HENBIT (*Lamium amplexicaule*)

This attractive weed has bright-purple flowers and
nettle-like leaves. Young plants have edible tops that
are good in salads or stir-fries, but pluck off the tops
to avoid tough stalks. If finely chopped, henbit can be
used in dressings and sauces for mild mint flavour.

NETTLE (*Urtica dioica*)

When stinging nettle appears down by the creek
it's time for a spring tonic, because steamed nettle
greens are full of iron, vitamins and chlorophyll,
which add pep to your step! Stop harvesting when
nettles set seed, as they develop gritty particles that
irritate the urinary tract. The stinging hairs collapse
when the greens are cooked, but until then I handle
stinging nettles with respect using gloves and tongs.

Nettles are cooked and used like spinach in a
multitude of dishes, and the leaves can be dried to
make a pleasing tisane.

In Europe, dock leaves are traditionally used
as a remedy for "nettle burn" and relieve
the itchiness and discomfort when rubbed
into the area. Broad-leaved dock (*Rumex
obtusifolius*) often conveniently grows beside
stinging nettle.

PURSLANE (*Portulaca oleracea*)

Golden purslane (*Portulaca oleracea sativa*) is not
your basic garden weed, but a tender annual with
tangy flavour and crispy texture, packed with omega-3
fatty acids. It can be direct seeded or transplanted
when the soil is warm. Space 6 in. (15 cm) apart to
allow the low, bushy plants to spread, and pick leaves
as needed. This succulent edible prefers summer heat
and golden plants look great growing along sunny
borders.

Golden purslane.

Spring Tonic Nettle Soup

1 chopped onion (or 4 chopped leeks)

1 Tbsp. (15 mL) butter with a drizzle of olive oil

2 bay leaves

4 medium potatoes, chopped

4 cups (1 L) tender nettle tops, rinsed in large bowl

Salt and pepper to taste

1 cup (250 mL) milk and 1 cup (250 mL) light cream or 2 cups (475 mL) milk or soymilk

1 bulb roasted garlic (optional)

Sauté the onions (or leeks) with the bay leaves in butter and oil until softened. Add potatoes, just cover with water and season with salt and pepper. Bring to a boil and reduce heat, cooking only until the potatoes are soft. Add the nettles using tongs, and allow to cook for 10 minutes until the greens are wilted. If adding roasted garlic, squeeze the cloves in now. Remove bay leaves.

Purée everything in a blender until smooth and return to the heat while slowly adding dairy or soy and stirring while the soup heats up. Do not allow to boil, or the soup will curdle. Garnishing options: parsley, yoghurt or croutons.

Nettles.

Golden Purslane Salad

Mix well:

2 cups (475 mL) young purslane, washed
and chopped

1 large tomato, chopped

1 Tbsp. (15 mL) salt

2 Tbsp. (30 mL) cilantro, finely chopped
Leave to marinate for a few hours. Drain.

Dressing

Whisk:

3 Tbsp. (45 mL) olive oil (or walnut oil)

2 Tbsp. (30 mL) red wine vinegar

1 Tbsp. (15 mL) lemon juice

2 Tbsp. (30 mL) Dijon mustard

Salt and pepper to taste.

Garnish with walnuts (optional).

The Ode to the Dandelion

Now I live on a nice street, as nice as nice could be,
And everyone has green lawns, that's all except for me,
For my lawn is a haven for every flower you've seen
I like to see the colours, mixed in with the green.
There's one flower that is special,
It smiles at me each day, and every time I see it
It blows my blues away.

I thought I'd write a song to show it just how much I
cared
And now I'll share with you the song that I have
prepared.
It's the ode to the dandelion,
Yes the ode to the dandelion;
That pretty yellow flower that feeds the bees,
The suburban gardener's nightmare weed,
The miracle plant for vitamin C
The dandelion!

Well all my friendly neighbours were not pleased to see
The flowers on my lawn that made me skip with glee.
They said they were a danger, a hazard to our town,
They sent a lawyer's letter and said they'd mow them
down!

Now I'm not one for conflict, I like a peaceful scene,
And rarely am I angry or particularly mean,
But when you try to tell me that a flower is a disgrace,
I have to say you zap the smile that's always on my face.

I thought I'd have a party, so everyone could see
That dandelions are healthy, and tasty as can be!
I'd make some soup and salad and canapés to die,
And best of all I'd make some wine to help the night go
by!
So all my friendly neighbours
Poured in through the garden gate,
They munched and scrunched and slurped and slopped
Until the hour was late.

And as they tripped and tumbled way off down The
Garden Path,
I heard the strains of this fine song that went right to my
heart.

It's the ode to the dandelion,
Yes the ode to the dandelion.
That pretty yellow flower that feeds the bees,
The suburban gardener's nightmare weed,
The miracle plant for vitamin C
The dandelion!

Words and music by Rosie Emery

RHUBARB

Though technically a vegetable, rhubarb stalks are used in fruit pies, cakes, preserves and other desserts. Good news for weight watchers, rhubarb is low in calories, only 10 calories in 4 oz. (113 g) of fruit. The problem is the sweetener! TIP: Cooking rhubarb with the herb sweet cicely means you can cut back on sugar.

Rhubarb grows best in full sun or light shade, in fertile, moist loam soil. It is either green or red-stalked, the latter being sweeter, but less productive, and less suited to forcing. 'Victoria' and 'Glaskin's Perpetual' are green-stalked, 'Valentine', 'Canada Red' and 'Cherry Red' are red-stalked.

Harvest stalks of 1 to 2 ft. (30 to 60 cm) by pulling them off the crown with a twisting motion, rather than cutting them off. By mid summer stop harvesting, as mature rhubarb has increased levels of oxalic acid, a toxic substance that interferes with iron absorption. Allow the last leaves of the season to feed the roots.

Clean rhubarb should be stored in a cool place such as a refrigerator and also freezes well. Chop into 2-in. (5-cm) chunks, place on cookie sheet and freeze overnight, put individual chunks into freezer bags, record year, and use as needed.

For best production, roots should be divided every three years. Rhubarb should be divided when dormant, after leaves have died back or the soil has warmed in spring. With a large shovel dig out the whole root or remove only part of the root. TIP: When dividing the whole root, a sharp axe does an admirable job! Replant larger chunks of root 3 ft. (90 cm) apart, with the crown just below the surface. Rhubarb is a gutsy feeder, so feed it twice a year, in early spring and again in late fall.

Harvesting lightly the first year after dividing allows the plant to focus energy on developing a new root system. Plants come into full production in the third year and can continue for 15 to 20 years. Rhubarb does not seem to be troubled by diseases and pests, but be sure to compost dead leaves and stalks to prevent disease from overwintering. Allowing plants to go to seed reduces production, so unless you are saving seeds remove flower heads as they appear, and redirect the plant's energy from seed production to fruit production.

Above: Rhubarb is a very productive plant when fertilized well.

Left: Force tender stalks of rhubarb by covering with a terra-cotta pot.

43

MILDRED'S NORWEGIAN FRUITCAKE

Preheat oven to 350°F (175°C)

Lightly grease a 9 by 13 in. (23 by 33 cm) baking pan

1 cup (250 mL) sugar

¾ cup (180 mL) butter

Beat until creamy in texture

Beat 2 large eggs or 3 small eggs, and blend in (using a wooden spoon always works best for me!)

Sift:

1½ cups (350 mL) unbleached flour

1½ tsp. (7.5 mL) baking powder

Pinch salt (if using unsalted butter)

Add the flour gradually and blend in to make a smooth batter. Spread into the baking pan using a spatula. Choose fruit in season: rhubarb chunks with orange peel, blueberries with lemon peel, raspberries, strawberries, cherries, blackberries, pear slices, apple slices, etc. Press berries or fruit slices generously into batter. Sprinkle with cinnamon sugar (optional).

Turn oven down to 325°F (160°C). Bake 30 minutes until lightly brown on top and firm in the centre. Serve warm or cool. Great with whipped cream, ice cream or yoghurt!

'Glaskin's Perpetual' rhubarb in seed.

Seed Saving

Rhubarb (Polygonaceae family) is normally propagated by root division and not from seed because seeds display diversity and do not grow true to type. If growing from seed only select those plants displaying the desired characteristics of the variety. Usual seed life is one year.

March

SPECIAL TEAS

Compost Tea

Can you believe there's something even better for the garden than compost? It's compost tea—made from extracts of quality compost and containing high levels of beneficial micro-organisms, nutrients and organic matter. Compost tea is the fastest way to bring the benefits of compost to soil when there's no compost available. It can be used as a liquid fertilizer on a regular basis, or as a more potent aerobic brew. Compost tea should smell sweet and earthy, indicating the presence of aerobic micro-organisms ("the good guys") at work. If the tea smells noxious then it's the anaerobic micro-organisms ("the bad guys") at work. Your nose will tell you whether you've got a good batch or not!

USE COMPOST TEA TO:
- Stretch the benefits of compost.
- Help suppress foliar disease, such as black spot and powdery mildew.
- Increase the availability of nutrients to plants.
- Speed up the control of pathogens.
- Increase yields.
- Enhance soil bio-fertility.
- Reduce transplant shock.
- Activate compost piles.

- Restore populations of micro-organisms to degraded soils following application of pesticides and synthetic fertilizers.
- Reinvigorate the lawn—dilute 1:3 with water and spray.
- Assist growth of hedges, shrubs and trees—apply as a soil drench diluted 1:10 parts water.

TO MAKE A BARREL OF COMPOST TEA:
1. Half-fill a 45-gal. (205-L) food-grade barrel with water.
2. Scoop one 5-gal. (23-L) food-grade bucket of high-quality compost (i.e., Super-Duper) into a burlap bag and tie tightly with twine.
3. Place the "giant teabag" into the barrel of water.
4. Leave to brew for one week. TIP: if you live in the city de-chlorinate the water in the barrel for 24 hours prior to adding the teabag. Chlorine destroys microbes.
5. After one week, strain the teabag out of the barrel and add the compost back to the pile.
6. Dip a 2-gal. (9-L) watering can into the barrel and use undiluted as a liquid fertilizer wherever needed. The tea is good unless it turns anaerobic.
7. Make a fresh brew whenever you need one.

"SUPER-Brewed" Compost Tea

A well-oxygenated "brew" results in a more potent tea that contains billions of living beneficial micro-organisms. Don't be put off by comments about a "witches brew"—as you will find the results to be magical!

TO MAKE A BARREL OF "SUPER-BREWED" COMPOST TEA:

1. Fill a 45-gal. (205-L) barrel three-quarters full with water. If using chlorinated water, let sit for 24 hours.

2. Add two 5-gal. (23-L) buckets of high-quality compost.

3. Use a wooden pole or an old broom handle to vigorously stir the contents of the barrel often. Stir fast in one direction, and then in the other, so that compost settled on the bottom of the barrel is suspended in the water. The more the brew is oxygenated the more potent it becomes; micro-organisms respond to oxygen by multiplying like mad, evidenced by lots of bubbling on the surface of the tea.

4. Add one cup of brewed compost tea to a 2-gal. (9-L) watering can and use to feed plants throughout the season. Dilute 1:10 parts water for a soil drench, or use a more concentrated dilution of 1:3 for a foliar spray. Brewed compost teas should ideally be used fresh, 24 hours after brewing, definitely no more than three days old.

Compost tea being served.

Variegated golden comfrey.

Comfrey (or Nettle) Concentrate Tea

Comfrey and nettles can be turned into a liquid concentrate rich in nitrogen, potassium and potash—liquid gold for garden plants.

USE COMFREY OR NETTLE CONCENTRATE TEA TO:
- Provide a regular feed to outdoor planters.
- Activate and enhance the compost heap—simply water onto the pile.
- Feed fruit bushes—water in before fruiting.
  Note: Do not use regularly on acid-loving plants.

TO MAKE A COMFREY OR NETTLE CONCENTRATE TEA:

1. Drill a ¼-in. (6-mm) hole in the bottom of a 5-gal. (23-L) container with a fitted lid.

2. Place a piece of wire mesh over this hole to prevent blockage.

3. Stand the container on top of bricks, so that a collection bottle fits under the hole. Pack in enough comfrey (or nettle) leaves to fill the container. Do *not* add water.

4. Put the lid on tight.

5. The leaves will slowly decompose into a black liquid. This liquid can be stored in stoppered bottles in a cool and dark place for up to a year.

6. Always dilute the concentrate before use. If it is black and strong, dilute 1:20; if it is brown and thin, dilute 1:10.

Fill a plastic bottle with compost tea, poke a nail through the bottom, and 'drip feed' pole beans. Kristin Ross photo

SEEDING THE GREENHOUSE

The "primary seeding" at The Garden Path happens at the beginning of March, and involves extensive preparation. The greenhouse is emptied of plants (which go into a cold frame to be hardened off) and is thoroughly cleaned, with special care taken to get into the corners and on top of ledges. Glass panes, the floor and all work surfaces are scrubbed with a 1:10 dilution of hydrogen peroxide to get rid of algae, botrytis, overwintering bugs, spores and egg masses.

The cool-weather seeds are sown first—lettuces, leeks and onions, globe artichokes, herbs, parsley, kale, chard, spinach, peas, chicories and all the brassicas (e.g., broccoli, Brussels sprouts, cabbage, cauliflower, kohlrabi and cabbage).

Organize seeds by filing them alphabetically in a shoebox behind marked cards. Create sections for cool-weather seeds, seeds that require light for germination, winter vegetables or seeds that need warmth for germination.

All the seeds, except for heat-loving plants such as beans, squash, melons, basil, sunflowers, zinnias and cleome, are started in what I refer to as the "primary seeding." Tomatoes, peppers and eggplant all need a long growing season, so I seed them at the same time as the cool-weather seeds. The eggplants and peppers grow on heater cables as they need 70 to 75°F (21 to 24°C) for germination; providing bottom heat means they germinate in 1 to 2 weeks instead of 4 to 6 weeks.

To get a head start on cool-weather plants, lettuces, peas and leeks are germinated inside the greenhouse (cold frames also work), but once the seeds have germinated and are about 1 in. (2.5 cm) tall, they are grown outdoors until transplanted into the garden. Being prepared to cover young plants when the weather misbehaves is a "plant saver," so I built a cold frame using recycled wooden pallets. Wrapping the pallet system with sections of 6-ml polyethylene vapour barrier protects against unexpected frosts. This "cold frame" comes in very handy when hardening off plants.

Above: Flats of vegetable seedlings in the greenhouse.

Top left: Leek and onion seedlings.

Left: Recycled pallets offer seasonal protection.

Pricking Out Seedlings

Prick seedlings out into their own 4-in. (10-cm) pots when the first set of true leaves develop. Handle seedlings with care by their seed leaves. Use a pre-moistened lightweight mix. Make a small hole for the seedling using a dibber or a chopstick. Lower the seedling in, firm gently and water again. Keep newly transplanted seedlings in cool shady places, out of sun for a few days, where they can recover from transplant shock. Then move them to a brighter location.

Disease Prevention

Here's my mantra: "To prevent disease remove disease," and this goes for the greenhouse and the garden. The confined environment of a damp greenhouse is perfect for breeding fungal spores and pest problems, so check it out regularly. Remove dead plants or decaying leaves and inspect plants for aphids, fungus, gnats and whiteflies. Space container plants so they have enough room to get sufficient air and light. Water greenhouse plants only when needed; and preferably in the morning, so that they don't sit wet and cold at night.

Problems?

SEEDS DID NOT GERMINATE?

- The seeds may no longer be viable. Check the date on the seed package. Do a viability test by sowing 10 seeds on a dampened paper towel. Fold over, and keep damp for a week or so. Check to see how many seeds have sprouted; 3 out of 10 indicates only a 30 percent germination rate, in which case I'd recommend buying a fresh packet of seeds! A germination rate around 65 percent indicates acceptable seed viability.
- The seed may need longer to germinate. Check a germination guide before you give up. As an example, parsley seed requires 21 to 28 days.
- Some seeds need light for germination. This means sowing them on top of seeding mix and not covering them. Read seed packets to see if light requirements are specified. Usually it's the tiny

seeds that require light to germinate—and when you follow the depth principle of covering seeds three times their size, this makes perfect sense.

- Temperatures may be too cold. "Heat-lovers" like peppers, basil and tomatoes require temperatures around 75 to 85°F (24 to 29°C) for germination.

SEEDLINGS ARE YELLOW?

- Usually this indicates a lack of nutrients in the growing medium. The speediest remedy to green up seedlings is a feeding with liquid fish fertilizer.

SEEDLINGS ARE TOO SPINDLY?

- There's not enough light. Increase light by moving pots closer to a bright window or use grow lights. Rotating seedlings helps straighten them. You can plant spindly seedlings deeper to compensate for weakness.

SEEDLINGS ARE GROWING TOO SLOWLY?

- It could be overcrowding. Consider sowing seeds less thickly. Transplant seedlings into individual pots to relieve stress.
- The growing medium may have insufficient nutrients to supply all seedlings. Feed with liquid fish fertilizer.

SEEDLINGS COLLAPSING AT SOIL LEVEL?

- This is called "damping off" and is caused by soil-borne fungus, and aggravated by overseeding in warm, moist conditions. Try not to overwater. If "damping off" affects your seedlings, you'll need to start over, as there is no hope for them!

SEEDLINGS ARE BEING EATEN?

- You've got a critter! Check for slugs or sowbugs that love tasty young seedlings. Play "hide and seek" with the culprit until you find it.

SEEDLINGS ARE WILTED?

- Are seedlings rootbound? When there are more roots than growing medium in the pot, the plant dries out fast. Pot seedlings on into bigger pots.
- Perhaps the medium is too free-draining? Change the mix so that the seedlings do not dry out.

10 GOLDEN RULES FOR GROWING INCREDIBLE EDIBLES!

1. Seed Selection

In answer to the question "What shall I grow?" ask yourself what you and your family most like to eat. There's no point planting a row of space-hogging cabbages if no one in the family likes cabbage. If you consider the economic factor, it makes sense to grow food that costs more, especially when space is an issue. Also, check the number of days to maturity and select plants that will mature and produce in your garden's microclimate.

2. Soil

Most vegetables grow best in full sun and prefer well-drained fertile soil with a pH of 6.0 to 7.5. A gently sloping site with full southern exposure would be ideal, but any site free of large tree roots, receiving at least 7 to 11 hours of sun a day could work. Adding organic matter builds humus in soil, which increases its ability to hold moisture and nutrients. My four secrets of successful soil building are compost, manure, leaves and seaweed. If you add these amendments to soil every year I guarantee you will notice an incredible difference in food quality and quantity.

3. Fertilizers

Another mantra to remember is "it's all about the microbes!" Slow-release, natural-source fertilizer nourishes the teeming microscopic soil life that makes nutrients available to plants. To make your own granular organic fertilizer with little expense, purchase the ingredients in bulk at a farm-supply store. Basic recipe: Mix four parts (by volume) seed meal (N) with one part dolomite lime (pH), add one part rock phosphate (P) and one half-part kelp meal (K).

4. Companion Planting

Diversity is the key to maintaining health and balance in the garden. Communities of plants work together to keep bugs at bay, attract pollinators and improve plant growth. Large-scale monocultures offer a shining beacon to pests and disease, which is why they require the repeated use of increasingly toxic pesticides. When we go back to small-scale diversified food production, including hedgerows, flowers, grasses, herbs and berries, Nature will take back the control of potential problems, and we will garden in co-creation rather than against Her.

Incredible winter squash.

5. Crop Rotations

When the same species of plants are grown in the same place year after year, it's just a question of time before problems arise. After seven years, clubroot develops in brassicas; after 10 years, white rot shows up in garlic; weevil populations explode where peas and beans are always grown; if blight occurs it is passed on to all members of the *Solanaceae* family. Moving plants around breaks the life cycle of these common pests and diseases, because host plants are no longer present.

6. Pest Prevention

Deer, rabbits, birds and raccoons can play havoc in food gardens. Deer have a broad range of tastes from fruit trees to broccoli. Raccoons and birds can cause a ripe corn or cherry crop to disappear overnight. Netting and other physical barriers work well to prevent this. In my experience the only way to keep deer out is to use an 8-ft.-tall (2.4-m) fence.

"An ounce of prevention is worth a pound of cure" is another one of my gardening mantras. For prevention, observation is key, followed by identification. Always know what you are destroying and use the least toxic method possible.

7. Seeding

Over the past 20 years as a professional grower I have observed progressive cooling in spring. Whereas March/April used to be planting months, we now wait until June before conditions settle, and sometimes the conditions never settle! Instead of direct seeding I now grow most of my seedlings in a greenhouse and transplant them out when the conditions are right. With current fluctuations in climate, gardeners need to be more flexible and throw out old planting formulas. Instead I take a look out of the window, and entertain thoughts such as "If you need a coat, it's way too cold for basil!"

If you don't have the luxury of a greenhouse there are many ways to improvise using recycled wood and glass windows for cold frames. Container gardening is a good way of surviving poor summers for many heat-loving plants such as tomatoes, peppers, cucumbers, eggplant and basil. You don't need a garden to grow food—many edible plants fare very well in planters.

8. Weed Control

In spring the best time to weed is when the soil is still moist, and you can pull or dig established weeds out easily. If you can time it, weed just after heavy rainfall, because then the weeds almost jump into your hands—schlock! It's then that I roam around the garden pulling up the more deeply rooted perennial broadleaf weeds such as buttercup and dandelion. At the end of the season I aim to smother weed seeds with thick layers of organic mulch or compost—what I refer to as an "Organic Weed and Feed."

9. Saving Seeds

If you want to save seeds, start with open-pollinated varieties that have not had their genetic makeup changed by hybridization or genetic modification. Plants adapt to cultural conditions, therefore organic seeds will perform best for organic gardeners, and regional seeds will have an edge over seeds grown in other climates. If I purchase seed from Italy, I grow it out the first year, but access it in the second year, using the seeds I have saved, because it's then the plant shows its full potential. TIP: Always collect seeds from the recommended minimum number of plants in order to preserve the genetic diversity of the strain.

10. Winter Gardening

It seems a shame to leave beds empty from October to April when there are so many food plants that can be harvested through the cold season. There's nothing like eating food from the garden on a blustery winter night. In severe weather, cold frames may be necessary for protection, but generally plants are cold-hardy enough not to require this. TIP: When purchasing seeds for the start of the season, order winter vegetable seeds at the same time to insure you have the seeds you need at sowing time in summer.

THE A TO Z OF VEGETABLES

ARTICHOKE (GLOBE)

Globe artichokes (*Cynara scolymus*) are native to the Mediterranean, but given the right situation can be long-lived in temperate climates too. In Italy both purple and green varieties are favoured, but while the flavour of purple artichoke hearts is said to be superior, they are not as reliably hardy as the green varieties in my garden.

Globe artichoke plants grow to 5 ft. (1.5 m) tall, and can spread to 6 ft. (1.8 m) across. They prefer full sun, requiring a minimum of 10 hours of sunlight a day. They are heavy feeders, needing soil with plenty of organic matter, so feed generously. Mulching with seaweed in winter or adding granular seaweed in summer adds potassium, which boosts flower production and hence the number of hearts to be harvested.

Globe artichokes are frost-resistant perennials, but will not survive winters with deep-ground freezes. Cut them back to the ground in November, then cover thickly with mulch, which feeds the soil and protects the roots from freezing. Uncover the plants in spring.

I grow 'Green Globe' artichokes, an open-pollinated variety for seed saving, with 180 days to maturity. 'Green Globe' grows so fast you can actually harvest an edible artichoke in September from a March seeding! Better harvests follow in the second and third years, but by the end of the third season the plants may be crowded and need dividing.

Flowers appear from summer to late fall, on tall sturdy stalks with numerous branches. When they open to reveal purple thistledown they become very attractive to bees, which provide the pollination for seed production. The flower buds are layers of edible bracts that are fleshy at the base. This base is good for eating, but it's the heart of the bud that is sought as the main delicacy. Flowers should be harvested before the buds open.

*Above: Artichoke (*Cynara scolymus*) flowers in bud.*

Right: Artichoke thistle flowers are highly decorative.

Propagation

Division is the recommended way to propagate artichokes, because when grown from seed they do not always come true. To divide, remove young offsets in spring, and set them out or pot them up. Leaves always go into serious wilt, but do eventually recover. Artichokes have sensitive taproots and do not transplant well at any stage. For this reason it's best to start seeds individually in pots or soil blocks, so they can be transplanted with the minimum of root disturbance.

Seed Saving

(See "Cleaning Seeds" in October.)

For selective breeding purposes, it's exciting to grow from seed and select plants with the largest number of good-sized buds. Why not try adapting a variety to your garden?

The heads to save seeds from are those with the largest buds; cut off smaller buds on the same stalk to direct energy to ripening these seeds. White thistledown and hardened bracts, faded to brown, indicate that seeds are ready to harvest.

TIP: Don't confuse globe artichoke (*Cynara scolymus*) with its relative, cardoon (*Cynara cardunculus*). Cardoon and globe artichoke cross-pollinate if they are flowering at the same time, because their purple thistles are very attractive to pollinating bees. Usual seed life: 5 years when stored correctly.

ARUGULA

Arugula (*Eruca sativa*) germinates in cool conditions, so can be seeded twice a year, in early spring and again in fall. TIP: When broadcasting seeds scatter cautiously and evenly, taking care not to overseed. When plants are in competition from overcrowding they don't produce well. Thin the young seedlings for milder-flavoured rocket greens. If you like things spicier let plants mature, when mustard "heat" develops in the leaves. I love the fresh bite that arugula (sometimes called rucola, rocket salad or

Rucola, Italian arugula.

cultivated rocket) adds to sandwiches and salads, or when it is sautéed gently and then tossed with pasta.

Seed Saving

Arugula belongs to *Brassica hirta*, the white-flowered mustards. These biennials produce greens all season long. The following spring they bolt to seed when the soil warms up, and produce pretty black and white flowers, much admired in my garden. Flowers require insects for pollination, as they are self-incompatible. The seed pods are small, with about four round brown seeds in each. Arugula does not cross-pollinate with other brassica species, but it will cross with other varieties of white-flowered mustards within ½ mi. (800 m). Usual seed life: 2 years.

Perennial Arugula

Arugula sylvetta is a wild perennial Italian species, which for some has a preferred flavour. It's a compact sub-shrub with sprays of finely divided leaves. It only takes one plant to provide all the leaves you'll ever need. *Arugula sylvetta* is drought tolerant and cold hardy, but watch out—it self-seeds very readily. My advice is to not let it go to seed. Cut it back before the tiny yellow flowers mature into seeds, as it easily becomes a pest. Caution is required when you introduce wild plants into cultivated gardens!

Hey Presto! Arugula Pesto

2 cups (475 mL) young arugula (rocket) leaves

2 cloves garlic, peeled

½ cup (125 mL) chopped almonds, walnuts, cashews or pine nuts (your choice)

½ cup (125 mL) olive oil

½ cup (125 mL) fresh grated Parmesan cheese

½ tsp. (2.5 mL) salt (or to taste)

Whirl arugula, garlic and nuts in a food processor until well blended. Add the olive oil through the funnel in a slow steady stream, until a smooth paste has formed. Add the Parmesan and mix in. Cover with a thin layer of olive oil to prevent discolouration, and refrigerate in an airtight jar. Good for 2 weeks. Alternatively, freeze in ice-cube trays, and use cubes as needed.

Above: Flowers of arugula are very ornamental.

Left: Arugula sylvetta, *perennial arugula.*

ASPARAGUS

Asparagus is a perennial vegetable that requires patience for good yields, but is worth waiting for. An asparagus bed should preferably be prepared in fall, in preparation for spring planting. Dig it over to remove weeds and rocks and enrich the bed with Super-Duper compost. Once planted, asparagus roots remain undisturbed, where they produce increased harvests of spears each spring for years to come.

Spring is the time to plant asparagus "crowns." Select a permanent site in full sun, where 5-ft.-tall (1.5-m) ferny fronds won't cast unwanted shade on plants nearby. Space roots 2 ft. (60 cm) apart in rows 3 ft. (90 cm) apart. The crowns should be splayed over a raised mound set in a deep trench, and the trench carefully filled with soil around the roots, tamping it down to get rid of air pockets.

You can grow from seed, but it takes a few seasons to establish and identify the male plants from the female. It's much faster to start with two-year-old roots, preferably from male plants, which produce larger spears than females. You'll get a few meals of asparagus the first year after planting two-year-old roots, but it won't be until the next year that you will start to get better harvests. Nine years after planting, we enjoy feasting on asparagus for four to six weeks in early spring, as tender new shoots quickly grow to replace the harvested ones.

Harvest asparagus by snapping the spears off by hand, at the point where they break the easiest. This way the whole spear will be tender to eat. I harvest the fattest, most tender spears just before bud break, after which they become more fibrous and tougher to eat. My favourite way to eat asparagus is steamed for 10

Asparagus fronds in fall feed back roots.

Asparagus spears appear in early spring.

minutes and either tossed in lemon juice or dipped in butter or both!

It's best to stop harvesting in July to leave some fronds to develop. These tall feathery fronds replenish food in the roots, resulting in better production the following year. At the end of the season, when asparagus fronds turn yellow, cut them down and compost them, to avoid attracting asparagus beetle. Mulch the bed with Super-Duper compost, or aged manure and leaf mulch, and be sure to add dolomite lime, which asparagus loves.

If spears turn yellow and the outside of the stem is nibbled you've got asparagus beetles. The beetle and its grubs eat the stems and the leaves. If this happens, don't compost; instead, bury the plants. Handpick beetles as they appear in spring, and spray the plants with neem oil to make them taste awful.

ASPARAGUS PEAS

Asparagus peas (*Lotus tetragonolobus*) are small, low-growing bushy plants that are highly ornamental with bright flowers that can only be described as fire-truck red. Picked when young and tender, the winged seed pods of asparagus flavour are

eaten lightly steamed or raw with dips, but you will need a decent number of plants to get enough for a meal.

Start seeds indoors eight weeks before setting out, once all danger of frost has passed. Sow directly in the garden once the soil has warmed up, and thin the plants to 6 in. (15 cm) apart. The flowers are self-pollinating so there are no concerns about cross-pollination. Usual seed life: 2 years.

Asparagus pea.

BEANS

Beans have played an important role in the human diet since the dawn of agriculture because they are a good source of protein. Roughly 6,000 years ago the invention of pottery in South America enabled dried beans to be cooked and quickly they became a staple of many traditional diets. Heirloom beans have been handed down through generations and transported all over the world in the pockets of migrants, who took their precious seeds with them. Many have stories to tell, like the 'Cherokee Trail of Tears', brought from Tennessee to Oklahoma by Cherokee Indians in the terrible winter of 1838 to1839, and the 'Lazy Housewife' pole bean, introduced by Burpee in 1888, which is so prolific and stringless that it actually lives up to its name!

While beans in combination with grains, seeds or nuts provide complete dietary amino-acid (protein) balance; soybeans are the legume that contains all eight essential amino acids the body cannot manufacture itself, which makes them a complete protein and extremely valuable food source.

Beans are a source of "slow-release" carbohydrate, which controls diabetes by regulating blood-sugar levels. They are low in fat (apart from soybeans) and also provide dietary fibre, which lowers blood lipids and cholesterol levels. Beans are rich in iron, calcium, phosphorus and other minerals, and vitamin A and many B vitamins. Beans are low in cost, do not need preserving, and lose very little nutrient in processing—although nothing beats the flavour of beans from your own garden.

Legumes grow best in the presence of bacteria, with which they have a symbiotic relationship. Rhizobia bacteria live in the root nodules fixing atmospheric nitrogen and adding it to the soil, which benefits the plant. Where legumes have not grown

Amethyst purple bush beans.

before, using a soil inoculant of rhizobacteria will benefit growth in the first year. After this, bacteria grow on for years. You can purchase bacterial inoculant through seed catalogues; it consists of extremely fine black powder and is used to coat soaked seeds with just before planting. TIP: After harvesting, don't pull the roots of legumes out of the soil. Instead cut them off at ground level, leaving the bacteria in the root nodules in the soil.

Pole beans or bush beans are tender annuals, warm-season plants that need to be planted after all danger of frost, in a site that ideally receives full sun. The best timing for seeding is just after heavy rainfall, followed by a long, warm, dry spell. Warm soil over 75°F (24°C) is needed for germination; in cool soils below 55°F (13°C) seeds will not germinate and will rot. Due to the unsettled nature of spring these days,

I prefer not to leave germination to chance, so I start beans indoors and transplant established seedlings into the garden in June. TIP: Beans do not survive transplanting well, so plant seeds into pots or soil blocks individually, so that roots are not disturbed when planting out.

Plant bush beans 6 in. (15 cm) apart in the row, the rows 2 ft. (60 cm) apart. For continuous harvests plant at 3-week intervals. For pole beans plant 4 to 6 seeds around each post of a teepee, or sow them at 3-in. (8-cm) intervals along a support system (fencing, bamboo or strings) and thin to the strongest plants. Teepees are easy to construct using jute twine, and make an attractive feature in the garden. Climbing pole beans yield up to three times as many beans as bush beans, and take up a fraction of the space, but they mature later in the season.

Runner Beans

Runner beans are actually perennials, although they are almost always grown as annuals. Most gardeners don't know that if you dig up the roots before winter and store them in a damp, frost-free place, they can be replanted the following spring after danger of frost. Underground storage organs are what distinguish runner beans (*Phaseolus coccineus*) from pole beans (*Phaseolus vulgaris*), this and the fact that the beans are bigger. In some parts of the world it's the green snap beans that are favoured, whereas in others it's the shelled beans.

Soybeans

Soybeans grow on short sturdy bushes that are drought tolerant once the deep taproot gets

'Lazy Housewife' Bean (1882)

'Lazy Housewife' beans date back to 1882, and got their name because they are prolific, and set beans in easy-to-pick clusters. In 1907, 'Lazy Housewife' was the third most popular bean in the US, with Burpee's 1888 catalogue declaring "they are broad, thick, very fleshy and entirely stringless! Many persons have testified that they never ate a bean quite so good in distinct rich flavour." 'Lazy Housewife' also produces first-rate shelled beans if the pods are left to ripen longer.

'Painted Lady' Runner Bean (1753)

This heritage bean is also known as the 'York and Lancaster' bean. It has flowers that are half red and half white, that attract hummingbirds and admiring glances alike. This is where a 10-ft. (3-m) teepee comes in handy. Plant 6 seeds around each pole, and thin to the strongest plants, or just let them battle it out! Harvest young beans anywhere from 70 to 90 days, depending on the weather. The more you pick, the more they produce, and it's best to harvest the young beans before they get stringy.

'Lazy Housewife' pole beans.

'Painted Lady' runner beans.

established. Seeds germinate at 60°F (16°C), so warm days and cool nights are important at the time of sowing. Eating fresh green edamame beans out of the pods, after boiling for 5 minutes in salted water, is a gourmet treat. You can also freeze them. Yields are not as high as for other beans, because soybeans only produce 2 to 3 beans in each pod. TIP: Keep weeds down in the early stages of growth, as soybeans are slow to establish and do not appreciate competition.

Lima Beans

Limas need warmer soil than soybeans for germination, and can be eaten fresh or dried. Cultivation is basically the same as for soybeans, except that limas need a longer growing season. If plants turn yellow it's a sign that you are overwatering. These beans are good producers—my friend Dan Jason can get 10 lb. (4.5 kg) of lima beans from a 50-ft. (15-m) row.

'Winifred's' garbanzo beans.

Garbanzo Beans and Lentils

Both these beans germinate well in cool moist soils, and can be grown like peas as soon as the soil can be worked in early spring. Garbanzos (also called chickpeas) grow 2 ft. tall (60 cm) with surprisingly attractive foliage and tiny, pretty pink flowers.

Lentils are small branching plants that grow in tufts about 1 ft. (30 cm) off the ground. Small white or blue flowers come before seed production, usually 2 seeds in each flat pod. Different cultivars of lentils and garbanzos do not cross-pollinate with each other.

THE LEGUMINOSAE FAMILY

Legumes are nitrogen fixers, adding nitrogen to the soil. Beans are grown as fresh snap beans or dried beans, and sometimes the plant provides both.

White beans:
- Cannellini
- Great northern
- Navy
- White kidney

Red beans:
- Mexican
- Pinto
- Red kidney

Black beans:
- Black-eyed beans (also called peas)

Various:
- Garbanzo beans or chickpeas (*Cicer arietinum*)
- Lentils (*Lens culinaris*)
- Lima beans (*Phaseolus lunatus*)
- Soybean (*Glycine max*)

Seed Saving

The beauty and diversity of bean seeds makes them very desirable to collect. Grassroots networks of seed savers around the world maintain thousands

Beans Baked in a Bottle

Serve with a baguette and glass of wine
Serves 6

2 cups (475 mL) dried cannellini, navy or
   small lima beans
1 Tbsp. (15 mL) flour
3 sage leaves
2 garlic cloves, chopped
1 Tbsp. (15 mL) olive oil
Hot water
Dressing:
½ cup (125 mL) olive oil
¼ cup (60 mL) balsamic vinegar
3 Tbsp. (45 mL) liquid honey
2 tsp. (10 mL) Dijon mustard

1 tsp. (5 mL) salt
½ tsp. (2.5 mL) pepper

Soak beans in 5 cups water with 1 Tbsp. (15 mL) flour for 8 hours or overnight.

Preheat oven to 325°F (160°C)

Drain and rinse the beans, and pour into a 1-qt. (1-L) mason jar. Add the sage, garlic, olive oil and enough hot water to fill the jar ¾ in. (2 cm) above the beans. Put the jar in the hot oven and cover the top with foil. Bake the beans until tender, for approx. 2 hours. Turn beans out of the jar and mix the beans with the dressing. Serve warm.

of varieties of beans. Saving beans is a good place to begin because they are self-pollinating, which means they have "perfect" flowers with both male and female reproductive parts inside. Neither insects nor wind are required for pollination, and because there are no concerns regarding out-crossing with other beans, you can grow a large number of different varieties at the same time. TIP: You can only grow one variety of lima bean at a time, however, as they will cross-pollinate within a mile of each other.

To be on the safe side I plant a different crop (e.g., tomatoes) between rows of bush beans, and space pole-bean teepees a minimum of 30 ft. (9 m) apart. To collect seeds leave beans to dry on the bushes, and harvest by pulling up the whole row of plants at once. Usual seed life: 3 years.

BEANS (BROAD)

Buttery without the cholesterol, broad beans are a special treat. *Vicia faba* is the botanical name for this legume member of the pea family Fabaceae. The genus *Vicia* indicates fava beans are vetches,

nitrogen fixers, which means they can be grown as cover crops that add both nitrogen and organic matter to soil. They also have deep taproots that break up compacted soils. I love the fact that I can grow a crop of beans and improve my soil at the same time! When grown as a cover crop, plants are turned under before they set seed, and allowed three to four weeks for breakdown before the area is replanted.

Being a cool-weather crop, favas can be planted in November or the following year in March. In wet winters, there's a good chance seeds will rot in cold soils. For this reason, I stopped planting in November, and now wait until March. This way I get 95 percent germination, and the only difference is that I harvest beans later—in July/August now, instead of in May/June.

Plant 4 in. (10 cm) deep, 6 in. (15 cm) apart in the rows, the rows 9 in. (23 cm) apart. TIP: Experiment and keep 50 percent of your seeds back for spring planting, and decide which strategy works best for your microclimate.

Large, fur-lined pods are produced in pairs on tall stalks; seeds can produce up to 3 stalks with several

'Sweet Lorane' small-seeded favas are very productive.

Crimson-flowered broad beans (1778).

pairs of pods on each, what I call a good harvest. I wrap jute twine around the bean patch in mid May to prevent the heavily ladened stalks from falling over. In 2009, crimson-flowered favas seeded as a 20-by 4-ft. block (6 by 1.2 m) yielded 8 lb. (3.8 kg) of dried beans.

Bean weevils may be a problem in early spring— you'll know by notched edges on seedling leaves. Weevil populations build up over years of growing beans, so I make sure I rotate crops yearly. A few sprays of neem oil (or an application of neem seed cake, which acts as a systemic) stops weevils from eating bean plants, and allows the plants to outgrow the ground-dwelling insects' attacks.

Black aphids can be a problem for beans in late spring, when they colonize tips of tall plants. (The only benefit is that the aphids attract ladybugs, so you could regard this as a good "lure" situation.) If aphid colonies build up, I snap infested tops off the stalks; aphids don't fly, they crawl, so it takes a long time for colonies to re-establish. Removing the tip signals the plant to set seed and matures the beans. In the beginning aphids do not affect the quality or production of beans, and are just an eyesore, but if

left to smother the plant they could weaken it beyond recovery.

Broad beans are harvested for fresh eating when the seeds swell in the green pods. Properly cooked, fresh-shelled favas have a sweet, buttery "melt-in-the-mouth" appeal. Freeze any fresh beans that you don't eat; just throw them still frozen into boiling water for 10 minutes, after which they taste as good as fresh. Drizzle with olive oil, lemon juice, minced garlic or herbs of your choice—yum!

They can also be harvested as dried beans, when the pods are black and the beans inside hardened. To eat the dried beans they need to be soaked overnight, and then cooked for about 75 minutes.

Favas have no cholesterol and little oil, but they are high in carbohydrate and protein, averaging about 30 percent protein.

Favas are large-seeded (e.g., 'Green Windsor', 'Mr. Barton's', 'Aquadulce') or small-seeded (e.g., 'Sweet Lorane'). Fava beans have pretty black and white flowers, with the exception of one variety, the small-seeded crimson-flowered broad bean that dates back to 1778. Apparently all favas were originally crimson-flowered before plant breeders started creating new varieties.

I got a few precious seeds of the crimson-flowered broad bean in 1997 from the Henry Doubleday Heritage Seed Library in the UK and have been growing them ever since. I know that by planting and sharing these seeds, I am ensuring this bean will be around for future generations. Growing heritage plants preserves our plant heritage, as well as genetic diversity for future generations.

Seed Saving

Even though these beans are capable of self-pollination, they carry flowers attractive to pollinating bees, so it is possible that different strains of favas could cross up. In my experience, 50 ft. (15 m) of separation between different cultivars has been sufficient to prevent accidental crossing. However, if you get an "off type" the next year, it will need to be "rogued" out. The lower pods on the stalk are the first to mature seed. Usual seed life: 3 years.

BEETROOT

Beetroot (*Beta vulgaris*) was domesticated as either a garden vegetable (chard and sugar beets) or for fodder (mangels). We eat beets in a variety of ways—grated on summer salads, boiled and sliced, hot or cold, oven-baked with other roasted vegetables, with olive oil and balsamic vinegar, and pickled. TIP: Because of their high sugar content, beets are not recommended for diabetics.

Beets prefer rich, well-drained sandy loam that has been well manured and dug over. TIP: Add manure in the fall, as fresh manure causes the roots to fork. Beets are best seeded in drills for ease of hoeing, and to better distinguish emerging seedlings from weeds. Dig a shallow trench and add potash by sprinkling the bottom of the trench with granular kelp or wood ash; if your soil is poor in phosphorus add granular rock phosphate for root development. If beets are not sweet, it may be due to a lack of boron in the soil;

boron can be supplied by sprinkling borax very lightly over the soil at the rate of 1 tsp. (5 mL) per sq. yd. (.84 sq. m)

RECOMMENDED VARIETIES

'Lutz' or 'Winterkeeper': large beets and nutritious greens.

'Golden Detroit': orange beets turn golden-yellow when cooked.

'Bull's Blood': smaller beets with red/purple baby leaves.

'Detroit Dark Red': good storage beet, sweet flavour, lots of greens.

Direct sowings of beets can be made in succession from late March until early August. Sow every three weeks from early spring to ensure continuous harvests. Plant seeds 1 in. (2.5 cm) apart, and thin the seedlings to 4 in. (10 cm) apart. Young seedlings withstand transplanting well, and using a dibber makes it really

Dibber and beet seedlings.

quick. Simply moisten the soil, and make a block of holes, 4 in. (10 cm) deep and 4 in. (10 cm) apart, using the dibber. Drop rooted seedlings into the holes, and use a rake to cover them. TIP: Beets thrive interplanted between other crops, but don't grow well if overshadowed—planting them out in the open works best.

Harvest root crops later in the day. Plants gather their vital life force from photosynthesis during sunlight hours, and at the end of the day redirect this force from their leaves to their roots. Root crops harvested later in the day have been shown to have better keeping qualities.

Beets are biennial—forming fleshy roots in the first year, setting seed in the second. Beets can be left in the ground, and mulched with straw or leaves, to get them through the winter in milder climates. In regions where they will freeze if left in the ground, they need to be dug up and stored. Beets store better than other root crops; cut tops at 1 in. (2.5 cm) above the crown, wash them and dry them before storage. Store between layers of clean dry sand in a place cool and dark enough to stop the roots from sprouting over winter. For seed, select the best beets for replanting.

Seed Saving

When beets go to seed, a tall ribbed stalk grows, bearing glomerules, clusters of light-brown seeds. Beetroot is pollinated by insects, and beet pollen is very fine, travelling far on the wind. Beets are in the Chenopodiaceae family, and will cross with other members of this family (e.g., chard, spinach and other sugar beets). For this reason, they must be isolated by ½ mi. (800 m) from any of these plants that are flowering at the same time.

In milder winters the roots will survive under protective mulch, and will set seed as soon as the ground warms up in early spring. In cold climates the

'Lutz' or 'Winterkeeper' beets.

roots have to be lifted and stored in order to save seed. To preserve the diversity of the strain, at least 12 plants must be selected to save seed from. Cut stalks down and strip the brown glomerules off by hand, wearing gloves. Stalks can be dried to ripen seeds if necessary, as long as the green glomerules have started to turn colour on the stalk. Sieve to remove dust and debris, and store the cleaned seeds in an airtight container in a cool, dark place. Usual seed life: 4 to 6 years.

BEET AND CHIVE DRESSING

Makes 2 cups (475 mL)

4 large or 6 to 8 small beets, cooked, peeled and chopped into ½ in. (1 cm) cubes.

¼ cup (60 mL) beet liquid reserved and processed in a blender with the beets until smooth.

Add:

2 Tbsp. (30 mL) vinegar

2 Tbsp. (30 mL) finely chopped chives

6 Tbsp. (90 mL) mayonnaise

BROCCOLI

Broccoli belongs to the Brassicaceae family (Cruciferae), along with cabbage, mustards, kohlrabi, Brussels sprouts, turnip, rutabaga, cauliflower, kale and collards. These cool-weather biennials grow best with cool days and cool nights, which means plentiful harvests of broccoli in spring and fall, in climates where soil does not freeze in the winter.

One head of steamed broccoli provides 3 g protein, 5 g dietary fibre, 75 mg vitamin C, and 1300 IU of beta carotene—with only 40 calories.

Broccoli for summer and fall harvest can be seeded indoors in March/April, but can also be direct seeded into the garden as soon as the ground warms up. Prepare soil by adding dolomite lime to sweeten it, and to discourage clubroot (see "Pests of Brassicas"). Broccoli plants are like tomatoes and will root along buried portions of the stalk, so bury plants deeper when you transplant. Allow 18 in. (46 cm) space for plants, with 2 ft. (60 cm) between rows. Brassicas are heavy feeders, so add screened compost to the planting hole or a balanced organic fertilizer NPK: 6-8-6 approx.

Sprouting Broccoli

Sprouting broccolis need a period of vernalization (200 days) to produce side shoots the following spring. Plants grow very slowly over winter months, and then grow fast when temperatures climb in spring. As soon as the main head is harvested, side shoots form in axils along the stalk to provide continuous harvests of broccoli shoots. TIP: Soak broccoli inverted in warm water before cooking so that any worms crawl out!

Start seeds in June/July for harvests the following spring. Seeds can be grown outdoors in summer, keeping them out of the hot sun. Keep seedlings off the ground for protection against slugs, earwigs, sowbugs and cabbage worms. Check for signs of damage often to control insect problems before they get established.

'Green Goliath' broccoli.

'Purple Sprouting' broccoli.

63

'Nine Star' Perennial Broccoli

This hardy perennial vegetable overwinters for harvests the following April/May/June. It produces large snow-white heads followed by good-sized white shoots for the next six to eight weeks. These sweet tender shoots make a delicious side vegetable when lightly steamed. The seeds can be direct seeded by June, or grown from transplants planted by the end of August. After harvest, simply cut the stalk back, which makes it regrow for another season of production. Expect good yields up to four years with this variety.

RECOMMENDED VARIETIES

'Green Goliath': Open-pollinated variety for huge yields of good-sized heads in summer/fall. Does not reliably overwinter.

Romanesco: Chartreuse-coloured buds spiral around 10-in. (25-cm) heads. Fantastic for veggie dips!

Broccoli Raab: Fast-growing plants in spring provide nutritious shoots of good flavour. Steam, stir-fry or sauté with your favourite sauce.

Italian Green Sprouting: A multi-cut variety with prolific production of heads and side shoots. Fast-maturing, only 50 days from spring and fall sowings.

Purple Sprouting: Overwinters to produce sweet purple shoots in spring for 6 to 8 weeks. Flowering shoots are tender and edible, and can be harvested until the yellow flowers open.

'Nine Star' Perennial White Sprouting: See above.

Seed Saving

Broccoli (*Brassica oleracea* var. *botrytis*) is self-incompatible so must be insect-pollinated. Save seeds from a minimum of six plants to preserve genetic

'Nine Star' perennial broccoli.

diversity. *Brassica oleracea* cross with other members of the same family flowering within 1 mi. (1.6 km). After the yellow flowers fade, seed pods will develop with small, round light-brown seeds. When stalks turn light brown, cut and dry them in paper bags or buckets. Thresh them against a wheelbarrow to collect the seeds, screen and winnow away remaining dust. Usual seed life: 4 years.

Pests of Brassicas

Members of the Brassicaceae family require similar cultural methods and are attacked by the same pests and diseases. Prevent problems by removing older and yellowed leaves from plants in October, which may carry disease and insect eggs, and by keeping an eye out for the following problems.

Aphids can sometimes be a problem on brassicas, but if spotted in time can be dislodged with a blast of water from the garden hose. Attracting predators such as ladybugs, lacewings or parasitic wasps will prevent the build-up of aphid colonies. Insecticidal soap sprays help if a jet of water does not do the job.

Cabbage white butterflies flit about in summer, and lay eggs on the undersides of the leaves; these hatch into hungry green worms that munch raggedy holes into the leaves. Floating row covers can be used as prevention. Insecticidal soaps or neem oil sprays also help. Side-dressing with neem seed cake works as a systemic insecticide.

Flea beetles are shiny, black beetles that hop and feed on leaves of cabbage plants, leaving tiny round holes behind. Break the life cycle of this pest by not planting brassicas between April and June when the adults emerge. A soil drench using parasitic nematodes will work to eliminate this pest, and covering brassicas with floating row cover deprives pests of contact with host plants. A side dressing with neem seed cake, which acts as a systemic insecticide, is also effective.

Cabbage maggots may be a problem. Adult flies lay eggs in spring near cabbage plants. These hatch into larvae that spend the next few weeks boring into the roots, stunting the plant and destroying the harvest. Wilting at midday is the first sign of this problem. Remedies include applying parasitic nematodes to the soil while it is warm and moist. Floating row covers will prevent the adult from laying her eggs on the plants. Wood ash piled around the base of the stalk also works for moderate problems with cabbage maggots.

Cutworms chew plants off at the soil line. If cutworms are a problem, use collars around the base of newly transplanted seedlings to protect them. Slip a 4-in. (10-cm) cylinder made from an open-ended yoghurt tub or old tin can (with both ends cut off) over the seedlings. Push the collars at least 1 in. (2.5 cm) deep into the soil. Biological nematodes may need to be applied in spring to destroy heavy infestations of cutworms. Cultivating the soil brings cutworms up to the surface where birds will eat them.

Cabbage loopers result when grey moths lay green eggs on the underside of leaves. Caterpillars (of about 1½ in./4 cm and with two white lines down the side) chew large raggedy holes in the leaves, and can destroy the whole plant. Loopers move by looping their bodies. Control by handpicking, attracting parasitic wasps, or using sprays of insecticidal soap.

Slugs and snails love all members of the cabbage family. They rasp holes in leaves and may demolish seedlings. Lay a wooden board down and inspect underneath weekly for slugs and egg masses. You'll be amazed how many you find! Protect seedlings with wide bands of wood ash (uncontaminated) around the base.

Clubroot is a slime mould fungus that is attracted by plants in the Brassicaceae family. Crop rotations for members of this family are vital because clubroot persists in soil for seven years. Plants are affected by wilt in the day, and eventually yellow and die off. If you pull the roots up, you will see knobby distortions on them that look like fingers and toes. This fungus thrives in acidic soils, so you can control it by adding lime to adjust the pH to 7.5. Remove and destroy infected plants; bury them, do not compost them. TIP: Try destroying clubroot spores by "cooking" the soil; use black plastic to cover affected areas in July and August. If successful you should be able to plant a disease-free crop of brassicas afterwards.

NEEM SEED CAKE

Neem seed cake is the by-product of neem oil extraction and has been found to act as both a fertilizer and a systemic insecticide. This year I experimented by side-dressing brassicas with it, and found that plants grew like crazy with no damage from flea beetles or cabbage worms.

BRUSSELS SPROUTS

Brussels sprouts belong to the Brassicaceae (Cruciferae) family, along with broccoli, cabbage, mustards, kohlrabi, turnip, rutabaga, cauliflower, kale and collards. These cool-weather biennials grow best around 60°F (16°C), as cool temperatures are important for quality sprouts. "Little cabbages" grow from buds in the crook of the leaf base and stalk. One stalk can produce 75 to 100 sprouts. Frosts make the "little cabbage" heads grow tight and sweet, so that kids may actually enjoy homegrown sprouts that are full of beta carotene and vitamin C.

I seed Brussels sprouts indoors in March for transplants; but they can also be direct seeded in the

Brussels sprouts are sweetest after heavy frosts.

garden as soon as the ground warms up. Brussels sprouts are heavy feeders, so add screened compost to the planting hole, or a balanced organic fertilizer NPK: 6-8-6 approx. Plants need 18-in. (46-cm) spacing to allow room for the 3-ft.-tall (90-cm) plants to grow.

The important thing is to get plants established in time to serve Brussels sprouts for Thanksgiving! They take around 120 days to mature from transplanting, so get them in the garden by May for an October harvest.

For pest prevention, see "Pests of Brassicas."

TIPS FOR SUCCESS
- Prepare the soil by adding dolomite lime to sweeten it and discourage clubroot.
- Soils with high-nitrogen content result in loose-leaved sprouts that do not "bud up,"

so do not add high-nitrogen fertilizer after spring.
- Snap the top off stalks in fall to encourage development of upper sprouts.
- Leave stalks in the garden through winter. Harvest by twisting individual sprouts off the stalk, starting at the base.
- Prevent problems by removing older yellowed leaves from plants in October. They may carry disease and egg masses of the cabbage white butterfly.
- If seed saving, take the bottom sprouts at the start of the season, save the middle ones (the best for seed saving), and skip to the top of the stalk for the rest of the season.

Seed Saving

Brussels sprouts (*Brassica oleracea* var. *gemmifera*) are self-incompatible and must be insect-pollinated. Therefore, more than one plant is necessary to save seed. Ideally, collect seeds from a minimum of six plants to preserve genetic diversity. Brussels sprouts will cross with other members of *Brassica oleracea*—cabbage, broccoli, kale, cauliflower, or kohlrabi flowering close by. You'll need 1 mi. (1.6 km) of separation to prevent this.

As long as the temperature does not drop below 14°F (-10°C) during winter, Brussels sprouts survive. In spring sprouts not harvested split open and send out a flower stalk. TIP: You can knife a shallow cross into the top of the sprout to stimulate this. After the yellow flowers fade, seed pods will develop small, round light-brown seeds. When the colour turns to light brown, cut down stalks to dry them in paper bags or buckets and thresh them against a wheelbarrow to collect the seeds. Screen and winnow away the dust. Usual seed life: 4 years.

CABBAGE

Cabbages belong to three distinct groups—spring, summer and winter—which refer to the time of harvest and not the time of planting. There are two distinct categories of cabbages—heading cabbages (*Brassica oleracea* var. *capitata*) or non-heading cabbages (*Brassica rapa* var. *chinensis* and var. *pekinensis*). Non-heading cabbages have clusters of wrapped leaves, rather than a tight ball head. There are three types of heading cabbage—green, red and savoy. Savoy cabbages have crinkled leaves with mild flavour and are extremely winter hardy. Homegrown cabbage, harvested fresh from the garden, tastes like a different vegetable than the cabbage you buy in the store.

Cabbages are biennials that thrive when the air is cool and moist. Summer cabbage is seeded indoors in March, but can also be direct seeded into the garden as soon as the ground warms up in early spring. Winter cabbage seedlings can be started in spring, and transplanted around the garden in July/August, filling in spaces where earlier crops of lettuces, bush beans, potatoes or garlic have been harvested.

Chinese cabbages (*Brassica rapa*) grow fast and will go to seed if sown too early. It's best to wait until mid June to sow these cabbages outdoors, where they form medium to large heads of sweet, pale-green leaves that can be eaten raw or lightly steamed. They are not winter hardy, so make successive sowings from June onwards for good harvests before winter.

Prepare soil by adding dolomite lime to lower the pH, as well as to discourage clubroot (see "Pests of Brassicas"). Add screened compost or a balanced organic fertilizer (NPK: 6-8-6) when transplanting. Cabbage plants, like tomatoes, root along portions of the buried stalk, so bury seedlings deeper when transplanting. Allow 18 in. (46 cm) of space between plants, and 2 ft. (60 cm) of space between rows. Cabbages are heavy feeders, so to encourage the formation of good-sized heads mulch between rows of cabbage in summer with a generous application of aged manure or Super-Duper compost.

Recommended Open-pollinated Varieties

'Early Jersey Wakefield': This heirloom cabbage has been grown in the Howe Sound region since 1890. A summer cabbage with pointy heads of medium size and fine flavour, that takes two months to mature from transplant.

'First Early Market': A non-heading spring cabbage with smaller conical wrapped heads; overwinters for tasty greens the following spring.

'Red Express': Early, smaller, uniform red cabbages with good colour throughout. TIP: Plant a block of these at 8-in. (20-cm) spacing for a knockout display in the garden.

'Danish Ballhead': A tender general-purpose cabbage perfect for coleslaw, sauerkraut and cooking. Large 9-in. (23-cm) heads are well wrapped for protection through winter.

Seed Saving

Cabbage (*Brassica oleracea*) is self-incompatible, so plants need insects for pollination. Choose your best 6 to 12 cabbages to save seed from in order to preserve genetic diversity. *Brassica oleracea* will cross with other varieties of the same genus if flowering within 1 mi. (1.6 km). Chinese cabbage (*Brassica rapa*) and Asian greens (*Brassica juncea*) must also be separated by a mile. Sometimes a deep-cut cross made in the head is

Jennifer and her giant 'Derby Day' summer cabbage.

'Red Express' cabbage.

needed to allow the seed stalk to emerge. After the yellow flowers fade, seed pods develop with small, round reddish-brown seeds. Harvest stalks when pods are just turning colour, and dry in bags or buckets. Thresh against a wheelbarrow to release the seeds; screen them and blow away any remaining dust. Usual seed life: 4 years.

APPLE GINGER KIM CHI

10 cups (2.4 L) (1 medium head) green cabbage, very thinly sliced using a mandoline

⅓ cup (80 mL) coarse sea salt
Toss the cabbage with the salt, coat well and leave overnight to sit.

Drain off the resulting liquid.

1 cup (250 mL) onion, thinly diced

4 green apples, grated

2 Tbsp. (30 mL) ginger, finely minced

1 cup (250 mL) carrots, grated
Add the above ingredients, toss and let sit again for a few hours. Drain juices.

Put the kim chi into a quart glass jar (or ceramic crock), stuffing the jar as tightly as possible, leaving ½-in. (1-cm) space at the top. Leave to ferment anywhere from 7 to 10 days at 50°F (10°C), draining liquid off as necessary. When fermentation stops, the kim chi is done. Store in the fridge for up to 6 months, or process in a water canner for 25 minutes in water at a rolling boil.

CARDOON

Cardoon (*Cynara cardunculus*) is a striking perennial and relative of the artichoke, considered a delicacy in Italy. It is the young celery-like stalks that are edible, marinated or steamed, not the flowers as with globe artichokes. Clumps of serrated silvery leaves emerge in January, and stunning purple thistle-like flowers appear in July. TIP: When they reach 2 ft. (60 cm) tall, wrap newspaper around the plant and harvest more tender "blanched" stalks later. Cardoons grow fast, reaching 6 ft. (1.8 m) in height, so make sure you have room when you plant them. Cardoon is winter hardy, and can be propagated by division of young offsets in spring; offsets need to be divided every three years. Cardoon transplants can also be started from seed indoors. For seed-saving tips, see "Artichoke." Usual seed life: 7 years.

*Cardoon (*Cynara cardunculus*) is spectacular dried for floral arrangements. Kristin Ross photo*

CARROT

Carrots hail from Afghanistan, where they were grown in all colours from purple to red to yellow. The first orange carrots came from Holland in the seventeenth century. When you see the list of varieties below you'll know that there's no excuse to become bored with carrots! TIP: Carrots are high in beta carotene and minerals, but only if you do not peel them, as most of the nutrient is in the peel or just under it.

Recommended Open-pollinated Varieties

'Yellowstone': A sunny-yellow carrot that grows to 10 in. (25 cm) long in light sandy soils.

'Atomic Red': Red-skinned, with orange flesh and yellow core, tapered to 9 in. (23 cm).

'Cosmic Purple': Danvers type tapered to 8 in. (20 cm) with deep-purple skin, orange flesh and bright-yellow core.

'Thumbelina': Thumb-sized orange carrots, which work well in containers.

'Scarlet Nantes': A classic among carrots, good flavour with almost no core. Nantes carrots have blunt rather than tapered roots.

Seed of Apiaceae (Umbelliferae) plants is slow to germinate, and must also be fresh for germination. Carrots are usually direct seeded in spring, as soon as the soil has warmed up. They need a fine-textured sandy loam; so heavy clay soils need to be lightened with organic matter—this should be added in fall, because newly manured soil causes roots to fork. Double digging and incorporating drainage material such as coarse washed sand creates a well-drained open soil that carrots thrive in.

For direct seeding, create shallow drills using a hoe and try carefully to broadcast the seeds at ½-in. (1-cm) spacing. After seeding, fill the drills with lightweight growing medium or coarse washed sand to help the tiny carrot seeds germinate. TIP: Take care not to compact the soil where carrots are to be grown, it causes the roots to fork.

Thin carrots when ¾ in. (2 cm) tall to 1 in.

(2.5 cm) apart. In areas where soil does not freeze, carrots can stay in the ground through winter, though they fare better under protective mulches. Beware that the more time root vegetables spend in the ground, the more likely you are to find wormholes in the crop when harvested.

'Scarlet Nantes' carrots

STORING CARROTS FOR WINTER

Dig carrots up on a dry day just after the first frost. Wipe off excess soil and cut the foliage to within 1 in. (2.5 cm) of the crown. Leave the roots exposed on all sides to dry, until the skin is toughened but the root is still firm. Carrots can be stored layered in damp sand, sawdust or peat moss in rodent-proof boxes kept in a cool, dark place. Removing any carrots that rot during storage helps preserve the rest.

Problems with Carrots

Wireworms: If plants start dying it could be wireworms. The damage is worst in gardens where grass sod has just been removed. These ½-in. (1-cm) yellow/brown worms are the larvae of click beetles that feed on grass roots; when starving they will attack the seedlings of corn, potatoes, tomatoes, lettuce, squash and peppers.

Carrots and potatoes act as lures for wireworms, and can be planted as effective monitors of potential problems. Crop rotations of root vegetables are important to break the life cycles of these pests. An application of parasitic nematodes when the soil is warm and moist can also effectively solve wireworm infestations. TIP: Never sow carrots on ground that has recently grown carrots, parsnips or any Apiaceae relations. Maggots or pupae of the carrot rust fly may still be in the soil, waiting for a new crop.

Carrot Rust Fly: The carrot rust fly is a shiny

A bed planted using the "Nifty Carrot Trick."

Harvesting the results.

THE NIFTY CARROT TRICK

1. Fill a 4-in. (10-cm) pot with sterile seed mix.
2. Sprinkle 12 to 15 carrot seeds evenly across the top. Cover lightly.
3. After seedlings establish, feed them with liquid fish fertilizer.
4. Plant blocks of carrots out after all danger of frost. Remove rooted plugs that are 4 in. (10 cm) tall, and plant them in the garden without disturbing the roots.
5. Plant plugs 6 in. (15 cm) apart in rows 6 in. (15 cm) apart. The carrots will outgrow the weeds.
6. Dig entire bunches of baby carrots by pulling up the foliage or harvest as individual carrots left to grow on until larger.

black fly that lays eggs in the soil. The eggs hatch into maggots that tunnel into the roots of carrots, parsnips, parsley and celeriac. Adults emerge in May to hang around until heavy frost. I prevent attacks by making it unnecessary to thin carrot seedlings. I now seed carrots in pots and grow them in small bunches using the "Nifty Carrot Trick" (see sidebar).

TIP: Create a physical barrier against the carrot rust fly by covering carrot seeds with horticultural fleece (Reemay™). Alternatively, confuse the fly by disguising the carrot smell with a stronger one. I have had great success mulching my carrot patch with organic coffee grounds (plentiful from local coffee shops).

Seed Saving

Carrots belong to the Apiaceae (Umbelliferae) family. These plants have flowers called umbels that are umbrella-shaped. Angelica, celeriac, chervil, coriander, dill, fennel, lovage, sweet cicely, parsley and parsnips also belong to the Apiaceae family.

Carrots are biennial root crops that unless grown in mild winter climates will need to be dug up, stored in damp sand, and replanted the following spring. They must have matured enough by the end of the first growing season to withstand storage over winter to set seed the following spring. Choose the most choice, "true to type" roots to replant. A minimum of six plants is needed to preserve the genetic diversity of a variety.

After all danger of frost in spring the carrots are replanted, where they put up a stalk with flowering umbels. Each tiny flower on the umbel needs to be pollinated by insects, in time to produce two seeds by the end of the second growing season. Different species do not cross with each other, but varieties of the same species will. Saving carrot seed is tricky due to the prevalence of wild carrot, 'Queen Anne's Lace', which cross-pollinates with carrots within a ½ mi. (800 m). TIP: Never save seed from plants that go to seed in the first year, as bolting to seed is undesirable for biennial root crops.

CAULIFLOWER

It is said that growing cauliflower is one of the simplest and one of the most difficult things to do. I think it's worth trying, because the flavour of fresh-cut cauliflower is "melt-in-the-mouth" unbeatable!

Cauliflower is grown for heads of curds, nestled inside large wrapper leaves. The extent to which the head is wrapped depends on the variety, but snow-white heads, 6 to 10 in. (15 to 25 cm) in diameter, are the ideal. Tying wrapper leaves up over the emerging head blocks out sunlight, which prevents yellowing. Some varieties are self-blanching, but often produce smaller heads.

Cauliflower can be grown in two distinct seasons. It can be seeded in late winter for a fall crop, or seeded in summer for a crop the following spring. The plants should be thinned to 18 in. (46 cm) with 2 ft. (60 cm) between rows. Cauliflower is a heavy feeder,

'Purple Cape' winter cauliflower.

The Garden Path Cauliflower Cheese

Preheat oven to 350°F (175°C)

Makes 6 servings

1 large head of cauliflower (4 cups/1 L),
  chopped into large florets

Steam for 10 minutes. Drain.

1 large onion, chopped

3 cloves of garlic, minced

2 bay leaves

½ cup (125 mL) green peas, fresh or frozen

2 Tbsp. (30 mL) butter or olive oil

*Sauté together for 5 minutes, until soft. Mix
with the steamed cauliflower.*

Cheese Sauce

Melt ¼ cup (60 mL) butter in a saucepan.

Remove the pan from the heat.

*Stir in 1 Tbsp. (15 mL) flour to form a smooth
roux, using a wooden spoon.*

*Slowly pour in 4 cups (1 L) milk, stirring
for a smooth consistency.*

*Add 2 cups (475 mL) of grated cheddar
cheese, stir until well blended.*

*Season with a dash of Worcestershire
sauce.*

*Remove bay leaf and pour cheese sauce
over the vegetables.*

Mix:

1 cup (250 mL) breadcrumbs

1 cup (250 mL) grated Parmesan cheese

*Cover vegetables with a layer of
breadcrumbs and Parmesan, and fresh
sliced tomatoes if handy. Bake about 25
minutes, until the top has browned.*

so add screened compost to the planting hole or a balanced organic fertilizer (NPK: 6-8-6). TIP: Prepare the soil by adding dolomite lime to sweeten it and discourage clubroot. In order to survive winter, 6-in. (15-cm) transplants need to be planted in the garden by mid August. Overwintering cauliflowers are easier to grow than spring varieties.

Root maggots may be a problem for cauliflower seedlings. For information on pest prevention, see "Pests of Brassicas."

GROWING TIPS

- Rich and moisture-ladened soil is key to growing the best cauliflowers.
- The growth of plants must proceed rapidly without being checked; the quick formation of curds is desirable.
- Cauliflower is the most delicate of the cabbage family and less tolerant to extremes of temperature.
- Mulching with aged manure in hot summers is invaluable for good-sized cauliflowers (or a drenching with manure tea).
- Keep soil moist at all times; frequent watering is essential.
- Pull roots up and do not compost; bury in a trench to avoid spreading clubroot.

Seed Saving

If plants are set out in the garden early enough they usually set seed during the first year. Whether seeds ripen or not depends on growing conditions. Select cauliflowers with the largest heads to collect seeds from. After the yellow flowers fade, seed pods develop with small, round brown seeds. TIP: Pinch out the top flowers to help produce larger seeds on the lower flowering branches.

Brassica oleracea var. *botrytis* is self-incompatible and must be insect-pollinated. Therefore you need more than one plant to save seed. Ideally seeds should be saved from a minimum of 6 plants to preserve the genetic diversity of cauliflower plants. Cauliflowers cross with cabbage, broccoli, kale, Brussels sprouts or kohlrabi of the same species. To prevent cross-pollination, ½ mi. (800 m) separation between these plants is required. When light brown, cut down seed stalks, and dry them in paper bags or buckets. Thresh the dried stalks against a wheelbarrow to collect the seeds. Screen and winnow to remove chaff and dust. Usual seed life: 4 years.

CELERY AND CELERIAC

Celery and celeriac are in the carrot family, Apiaceae (formerly Umbelliferae). Celery is grown for its stalks and leaves, while celeriac is grown for baseball-sized roots with a strong celery flavour but potato-like consistency. I have always had trouble growing celery that is palatable. It is often stringy and bitter. My neighbour had a bed full of the best-looking celery I'd ever seen, and when asked her secret, she said she bought organic celery at the supermarket, cut it off at the base and planted it. It actually rooted! Huh!

Celery/celeriac has a long 100-day growing season, and needs cool moist soil with high fertility to thrive. Because of this long season, transplanting is recommended. Start indoors three months before setting out. Seed is slow to germinate, taking 14 to 28 days, and requires warm temperatures of 70°F (21°C) for germination. Transplant 6-in. (15-cm) seedlings outdoors in warm soil, adding balanced organic fertilizer to keep soil fertility levels high.

'Tango' is an open-pollinated short-season variety of celery (85 days) that is ready to harvest 2 weeks earlier than other varieties.

Non-stringy stalks have good flavour and are self-blanching.

There was a time when celery was blanched by hilling up soil around the base. This method is no longer used as it allows soil to fall between the stalks, encouraging rot and causing problems with grit when eating. Today celery is grown in square blocks, 12 in. (30 cm) apart in rows with 12 in. (30 cm) between rows. To prevent sunlight from reaching the stalks, 12-in.-wide (30-cm) planks are placed against the celery, using 18-in. (46-cm) stakes on the outside to keep the boards from falling away.

'Mentor' celeriac.

Tips

- If direct seeding in warm soil, prepare drills in the garden. Fill these with coarse washed sand, and sow the tiny seed shallowly on the sand. Cover lightly and keep moist. Thin seedlings to 6 in. (15 cm) apart. Self-blanching celery is blanched by growing plants close together.
- Never sow celery/celeriac on ground that has recently grown carrots, parsnips or any Apiaceae

relative. Maggots or pupae of the carrot rust fly may still be in the soil.

- Cut the head off with a knife at the base leaving roots in place. The plant may withstand mild winters to produce leafy pickings in spring, perfect for soups and winter salads.
- Harvested celery stores up to two weeks in a cool fridge. If your celery wilts, cut the ends off the stalks and stand them in a glass of water in the fridge, where they will soon perk up.

Seed Saving

Celery (*Apium graveolens* var. *secalinum*) and celeriac (*Apium graveolens* var. *rapaceum*) are biennial plants belonging to the same species, so they will cross-pollinate. A distance of ½ mi. (800 m) from each other must separate celery species flowering at the same time.

In cold winters celery may need to be harvested and stored around 32°F (0°C), insulated by layers of damp straw, coco peat, sawdust or wood shavings or burlap bags. The plants are replanted the following spring, leaving 24 in. (61 cm) of space between them. They will bush out, and produce flowering stalks 24 in. (61 cm) tall. Ripe seed from umbels can be collected as it turns brown and hardens. Several harvests are needed for Apiaceae plants, because they ripen seeds over a long period. Usual seed life: 3 years.

COLLARDS

Collards are cold-hardy members of the cabbage family, Brassicaceae, and are basically thick cabbage leaves that grow in clusters on short stalks. Collards are large-leafed plants that provide sweet, nutritious greens in fall, winter and spring. Don't be put off this underrated vegetable, as winter collards steamed with a dash of butter are the REAL thing!

Plants can withstand winter conditions without

Three-Ways Leek and Celeriac Soup

1 large onion
3 cloves garlic, minced
2 large leeks, chopped
 Sauté in ¼ cup (60 mL) olive oil until soft.
 Toss with:
1 large (2 medium) celeriac root, chopped
4 potatoes, cubed
1 bay leaf
2 tsp. (10 mL) dill
1 tsp. (5 mL) celery seeds
Salt and pepper, Bragg's or soya sauce
8 cups (1.9 L) stock or water
 Bring to a boil; reduce the heat and cook, simmering gently, until the root vegetables are tender.

Now choose from the "Three Ways" of enjoying this hearty soup:

Remove the bay leaf. Take 50 percent of the soup and blenderize it until smooth. Add it back to the saucepan, blend and adjust the seasoning.

Remove the bay leaf. Blenderize the whole soup until smooth and pour back into the saucepan. Stir in your choice of dairy milk, soy, or yoghurt as you reheat the soup to your preferred consistency, but do not allow to boil. Adjust the seasoning.

Remove the bay leaf. Blenderize the whole soup until smooth and pour back into the saucepan. Reheat while stirring and adjust the seasonings.

'Champion' collards.

the genetic diversity of collard plants. They will cross with other plants of *Brassica oleracea*—head cabbage, broccoli, Brussels sprouts, kale, cauliflower or kohlrabi. You need 1 mi. (1.6 km) of separation to prevent cross-pollination from occurring.

Winter collards survive as long as the temperature does not go below 14°F (-10°C). After the yellow flowers fade, seed pods develop small, round light-brown seeds. When the seed pods turn brown, cut the stalks and dry them in paper bags or buckets. Thresh the dried stalks against a wheelbarrow to collect the seeds. Screen them and winnow the dust away to complete cleaning. Usual seed life: 4 years.

CORN SALAD

Valerianella olitoria (syn. *Valerian locusta*), also called corn salad, lamb's lettuce or mache, is a hardy winter salad green, harvested right through winter and spring. The first time I grew corn salad, I was surprisingly impressed by 3-in.-tall (8-cm) rosettes of leaves with mild nutty flavour, eaten fresh like lettuce in salads or sandwiches. Individual leaves can be picked or the whole central rosette can be cut off—and it will regrow. Many varieties of corn salad are grown in Europe, where it is cultivated as a greenhouse crop for market.

protection, and the greens get sweeter after hard frosts. The flowering shoots in spring are also delicious when eaten steamed. Collard greens are a good source of beta carotene and vitamin C, but I value them most as a great source of calcium. TIP: Harvest the leaves from the bottom of the stalk up.

Sow collards from April to mid July directly into the garden, or grow as transplants. Space 18 in. (46 cm) apart in the row, and give the soil a boost, as collards are heavy feeders and benefit from addition of screened compost or balanced organic fertilizer (NPK: 6-8-6). TIP: Prepare the soil by adding dolomite lime to sweeten it and discourage clubroot.

Collards have a waxy leaf surface that provides natural protection from pests that bother brassicas. Watch out for small holes in young seedlings that indicate flea beetles are at work. For pest prevention, see "Pests of Brassicas."

Seed Saving

Collards belong to *Brassica oleracea*. They are self-incompatible and must be insect pollinated, so you need more than one plant to save seeds. Ideally save seeds from a minimum of 6 plants to preserve

Corn salad frozen at 23°F (-5°C) thaws with no problems.

Above left: 'Wrinkled Crinkled Crumpled' cress (Lepidum sativum) is a half-hardy garden cress that does not bolt as fast as other cress. It has attractive frilly leaves and you can collect seeds that are good for sprouting.

Above right: Greek cress (Lepidum sativum) prefers warmer soils, as the name suggests. This plant is not about leaves but quality sprouting seeds. Once established, it bolts to seed quickly, but puts on a good show along the way.

Watercress (Nasturtium officinale).

Seeds sprout best from a direct sowing in cool, moist soils. Sow seeds thinly and evenly in blocks or straight rows. Space plants 4 in. (10 cm) apart, and eat any thinnings.

This is a vegetable that self-seeds and magically appears around the garden in early spring and fall, but is easy to weed out where not wanted. Dormant seeds of corn salad germinate after the first fall rains, and grow on to overwinter as hardy rosettes of nutritious greens.

Seed Saving

In spring when the ground warms up, corn salad puts on a growth spurt and sends out small blue flowers that go to seed. Small, pale-yellow seeds ripen unevenly. Place newspaper under the plants to catch the seeds as they ripen. Spread the seeds out on plates to dry, screen to clean and store in labelled airtight tubs. Usual seed life: 2 years.

CRESS

Cresses are often overlooked as good sources of nutritious greens. As a child in England, I remember Mother regularly buying cell packs of mustard and cress sprouts at the greengrocer's. These were a fixture for adding to summer salads and sandwiches. We'd put the cell packs on the windowsill above the kitchen sink, where we'd remember to water them and we'd cut the sprouts off with scissors. I really enjoyed the juicy, crunchy and spicy contribution the sprouts made.

MUSTARD AND CRESS SPROUTS
Make a 50:50 blend of mustard and cress seeds. Sow the seed mix over the surface of a cell pack filled with moistened, sterilized seeding mix. Keep in a bright location and water daily. When the seedlings are 4 in. (10 cm) tall, harvest for sprouts with scissors. TIP: Get kids to grow them—it's a great way of getting alive food into their diet!

Cress seed can be direct seeded outdoors, but sparingly, taking care not to overseed. The cooler the location the longer it takes to go to seed. Plant it in full sun or part shade, depending on whether you are growing for leaf or seed.

Watercress (*Nasturtium officinale*) sounds like an enigma, but this is a species that looks and tastes like watercress (also packed with vitamin C) but does not require a stream to thrive. It's a half-hardy annual with pretty white flowers. Sow a long row and enjoy lots of succulent greens in sandwiches (especially egg and watercress!) or in salads, soups and wraps.

Upland cress (*Barbarea verna*) is a hardy annual that pops up all over the garden in cool seasons. We enjoy small leafy pickings for salads and sandwiches all winter from these rampant self-seeding land-cress plants.

Seed Saving

Cresses belong to the Brassicaceae family. Different species do not cross-pollinate, but plants of the same species flowering at the same time must be separated by 1 mi. (1.6 km). Lie out on plates to dry small, hard, red-brown seeds, and winnow to remove any chaff. Usual seed life: 3 to 4 years.

CUCUMBER

Long English cukes are thin-skinned, non-bitter, 8 to 12 in. (20 to 30 cm), always straight, and often grown as a commercial variety. I grow long English cucumbers in recycled 5-gal. (23-L) black plastic pots in the greenhouse, two seedlings to a pot, and twist them around jute twine as they climb. The trick to growing straight cucumbers is that they need to hang down.

As for other squash plants, cucumbers need heat to thrive. Squash roots hate disturbance, so grow seedlings in individual pots. Wait until the soil is warm and the weather has settled before setting out transplants. Young plants should be hardened off for a period of seven to ten days before moving them outdoors. Place outdoors in the daytime and back under cover at night.

Japanese cucumbers are sweet, crunchy and prolific when grown in the garden or in a 2-gal. (9-L) pot. These cucumbers are eaten 6 in. (15 cm) long and are never bitter. The more you pick the more they produce. TIP: Top-dress container plants with compost in late summer to trigger plants to set more fruit.

Squash plants are heavy feeders. Before planting, work organic fertilizer into the soil and make a raised mound. If seeding directly, sow four seeds around each mound; thin to the best two seedlings. If using transplants tap the seedling from the pot, or soil block, and plant it on the mound with the minimum of disturbance to roots.

Natural-source fertilizers (contents: seed meals, gypsum, greensand, Sul-Po-Mag, rock phosphate, zeolite, kelp meal) break down slowly and feed your plants with trace

'Marketmore' has slender, crunchy dark-green cucumbers, perfect for slicing. Vines are short, so you can plant them closer together for abundant yields.

Lemon Cucumbers (1894) produce prolific and early harvests of 3-in. (8-cm) lemon-sized fruits. The vigorous vines need strings to climb up.

elements as they grow. It takes three to four weeks for granular fertilizer to break down and become available to plants, so help new transplants get established with a liquid feed of fish fertilizer (for leafy greens) or liquid kelp (for fruiting and flowering plants).

'Homemade Pickles' is an open-pollinated variety with small, medium-green cucumbers with white spines and crispy flesh. Smaller pickling cucumbers are better suited to cooler growing conditions by the ocean or water. For baby pickles, harvest when 2 in. (5 cm) in size or wait for the bigger ones.

Vertical gardening is a great way to save space when growing cucumbers and other squash. Make a rectangular wooden frame, 6 ft. (1.8 m) high and hammer nails along the top and bottom. Tie string or twine to the nails up and down the frame. Lean the frame against the wall of a garage or shed, and plant cucumbers along the base of a wooden planter box or into the soil. Tie vines clockwise onto this framework, so that fruits hang from the underside for easy harvesting. Once producing, cucumbers grow fast, and vines will stop producing if not harvested regularly. If left on vines cucumbers become bitter, so it's best to harvest them when they are ready; you can store them in a fridge.

THE INSTANT EYE-STRAIN REMEDY
2 slices cucumber

Lie down and close your eyes. Place one slice of cucumber over each eye.

Lie still. Enjoy your thoughts for a few moments.

You will see better and the strain will be gone!

Q Last year was the first time I grew cucumbers, and they turned out bitter. I heard that removing male flowers reduces bitterness, but when I poke around online, it says that outdoor cucumbers need to be pollinated, while hothouse cukes are hybrids engineered to have mostly female flowers, and they do not need pollination. What's your understanding of all this?

A The reason hybrid cucumbers for greenhouse production are engineered to have female flowers that don't need pollinating is that when flowers are pollinated they can develop bitter flavour. Some varieties are more bitter than others, some are burpless, so check seed catalogues when growing from seed.

Cucurbitacin B and cucurbitacin C are the names of the compounds that cause bitterness in cucumbers. Bitterness does not accumulate uniformly and the extent of bitter compounds varies from fruits. Bitter compounds are likely to be more concentrated at the stem end than the blossom end. If present, bitterness is found just under the skin and not deep in the flesh, so peeling often improves flavour.

Seed Saving

Cucumber (*Cucumis sativus*) has "imperfect flowers," meaning each plant has separate male and female flowers. In this case, isolation distances must be taken into account when planting related squash of the same species. These need to be isolated by ¼ mi. (400 m) to prevent insects spreading pollen from one variety to another. Some unique crosses will happen but the results may not be of good-eating quality!

To collect seeds, leave fruits to fully ripen on the

Lemon Cucumber Refreshing Raita

6 lemon cucumbers, quartered
2 tsp. (10 mL) sea salt
Slice extra-thin wedges from the cucumber using a mandoline or a sharp knife. Sprinkle the wedges with salt and leave to sweat for a few hours. Squeeze the liquid out of the cucumbers.
Add:
½ cup (125 mL) sour cream
2 Tbsp. (30 mL) fresh mint, finely minced
   or 1 tsp. (5 mL) dried mint
1 lemon, juiced
2 tsp. (10 mL) ground cumin
½ tsp. (2.5 mL) ground coriander
Blend well. Refrigerate.
This sauce is brilliant with anything curried!

vines. When the fruits turn pale-yellow, harvest them. In case of frost take fruit indoors, where it will carry on maturing and ripening seed.

Scoop seeds out of the flesh with a teaspoon, and put them in a bowl of water, so that good seed sinks to the bottom and dud seed floats to the top. Pour these off. Leave good seeds to ferment for a few days, so that the jelly around them dissolves. This fermentation process destroys seed-borne pathogens. Rinse under running water in a sieve, and spread the clean seeds out on plates to dry. Crumble apart any seeds that stick together with your fingers, and dry them again. Store dry seeds in an airtight tub, in a dark cool place. Usual seed life: 4 years.

EGGPLANT

Eggplants are very beautiful perennial plants with purple star-shaped blossoms, usually grown as annuals in cold climates. They appear in many ethnic dishes from around the world. The French serve them in ratatouille, Greeks eat them in moussaka, Italians use them in eggplant parmigiana, and in the Middle East you find a delicious dip called baba ganouji. The Italians grow varieties with white flesh, which they consider to have the best flavour, and the Europeans call them aubergines! The best news is that eggplants are low in calories with only 27 per cup, high in fibre and are a good source of vitamin B2.

Eggplants are tender warm-weather plants that produce best in hot summers, because they do not set fruit when temperatures fall below 65°F (18°C). It's best to choose varieties suited to your growing conditions, or create a microclimate under a plastic cloche and lock warmth into the soil by planting them through black landscape fabric.

To get around cooler summers I grow eggplants in 5-gal. (23-L) pots in the greenhouse; one plant per pot, in a 50:50 blend of screened compost: coir (coco peat) with a scoop of granular organic fertilizer mixed in. Bushy plants grow 2 to 3 ft. (60 to 90 cm) tall, and require the support of a stake or tomato cage once they set fruit. They can produce between 3 to 5 fruits per plant, depending on the variety. They are ready to be harvested when the skin is glossy, as dull skin indicates they are overripe, and may be tough or bitter.

Eggplants need fertile, well-drained garden loam, pH 6.0, in a site that receives at least 8 hours of sun a day. Seeds germinate at 75 to 90°F (24 to 32°C), so I start them with a source of bottom heat by placing seedlings on a propagation table lined with heater cables, with the thermostat set at 70°F (21°C). Bottom heat speeds up germination and growth considerably in long cool spring seasons. A heater pad or the top of a fridge works too. Harden seedlings off gradually, before setting them out after the danger of frost has passed.

A range of pests from aphids, beetles, cutworms,

Japanese eggplants are long and slender purple fruits, better suited to cooler growing conditions.

flea beetles and tomato hornworms can bother eggplants. They can also be infected by fruit rot and verticillium wilt, especially in cooler climates. Having said all this, the only problem I've ever had has been aphids, a problem easily remedied, so don't let knowing this put you off growing eggplants! The best way to avoid problems is to practise crop rotation, by not planting them where you have grown eggplants, tomatoes, peppers or potatoes the year before.

Seed Saving

Eggplants (*Solanum melongena* var. *esculentum*) are in the nightshade family Solanaceae, related to tomatoes, peppers and potatoes. They need a long hot summer to ripen seed. They are self-pollinating, but it's best to isolate different varieties of the same species by 30 ft. (9 m) in case insects cross-pollinate the large attractive flowers.

EGGPLANT PARMIGIANA

Serves 4 to 6

Preheat oven to 400°F (205°C)

1 medium eggplant, sliced ¾ in. (2 cm) thick

1 cup (250 mL) flour

1 egg, beaten with a little milk

Breadcrumbs

½ cup (125 mL) olive oil

6 oz. (170 g) tomato paste

Dash of red wine

1 tsp. (5 mL) oregano

¼ cup (60 mL) fresh minced parsley

2 cloves garlic, minced

Salt and pepper to taste

1 cup (250 mL) grated Parmesan

½ lb. (227 g) mozzarella, sliced

Dip the slice of eggplant in flour, then egg and then into the breadcrumbs, until well coated. Heat the olive oil in a frying pan and sauté until browned on both sides. Add extra oil to prevent sticking if needed.

Mix the tomato paste with a dash of red wine, oregano, salt, pepper, parsley and minced garlic. Arrange the eggplant slices in a baking dish. Place a mozzarella slice on each one and spread with 2 tsp. (10 mL) of tomato sauce. Top with grated Parmesan. Bake in a preheated oven at 400°F (205°C) for about 15 minutes and serve steaming hot accompanied by a side salad.

Leave fruits on the plant as long as possible to ripen seed, and allow them to get even duller after harvest. To collect the seeds cut the eggplants into 1-in. (2.5-cm) square cubes, and whiz them in a blender with water for a few pulses until they are macerated. Pour this into a basin and fill it up with water; mature seeds will drop to the bottom. Strain through a sieve and spread out on a plate to dry. Store in airtight containers in a cool, dry place. Usual seed life: 5 years.

ENDIVE

Wild chicories have been harvested in Europe for centuries, their slightly bitter leaves valued as a health tonic when added as wild greens into mesclun mixes. North Americans are slowly acquiring a palate for bitter greens, as demonstrated by the surge of dandelions and chicories starting to appear on restaurant menus.

The farmers' market in the centre of Rome overflows with chicories and endive.

Endives (*Chicorium endiva*) are cool-weather, hardy biennials that do best in spring and fall, and are grown like lettuce. Direct sow in spring after all danger of frost, or grow indoors six to eight weeks before transplanting out. Space plants 6 in. (15 cm) apart in rows. Dig screened compost and granular organic fertilizer into the planting hole to encourage growth. A feed of liquid fish fertilizer also helps, but watch out for slugs that may be attracted by it.

Direct sow endive again from late June to the end of August for zingy salad and sandwich greens from fall through early winter. Light frosts actually improve the flavour. In areas where the soil does not freeze in winter, endive can be left in the ground, but fares best protected from heavy winter rain. (See "Tips for Crop Protection" in August.)

Batavian escaroles are less bitter than endives, and are spreading plants with luscious, dark-green, smooth outer leaves and tender pale hearts. They are hardier than frilly-leaved endives.

'Frisee' endives are fast-growing leafy greens, with the centre of the rosette blanched white. The

ENDIVE DRESSING

In a blender, whiz:
½ cup (125 mL) virgin olive oil
¼ cup (60 mL) red wine vinegar
1 Tbsp. (15 mL) prepared mustard
3 Tbsp. (45 mL) cream
Fresh herbs and garlic, finely minced (optional)

Toss endive greens with dressing and coat well.

tender finely curled leaves have delicate flavour, and are a crispy and tangy addition to the salad bowl. The greens are also good lightly steamed or added to sandwiches.

Blanching reduces bitterness and can be achieved by covering plants with upturned terra-cotta pots, or anything that will block sunlight. Spacing plants close together increases self-blanching.

Seed Saving

Chicorium endiva is in the lettuce family Asteraceae. The plants are biennials that are self-pollinating, so they do not need insects for pollination. Endive does not cross with chicory and other endives.

Plants put up seed stalks covered in pretty bright-blue flowers. When stalks are dry, thresh them against a wheelbarrow, so that ripe seeds fall to the bottom. The seeds are beige and tubular and adhere to the stalk, which makes it trickier to collect them. A light hammering may be needed to release the seeds. Screen and winnow for the final cleaning. Usual seed life: 4 years.

Batavian escarole.

FENNEL

Finicchio fennel (*Foeniculum vulgare* var. *azoricum*) is a tender perennial grown as an annual and often confused with sweet fennel (*Foeniculum vulgare dulce*) grown for feathery anise-flavoured leaves and seeds. (See "F" in "Herbs.") Finicchio (or Florence fennel) is grown for crispy, anise-flavoured bulbs harvested at 3 to 4 in. (8 to 10 cm) across.

Fennel seedlings are slow to germinate and to establish, so it's best to start seeds indoors in spring for the fall crop, and transplant established seedlings outdoors when spring conditions have settled. Space seedlings 6 in. (15 cm) apart, in furrows 18 in. (46 cm) apart. TIP: Lining the furrows with screened compost gives the seedlings the best start. (See "Hoe a Row in Five.")

Fennel seeds freshen your breath, and also add wonderful flavour to tomato sauces. A tea made with fennel seed cures hiccups!

Seed Saving

Florence fennel belongs to the Apiaceae (Umbelliferae) family, together with angelica, chervil, coriander, dill, carrots, lovage, sweet cicely, parsley, parsnips and celeriac. These plants have flowers called umbels that are umbrella-shaped. It will cross with wild fennel within a ¼-mi. (400-m) range. Usual seed life: 4 years.

'Perfection' finicchio fennel.

FINICCHIO PASTA

1 large bulb of Florence fennel, thinly sliced with a mandoline
Sauté in olive oil with garlic, fresh herbs and a dash of white wine. Toss in your favourite pasta and go straight to Italian heaven!

GOOD KING HENRY

Chenopodium bonus-henricus, better known as Good King Henry, is a perennial vegetable with leaves that can be eaten like spinach, and whose shoots are a delicacy. Hilling up soil over the roots in early spring produces blanched shoots that appear two weeks before asparagus. If Good King Henry is well manured, it will yield an abundant supply of shoots. The shoots should be peeled, tied up in bunches like asparagus, and boiled in deep water until tender.

Seed Saving

As the weather warms up, plants bolt to seed. They produce multiple spires of clustered brown seeds. Wait for the spire to turn brown, cut the seed head off and dry in paper bags. Several harvests will be needed, as the seed ripens over a long period. Usual seed life: 5 years.

Good King Henry going to seed.

'Aunt Molly's' ground cherries.

GROUND CHERRY

Ground cherries (*Physalis peruviana*) are golden-orange pineapple-flavoured fruits that grow in papery husks. They can be eaten fresh, added to fruit salads, made into a sweet sauce or preserve, and used for garnish. When ripe they drop off the bush, so be prepared to pick them up off the ground. Grow the seeds in the same way as tomatoes, and plant the seedlings outside only after all danger of frost. Space the plants 2 ft. (60 cm) apart. There's no need to stake the sturdy 2-ft. (60-cm) plants, they can hold themselves up. They always produce good yields, unless it's a cool summer.

Seed Saving

The easiest way to collect seeds is to put ripe ground cherries in a blender with 1 cup of water and give it a few whirls to macerate the flesh and release the seeds. Put this mix into a bowl full of water, where the good seeds will sink to the bottom. Sieve seeds and spread out onto plates to dry. Crumble seeds apart with fingers before storing in airtight tubs. Usual seed life: 3 years.

HORSERADISH

This tough, gnarly perennial root vegetable is prepared as a mouth-searing relish enjoyed across Europe, North America and Russia, and considered by some as indispensable to roast beef. It's no relation to radish or the equine family, so how it gets its name is a mystery! The large coarse leaves are not eaten; all the value lies in the long yellow roots, which will fatten to 2 in. (5 cm) in diameter if grown in moist fertile soil.

At least 80 percent of the world's supply of horseradish comes from Collinsville in southern Illinois, which has the dubious distinction of being known as "The Horseradish Capital of the Galaxy!" Collinsville holds the two-day International Horseradish Festival every year, where they do crazy things with roots and judge entries such as horseradish-devilled eggs, horseradish-infused dill pickles and horseradish and shrimp gazpacho.

Horseradish is propagated by pieces of root, squared off at the top if ragged. Prepare the ground by digging to 12 in. (30 cm) deep and adding aged manure, compost or leaf mulch. Plant the square end of 6-in. (15-cm) pieces of root upright in 12-in. (30-cm) deep holes during early spring, where they form buds that will sprout. Grows well in part shade, and

*Horseradish (*Armoracia rusticana*) is a member of the Brassicaceae family.*

can tolerate poor soils. Watch out for spreading—in the right conditions horseradish takes over!

HORSERADISH SAUCE

1. Lift roots in November when the leafy tops die down.
2. Remove the outer skin with a potato peeler and cut away any imperfections.
3. Cut the root into small chunks, or shave off thin slices. Shavings can be dried in an oven and later ground as needed.
4. Grind up the root in a food processor. Caution! An enzymatic reaction releases thiocyanate, a substance that burns the nose and causes eyes to tear up.
5. Add a few drops of vinegar to each batch; horseradish will lose its bite in minutes without this addition of vinegar.

KALE

Kale cultivars (*Brassica oleracea*) fall into different varieties and subspecies, which include 'Curled Scotch', 'Tall Curled', 'Drumhead', 'Russian', 'Tuscan Blue', 'Labrador' and 'Asparagus'. Kale leaves range from slightly wavy to tightly frilled, and they come in a range of hues: dark-green ('Toscano'), blue-green ('Lacinato'), purple ('Red Russian') and magenta ('Redbor').

Kale is REALLY GOOD for you! It has the highest levels of beta carotene of all the brassicas, contains 10 times the vitamin A of lettuce and 3 times the vitamin C of oranges. It also has more B vitamins than whole-wheat bread, and more calcium than milk! Kale is freely available from the garden at any time of year. Chopped kale makes a fine addition to soups and casseroles and tastes great mixed with mashed potatoes.

In spring the tender shoots of flower heads can be eaten raw with dips, lightly steamed or in stir-fries. TIP: The shoots are the most tender while the flowers are still in bud, before they open.

Kale is one of the easiest brassicas to cultivate. It is extremely cold hardy, but also more tolerant of hot weather than other members of the cabbage family. Kales occupy their share of space in the garden, needing 2 by 2 ft. (60 by 60 cm) to grow to maturity—but I think they deserve it. The seeds are fast to germinate, taking from 7 to 10 days. Kale should be grown in firm ground because the sturdy stalks can reach 4 ft. (1.2 m) and plants can keel over in windy conditions.

Sow in spring for summer and fall harvests. Direct seed ¾ in. (2 cm) deep in drills. Add lime to the garden area prior to planting; kales prefer a pH more alkali than acidic. Thin seedlings to 4 in. (10 cm) in the row, and grow on until planted out. For harvest through winter, kale is best either direct sown in

Above: 'Redbor' kale.

Top left: 'Red Russian' kale.

Left: Kale in seed.

June/July, or seeded for transplants that will be in the garden by the end of August.

Winter vegetables survive freezing temperatures by pumping sugars into their cells, which acts as an antifreeze. After hard frosts kale tastes sweeter. Once harvested, sugars quickly convert back to starch, which is why store-bought can never match the flavour of fresh-picked.

Kale is relatively unbothered by insects, and does not get clubroot like other brassicas. Flea beetles can be detected by small holes in the leaves. Cabbage white butterflies can import cabbage worms that are detected by large ragged holes in the leaves. TIP:

Prevent disease by removing older outer leaves, which may be harbouring pests. For pest prevention, see "Pests of Brassicas."

Seed Saving

Kale (*Brassica oleracea*) is grown as an annual but may grow as a perennial in mild winter climates. Kale plants are self-incompatible, so they must be insect-pollinated. Ideally, save seeds from a minimum of 6 plants to preserve the genetic diversity of kale plants. Kale will cross with other *Brassica oleracea*—cabbage, broccoli, Brussels sprouts, collards, cauliflower or

Kale with Soy Ginger Dressing

½ cup (125 mL) vegetable oil

¼ cup (60 mL) rice wine vinegar

¼ cup (60 mL) sesame oil

¼ cup (60 mL) soya sauce

2 Tbsp. (30 mL) honey

2 tsp. (10 mL) Dijon mustard

2 cloves garlic, minced

½ in. (1 cm) ginger root, minced

Toss 4 cups (1 L) of shredded kale with soy ginger dressing.

Sauté in a wok or skillet until the kale has wilted. Serve hot.

Dressing keeps for weeks if refrigerated.

'Early Purple Vienna' kohlrabi.

Recommended Varieties

'Early Purple Vienna' (pre. 1885): Smaller size, with purple skin and white flesh, fast growing—60 days from seed to harvest. Sow early in spring and again in late summer, and space 6 in. (15 cm) apart in the row, the rows 18 in. (46 cm) apart. Best eaten when young and tender.

'Superschmeltz': A large white kohlrabi that is still tender at an enormous size. Sow mid summer, harvest fall through winter, 70 days from seed to harvest. Needs 12 in. (30 cm) between plants.

Seed Saving

Kohlrabi (*Brassica oleracea*) is a self-incompatible biennial that produces seed in the second year. It needs insects for pollination, and a minimum of 6 plants is required to preserve genetic diversity. In harsh winter climates, the only way to save seed is to dig the plant out after the first frost, clip the roots back to 6 in. (15 cm) and store in damp sand or sawdust at around 32°F (0°C) for the winter. Plant the best roots out again the following spring and allow to set seed.

In milder climates, kohlrabi should overwinter without any protection, but it's a good idea to provide a protective mulch just to be on the safe side. Kohlrabi cross-pollinates with other members of the

kohlrabi. Allow 1 mi. (1.6 km) of separation to prevent cross-pollination occurring.

After the yellow flowers fade, the seed pods develop small, round dark-brown seeds. When seed pods turn brown, cut the stalks and dry them in paper bags or buckets. Thresh them against a wheelbarrow to collect seeds as they fall. Screen and winnow the dust away to complete cleaning. Usual seed life: 5 years.

KOHLRABI

Kohlrabi (*Brassica oleracea* var. *gongylodes*) is probably not near the top of most people's list of favourite vegetables, but maybe they haven't given it a chance? It's a surprisingly tasty vegetable that tastes like sweet turnip eaten raw, cabbage heart when cooked, and is simply delicious steamed. The edible part is the swollen base of the stem, which forms above ground. The size of the swelling varies from that of an orange to a large ball; the colour of the skin fluctuates from white to purple to light green. Kohlrabi is a good source of vitamin C, calcium and iron.

same family; an isolation distance of 1 mi. (1.6 km) is required to prevent this. After the yellow flowers fade, seed pods develop small reddish-brown seeds. Harvest seed stalks when seeds are turning colour, and dry in a warm place. Thresh the stalks against a wheelbarrow to release the seeds; screen and blow away any remaining dust with a hair dryer. Usual seed life: 3 to 5 years.

Katie's Kohlrabi Salad

Serves 6 to 8

Make a few hours before to let flavours meld.

3 cups (700 mL) cooked beets, chopped into
   1-in. (2.5-cm) cubes

3 cups (700 mL) raw peeled kohlrabi,
   chopped into 1-in. (2.5-cm) cubes

2 cups (475 mL) apples, chopped into 1-in.
   (2.5-cm) cubes

DRESSING

¾ cup (180 mL) of plain yoghurt

1 tsp. (5 mL) of cinnamon

1 Tbsp. (15 mL) apple cider vinegar

1 tsp. (5 mL) honey

¼ tsp. (1 mL) salt

LEEKS

Leeks (*Allium ampeloprasum*) are related to onions, but have a small bulb and long white stalk of superimposed layers that flow into broad grey-green leaves. They have light onion flavour and can be used in any recipe as a substitute for onions. Leeks are an excellent source of dietary fibre, and an average leek contains only 38 calories, plus significant levels of manganese (15 percent) and iron (8 percent), with high amounts of folic acid, calcium, potassium and vitamin C.

Leeks need a long growing season, so should be started from seed early in the spring. They can be direct seeded into the garden in March/April, and later will need spacing to 6 in. (15 cm) apart to mature. I sow seeds into cell packs, and when the seedlings are the thickness of a skinny pencil, transplant them into the garden. TIP: Trim roots to 1 in. (2.5 cm) and tops to 6 in. (15 cm) before transplanting.

Transplanting Leek Seedlings

1. Mark a line in the garden and water the soil.

2. Use a dibber to make planting holes 6 in. (15 cm) deep and 6 in. (15 cm) apart along this line.

3. Drop one seedling into each hole so that the leek roots are at the bottom of the hole.

4. Water them in just so the soil settles over the roots.

5. Keep the leeks watered until they're established.

6. Each time you water, soil naturally fills the hole and creates the best part—the blanched white stems.

'Durabel' leeks and Ipomoea purpurea *'Grandpa Ott's.'*

Leek and Potato Soup

¼ cup (60 mL) olive oil
1 onion, finely chopped
4 cups (1 L) leeks, sliced lengthwise,
   chopped coarsely, washed
1 cup (250 mL) celery or celeriac, chopped
Sauté until wilted.
Add:
3 cups (700 mL) potatoes
2 Tbsp. (30 mL) thyme or dillweed
1 tsp. (5 mL) salt and 1 tsp. (5 mL) pepper

4 cups (1 L) vegetable stock
Cover and simmer (15 minutes) until tender.
Add:
1 bunch spinach, chopped
3 Tbsp. (45 mL) parsley, chopped coarsely
Purée the soup in a blender or with a hand blender.
Return to a low heat and stir in:
1 cup (250 mL) milk or soymilk (optional)
Adjust seasonings.

'Durabel' leeks are very ornamental when in seed.

Seed Saving

Leeks are biennial plants in the Liliaceae family, so they must get through winter before setting seed. Select 20 plants to save seeds from to maintain plant genetic diversity. The flowers are perfect, but require insects to ensure pollination, so leeks will cross with other varieties of leeks, but not with other onions. The isolation distance needed between varieties is 1 mi. (1.6 km).

The large seed heads develop in spring, but the seeds do not mature until late September/October. Seeds develop in small inflorescences on large globular seed heads and can take a long time to ripen. I harvest seed heads at the end of the season, and leave them to thoroughly dry in the greenhouse. I use sharp scissors to cut the dry seeds off into a bowl, and rub them between gloved hands to release them from the chaff. Hard black seeds are spread out on trays to dry thoroughly, and finally screened and winnowed to remove dust. Usual seed life: 1 to 2 years.

LETTUCE

Lettuces (*Latuca sativa*) are cool-season annuals that can be grown all season long if you choose the right varieties. When the weather goes over 65°F (18°C), lettuces bolt to seed, so the best varieties are those that hold longer in the garden before bolting. Lettuces make follow-on crops to peas, garlic, favas and winter vegetables. They can be grown from a direct seeding in spring or from transplants that need to be hardened off before planting out after danger of frost. If seeds are sown every 3 weeks, there will be continuous harvests of greens that can be gathered as full-sized lettuces, individual leaves or hearts, or as "cut-and-come-again" mesclun baby salad greens.

Mildew and fungal diseases such as "damping off" are the most common problems when growing lettuces. Fungal problems are usually an indication of overcrowding, lack of aeration or prolonged cool, damp weather. Remediate these problems and the disease should abate.

"Hoe a row in five" works great for lettuces (see May).

Lettuce Top Picks

VARIETY	SUMMER	WINTER
Green leaf	'Tango'	'Arctic King'
Red leaf	'Merlot'	'Rouge d'Hiver'
Oak leaf	'Salad Bowl'	'Brunia'
Butterhead	'Continuity'	'Kweik'
Romaine (Cos)	'Crisp Mint'	'Winter Density'
Crisphead	'Cardinale'	'Iceberg'

DIRECT SEEDING LETTUCE

1. Make a shallow furrow in the soil using a hoe.
2. If the soil is dry, water along the open furrow.
3. Sow lettuce seeds sparingly along the length of the furrow. TIP: Avoid overseeding!
4. Rake or hoe the length of the furrow to cover the seed ½ in. (1 cm) deep. If soil is heavy, use a sandy soil blend to cover seeds instead.
5. Water the furrow with a hose or a watering can.
6. When seedlings are 2 in. (5 cm) tall, thin to 9 in. (23 cm) apart for full-sized lettuces, 6 in. (15 cm) apart for medium-sized lettuces and 3 in. (8 cm) apart for thinning and "cut-and-come-again" greens.

Seed Saving

Lettuces (Asteraceae family) have "perfect" flowers (with male and female), which means they are self-pollinating. You can grow different varieties of lettuces without worrying about them crossing up. I grow other crops in between the rows of different lettuces, just to be on the safe side. Crossing doesn't happen often, but it does occasionally occur. When

Raspberry Vinaigrette Dressing

This salad dressing can be made a day in advance, but bring to room temperature before using.

¼ cup (60 mL) Dijon mustard
¼ cup (60 mL) raspberry vinegar
1 Tbsp. (15 mL) dried Herbs de Provence
½ tsp. (2.5 mL) pepper

½ cup (125 mL) grapeseed oil
½ cup (125 mL) extra virgin olive oil
12 raspberries (optional)

In a small bowl, whisk together the mustard, vinegar, herbs and pepper. Gradually whisk in the oils. Add fresh raspberries to the vinaigrette if desired.

saving seeds from rows of lettuce, compare plants and "rogue" out any that are different before they go to flower.

Lettuces produce large quantities of seed. Yellow-flowered seed stalks grow tall and may need support. Tall bamboo canes do the job admirably, pushed into the ground with the plants tied up using twine. You'll know the seeds are ready because feathery white parachutes appear. I collect lettuce seeds when these cover two-thirds of the head. Cut stalks down and invert into brown paper bags, where the remaining one-third of seeds will finish maturing as they dry. Bash seed stalks against a wheelbarrow to release the seeds, and screen to remove chaff and debris. A hair dryer on a cool setting is needed to blow fine particles away. TIP: Wear a bandana for this job! Usual seed life: 3 to 5 years.

MAGENTA SPREEN

Magenta spreen is related to lamb's quarters in the Chenopodiceae family. Greens of delicate flavour have brilliant magenta tips on young leaves, which makes them a choice selection for salad mixes. They can also be steamed like spinach. You can direct seed magenta spreen in full sun to part shade, from spring through summer. The seeds are tiny, so sow them sparingly, and only ¼ in. (6 mm) deep. You will soon be harvesting "cut-and-come-again" salad greens.

Being a relative of lamb's quarters means this plant self-seeds. If you let magenta spreen go to seed, it puts

up 6-ft.-tall (1.8-m) stalks with massive sprays of seed. TIP: Pluck off seed heads before this plant takes over the garden!

Pioneer women used magenta spreen for rouge or to colour lips. The powder lies on the skin for quite a while and doesn't stain.

Lamb's quarters are wild plants, regarded as common weeds in the garden, but one person's weed is another's gourmet salad green! Lamb's quarters are eaten like spinach, taste similar to chard or beet greens, and can be added to salads when picked young. Native Americans ground the seeds to make a flour. Quinoa is a lamb's quarter relative, grown for high-protein grains.

Magenta spreen or lamb's quarter greens.

MESCLUN MIXES

1. Blend a mix of suitable seeds (see below) or buy a packet of mesclun mix. Note that mustard greens and arugula add heat, while dandelion, chicory and endive add tangy bitterness.

2. Scatter seeds lightly over a prepared bed or a planter filled with screened compost.

3. Cover lightly and water in.

4. Keep soil moist once the crop starts to grow.

5. Harvest baby greens when 4 in. (10 cm) high by picking individual leaves or cutting 1 in. (2.5 cm) above ground with scissors.

6. After harvesting a patch, fertilize with liquid fish fertilizer. In 2 to 3 weeks another crop will be ready.

7. Keep the salad bowl full by broadcasting more seeds every 3 to 4 weeks from spring to fall.

SUMMER BLEND
Arugula, beets, chard, chervil, chicory, dandelion, endive, parsley, kale, land cress, summer lettuces, orach, sorrel, spinach.

WINTER BLEND
Arugula, chard, chicory, corn salad, dandelion, endive, parsley, kale, land cress, winter-hardy lettuces, mustard greens, Oriental greens, spinach.

MINER'S LETTUCE

Miner's lettuce (*Claytonia perfoliata*) is a 3-in. (8-cm) plant with succulent greens, and in the Portulacaceae family. Miner's lettuce grows wild in disturbed soil along roadsides, especially in sandy soil, and is often found growing in the shade. The flavour is bland, but the juicy leaves make a good addition to salads and sandwiches. Young leaves are best, as the older leaves become bitter in summer.

Mesclun mix.

Miner's lettuce.

When this wild species is cultivated in the garden, the leaves grow much larger, which makes them easier to harvest. Miner's lettuce is a half-hardy annual that grows well in the cool weather in early spring. The leaves form rosettes and the flowers are tiny and white. The flowers are self-fertile, so there is no concern about cross-pollination. It is easy to grow by direct seeding in the garden, but don't overseed, and just barely cover the tiny seeds.

Oca (New Zealand yams).

OCA (NEW ZEALAND YAM)

Oca (*Oxalis tuberosa*) are wrinkled tubers with fleshy pink skin. Oca has ornamental oxalis-like leaves that make an attractive groundcover. During summer, swollen stems (stolons) grow above ground and spread; when the days shorten, they go underground and swell into plump little tubers. There are many different species of oca around the world, prepared in different ways. In North America they are enjoyed as potatoes, as the fleshy tubers are a good source of carbohydrate. They can be drizzled with olive oil and roasted for 25 minutes, or tossed into winter soups and baked in veggie casseroles.

These tubers can multiply like mad! A friend reported that the planter in which she had grown oca the previous year was full of tubers in spring after being stored in the garage through winter.

Oca tolerates cool weather; the tubers can stay in the ground without freezing over mild winters, but the foliage dies down as soon as hard frosts appear. TIP: The longer the tubers stay in the ground the more likely they are to attract pests, so harvest when the foliage dies back and store in a dark cool place. The tubers don't shrivel in storage, but actually stay firm and can be eaten as needed through winter. For propagation select the largest tubers and plant out in spring after all danger of frost.

ONION

Onions are in the genus *Allium*. Alliums span the breadth of the world's cuisines and are added to many types of food. Onions are milder and sweeter when grown in hot climates, which explains why some people eat them like apples! The pungent odour of onions deters many pests, so it's a good idea to plant them liberally throughout the garden. They grow best in full sun in well-drained soils.

KNOW YOUR ONIONS
Onions are photosensitive, formation of bulbs depends on the length of the day.
Bulbing onions belong to one of three categories:
Long day: Produces bulbs after 15 hours of daylight.
Intermediate day: Produces bulbs after 13 to 14 hours of daylight.
Short day: Requires 10 to 12 hours of daylight; and is usually planted in fall for harvest in early summer.

Allium cepa can be grown from seed or from sets. Onion sets are produced by sowing seed very thickly, resulting in small bulbs. These bulbs are then stored and set out to grow into mature bulbs the following year. Onions started from seed tend to store better than sets.

Transplanting is recommended for shorter growing seasons, and for sweet-onion varieties. If growing from seed, start them 8 to 12 weeks before the last frost date. Set transplants out on the surface of the soil and do not bury them too deeply, because the bulb grows at the surface of the soil. The bigger the tops the bigger the bulb, so if you want big onions regular weeding is recommended—onions don't compete well.

Cutting onions diffuses a gas that causes eyes to tear. Placing upturned wrists under running water stops this reaction instantly.

Stop watering at the beginning of August so that bulbs can mature in dry soil. Storage onions are harvested a week after the tops fall over, and then need proper curing. When the outer skin becomes crispy to the touch the onions have been sufficiently cured. Kept in mesh sacks, in a cool place with good ventilation, and they should keep until the following spring.

Bulbing onions (Allium cepa) *curing in the sun.*

Botrytis and mildew are common fungal problems. Botrytis develops as blight on leaves, and persists as contagious sclerotia in soil. If symptoms appear, bury infected plant material immediately, and practise crop rotations to break the cycle of disease.

Caramelized Onions

4 cups (1 L) of onions equals 1 cup (250 mL)
   of caramelized onions
   Peel and slice 2 cups (475 mL) mild onions
in thick rings (yellow, white or red)
   Add:
2 Tbsp. (30 mL) brown sugar
1 tsp. (5 mL) salt
1 tsp. (5 mL) black pepper
½ tsp. (2.5 mL) paprika
¼ cup (60 mL) oil or butter

Heat oil or butter over medium heat in a frying pan, and add the onion rings while stirring. Turn the heat down, and cook on a low heat for 45 to 60 minutes, until onions turn a rich brown colour.

Shallots

Shallots (*Allium cepa* var. *aggregatum*) are a self-perpetuating crop if a small portion of the harvest is replanted each year. Shallots have finer, more delicate flavour, considered gourmet (according to the market price). They can be grown from seed in the same way as bulb onions, but are easiest grown from sets. Selecting the largest bulbs for replanting results in large shallots, which are easier to handle on the chopping board.

Scallions (Green Onions)

Allium fistulosum are multiplier onions, which do not produce bulbs, but divide at the base into clumps of onions that are easy to tease apart and spread around the garden. All you need is one to get started! The more tender white part of the stem can be increased by hilling soil up around the clumps of onions, or by laying onion offsets into trenches and covering them 6 in. (15 cm) deep. Green onions can be harvested as required by slicing them off at the base of the clump, without having to pull up the whole bunch.

Seed Saving

Alliums are in the Liliaceae family (formerly Amaryllidaceae) and grow as hardy biennials or perennials depending on the species. Crossing may occur between *Allium cepa* and *Allium fistulosum* because of insect pollination, so an isolation distance of 325 ft. (100 m) is recommended. Collect seeds from at least 20 plants of the same variety to preserve the genetic diversity of the strain.

Hollow flower stalks produce seeds in capsules, which turn brown as the seeds ripen. Small, hard black seeds do not all ripen at the same time, so when the seed head has turned brown, check to see if some of the seeds inside the capsules are black and, if so, harvest whole stalks, then leave them to dry in paper bags or buckets. Shake the bag or bucket to release the seeds from the capsules. Screen and winnow to clean. Usual seed life: 1 to 2 years.

*Above: Welsh bunching onions (*Allium fistulosum*).*

*Top left: French shallots (*Allium cepa *var.* aggregatum*) multiply rapidly.*

Left: Allium fistulosum *in seed.*

ORIENTAL GREENS

Oriental greens are short-season, cold-hardy vegetables, which grow fast (21 to 60 days) from seed. The secret to success is to grow them in nitrogen-rich soil for rapid development and harvest them before they go to seed. TIP: To stop Oriental greens from bolting, plant in the shade of tall plants such as sweet corn, sunchokes, sunflowers or pole beans. They make a good follow-on for earlier crops of peas, fava beans, lettuce and garlic. Best grown in moist soils, sow seeds ½ in. (1 cm) deep in rows 8 in. (20 cm) apart. Thin to 6 in. (15 cm) apart in the row. Seeds germinate fast (5 to 7 days).

Oriental greens fall into three categories

Brassica rapa **ssp.** *chinensis*: Leafy non-heading cabbage-type vegetables—e.g., bok choy, pac choi, joichoi and tatsoi (tah tsai).

B. rapa **ssp.** *chinensis* **and** *B. rapa* **ssp.** *pekinensis*: Leafy heading vegetables—e.g., Chinese cabbages.

B. juncea **and** *B. rapa* **ssp.** *nipposinica*: Leafy mustard and Asian greens (best sown late summer for a fall and winter crop).

MIXED MUSTARD GREENS
Eat young leaves in salads throughout winter. Make the mix as mild or hot as you like by choosing from the following:
Mild: 'Komatsuna', 'Mizuna', 'Mibuna', 'Tendergreen'
Hot: 'Osaka Purple', 'Giant Red', 'Southern Giant Curled'

Seed Saving

Harvest any plants that flower early (an undesirable trait). As long as plants are different species they will not cross-pollinate. Seeds are produced in small pods, harvested when they turn light brown on the stalks. Cut down the stalks and dry them in paper bags or buckets. Thresh stalks against a wheelbarrow to release the dry seeds, screen and winnow. Usual seed life: 3 years.

Mixed mustard greens.

Oriental greens seedlings.

PARSNIP

Parsnips (*Pastinaca sativa*) are hardy biennials grown for their large, creamy-white roots, which after a few hard frosts become sweeter than any other root crop. TIP: Slice them like potato chips and sauté them in butter.

Parsnips require a long growing season. Plant no later than the end of May for mature parsnips from October through winter. They are high in potassium and vitamins B and C.

Planting Tip: Parsnips need deep, loose, well-drained soil. Take a pointed crowbar and thrust it into the soil 18 in. (46 cm) deep, rotate several times to loosen the soil and make a hole 6 in. (15 cm) in diameter. Fill the hole with seeding mix and plant 3 parsnip seeds ½ in. (1 cm) deep into each hole. Seed must be fresh to germinate.

Seed Saving

Parsnips belong to the Apiaceae (Umbelliferae) family. These plants have umbrella-shaped flowers called umbels. A minimum of 6 plants are needed to preserve the genetic diversity of the variety. The largest umbels are the best from which to save seeds. Roots need to be dug up and the best selected for replanting 2 ft. (60 cm) apart. If this is not done the quality and size of roots diminishes.

Insects fertilize flowers, so different varieties of parsnip will cross with each other. When seeds turn brown cut the umbel off the stalk, and dry in paper bags or buckets. TIP: Seed drops quickly after ripening, so it's best not to delay. The large seeds are easy to clean by screening followed by a quick winnowing. Usual seed life: 1 year.

My friend Jackie grows giant parsnips!

Root Vegetable Casserole

Preheat oven to 375°F (190°C)
Makes 4 to 6 servings

1 large onion, chopped
4 cloves garlic, minced
2 cups (475 mL) celery diced (or celeriac)
1 large sweet potato, cut into ½-in. (1-cm) chunks
2 carrots, sliced
2 parsnips, sliced
4 cups (1 L) vegetable stock
1 Tbsp. (15 mL) curry powder
1 cup (250 mL) yoghurt, soymilk or rice milk
½ cup (125 mL) dried cranberries (or raisins)

Mix veggies with stock and curry powder in a large casserole dish with lid. Bake covered in a preheated oven for 45 minutes or until the veggies are tender. Stir in the yoghurt (or soy/ rice milk) and cranberries (or raisins) and return to the oven uncovered for another 25 minutes. Serve.

PEAS

Peas (*Pisum sativum*) are cool weather crops, which grow best in moist, well-drained sunny locations, pH 6.0 to 6.5. The soil should be rich in organic matter, but heavy applications of manure provoke lush foliage at the expense of peas. 1 lb. (454 g) of seed will plant a 100-sq. ft. (9 sq. m) area.

TYPES OF PEAS

Peas are either grown as shelling, edible pod or dried soup peas.

Shelling peas are harvested when the pods are well rounded but not leathery.

Edible pod peas are either snow or snap peas.

Snow peas (also known as mangetout) are edible pod peas, harvested when pods are full-sized and the peas have just begun to swell.

Snap peas are the sweet, tender pods with fully formed peas inside.

Dried Soup Peas are harvested when the peas have dried in the pods.

As long as the soil is moist there's no need to soak pea seeds before planting. If peas grow in cold wet soils, it's best not to soak them, as they may rot. Wait until soil starts to dry out before sowing outside. Seeds germinate within 2 weeks at temperatures between 50 to 70°F (10 to 21°C).

Once peas start producing, harvest regularly to keep them coming. I enjoy the early pickings for kitchen use, because I know the more I pick the more I get. Pinching tips off vines makes them bush out and increases yields. Juicy pea shoots are delicious in stir-fries and salads.

Peas are legumes, which enrich soil with nitrogen. If sowing where no legumes have grown before, coat the seeds with black powdered bacterial inoculant to aid growth (available through seed catalogues).

A Fence of Peas

Grow peas using fencing—any fencing material will do, even chicken wire. Metal stakes or strong bamboo canes are threaded through to support and "plant" the fencing, and two rows of peas are sowed, one row along each side of the fence. TIP: Push stakes well into the ground so that later the heavy fence does not fall over.

Why not grow peas with a twist? Plant sweet peas alternating with the peas in the row. This past summer I enjoyed a "hedge" with bumper crops of snap peas and gorgeous ultra-fragrant 'Matucana' sweet peas.

Hoe a Row of Peas in Five!

"Hoe a row in five" (see May) takes five minutes to plant a 20-ft. (6-m) row of peas, and no time at all for the peas to start climbing their supports. I sow eight seeds per cell pack, 1 in. (2.5 cm) deep and 1 in. (2.5 cm) apart, hoping that 6 germinate. When pea seedlings are 6 in. (15 cm) tall, I remove them from the cell packs as a solid block without disturbing the roots. TIP: Harden cell packs off before planting outdoors.

1. Hoe a shallow furrow.
2. Empty seedlings out of cell packs.
3. Place blocks of seedlings, end to end, along the length of the furrow.
4. Cover with excavated soil using the hoe.
5. Water in.

PEA ENATION

Pea enation is a coastal virus spread by the green peach aphid. It causes vines to yellow and die, and peas to look warty. Choose enation-resistant varieties if you are planting peas directly into wet, cool soils. Crop rotations are strongly advised to counter pea enation—don't repeat peas in the same area for four years.

Top left: 'Sugar Snap' peas.

Top: 'Sugar Snap' peas interplanted with 'Matucana' sweet peas.

Above: Peas in cell packs.

Left: Seeds ready for collection.

Seed Saving

Peas (*Pisum sativum*) are self-pollinating so you can grow different varieties close together, but it's best to leave a buffer zone of 30 ft. (9 m) between to be sure. Seeds don't ripen at the same time so regular collection is necessary. Pea seeds are smooth or wrinkled. Smooth seeds are good for drying, while wrinkled seeds are best for eating fresh or freezing.

Once pods have been shucked, make sure seeds are thoroughly dry by spreading them out flat. White egg masses on seeds means pea weevils have been at work. To solve this problem remove any infected seeds, and put the rest in the freezer in an airtight container. Store in a container or bag in a dark, cool, rat-proof place. Usual seed life: 2 years.

PEPPERS

Peppers (*Capsicum annuum*) are heat lovers and do not thrive until conditions have warmed up. In tropical climates they grow as perennials, but in unpredictable temperate climates gardeners grow them as annuals. Wait until peppers have ripened to red, yellow, chocolate or purple before harvesting, because the flavour and vitamin-C content increases dramatically when the colour changes.

Peppers have a long growing season, so seeds should be started early. Seeds germinate around 75°F (24°C), which means growing them under lights indoors or on top of bottom heat in the greenhouse. Peppers grow best at 70°F (21°C) during the day, so young seedlings also appreciate a source of heat until weather warms up. After hardening plants off, peppers can be grown outdoors once soil has warmed.

CREATE A MINI-GREENHOUSE FOR PEPPERS
1. Line the area peppers will grow with black landscape fabric.
2. Peg it down using 4-ft.-tall (1.2-m) cedar stakes, one in each corner.
3. Transplant pepper seedlings through X-slashes in the fabric.

'Italian Sweet' peppers.

4. Wrap 6-mil plastic around the peppers by stapling plastic onto the stakes.
5. Make a lightweight roof for protection during cold nights.

Peppers in 2-gal. (9-L) Pots

I have given up waiting for conditions to settle since growing peppers in 2-gal. (9-L) pots in the greenhouse. One plant per pot, grown in screened Super-Duper compost, provides all the peppers I need. Providing a bamboo stake or tomato cage supports the bushy plants. TIP: For longer fruit set, feed weekly in July with liquid seaweed or compost tea, or top-dress pots with screened compost mid season.

Take the Heat Out of Peppers

The seeds and placenta of peppers contain capsaicinoids, which give hot peppers mouth-searing pungency. Use hot peppers with extreme caution and treat them with respect. Don't rub your eyes after handling them or inhale too deeply around them, or you'll be sorry! If you've eaten a pepper that's too hot, don't drink water, which increases the heat—eat dairy products or starchy foods such as bread and crackers instead.

Garden Path Favourites

(Heat scale: sweet to hot = 1 to 5)

'Corno Giallo': (1) Tapered bright-orange sweet peppers, 10 in. (25 cm) long. Perfect for stuffing, drying and fresh eating.

'Pimiento': (1) Thick-walled, sweet juicy slicer for salads, sandwiches and baking.

'Italian Sweet' and 'Red Bull's Horn': (1) Thin-walled, tapered sweet red peppers, good for roasting and stuffing.

'Jingle Bells': (1) Small multi-coloured ornamental sweet peppers.

'Klari Baby Cheese': (1) The shape of baby Gouda cheeses, great for fresh eating, roasting and stuffing.

'Pepperoncini': (2) Long, thin-walled peppers perfect for pickling and drying.

'Tequila Sunrise': (2) Carrot-shaped deep-orange peppers with a kick, good for drying and roasting.

'Hungarian Black': (3) Small early black peppers, good for drying and roasting.

'Early Jalapeño': (3) Medium-hot peppers ideal for salsas and pickling.

'Habanero' and 'Scotch Bonnet': (5) Small peppers hot enough to blow your head off!

Above: Pepper seedlings on heater cable in propagation box.

Top right: 'Early Jalapeño' peppers.

Right: Peppers for seed saving.

Basic Hot Sauce

Using rubber gloves:

Cut the stems off a few hot peppers and blanch them in boiling white wine vinegar for 3 minutes. Put the peppers with ½ cup (125 mL) of hot vinegar and 1 tsp. (5 mL) of salt into a food processor and purée. Put into a sauce bottle for 3 days before consuming. The longer the sauce stands the hotter it gets.

Optional: Add sliced ginger, sugar, lime juice or minced garlic to the sauce before processing.

The Red-Pepper Jelly Test

On the left in the photo below is red-pepper jelly using peppers from my garden; on the right, red-pepper jelly using hydroponically grown peppers from the store.

Using the same recipe (next page) in both cases, this photo clearly demonstrates that something is awry in the hydroponic-pepper jelly. Research is showing that food plants grown under glass and out of soil are missing valuable phytonutrients that fight disease. Try this red-pepper jelly test for yourself to see the value of growing real peppers worth eating.

The red-pepper jelly test.

Red-Pepper Jelly

Makes 2 cups (475 mL) of lively relish

6 to 8 sweet red peppers

2 Tbsp. (30 mL) salt

1 cup (250 mL) red wine vinegar

2 cups (475 mL) sugar

Dash of hot pepper sauce or cayenne pepper to taste

Remove seeds from peppers. Grind peppers coarsely in food processor, or chop by hand. Place them in a bowl and cover with salt. Cover the bowl and leave overnight. The next day drain off half the liquid. Combine the peppers and remaining liquid with the vinegar, sugar and hot pepper sauce or cayenne in a saucepan. Bring to a boil, reduce to a simmer and cook for one hour until thickened, stirring occasionally. When thickened, and while hot, pour the jelly into sterilized Mason jars. Wipe any spillage from the rim, cover with a lid, and tighten the ring. The jars seal tight as the jelly cools. Store in the pantry. Keeps 3 months refrigerated.

Seed Saving

Peppers (*Capsicum annuum*) are in the nightshade family (Solanaceae) and are related to tomatoes, eggplants and potatoes. They need hot summers to ripen seed, which may mean growing them under a poly tunnel or in a greenhouse. They are self-pollinating, but it's best to isolate different varieties by 6 ft. (1.8 m), as peppers have large open flowers. Leave peppers to ripen on the plant for seed. To collect seeds, cut the peppers in half lengthwise, and scrape the seeds off the placenta. Lay the seeds out on plates to dry and then store in airtight containers. Usual seed life: 2 to 3 years.

POTATO

The potato (*Solanum tuberosum*) is one of the most diverse food crops in the world, first domesticated by humans ten thousand years ago. Potatoes originated in the Andes, but only arrived in North America with Irish settlers. The potato is best known for its carbohydrate content, approximately 1 oz. (28 g) in a medium potato. Potatoes provide vitamin C and B6, potassium, magnesium, phosphorus, iron and zinc. The nutrients of potato are evenly distributed between the flesh and the skin, so it's best to eat them unpeeled.

Potatoes are easy to grow and productive—a 30-ft. (9-m) row can yield up to 60 lb. (27 kg). Just 1 lb. (454 g) of seed potatoes can provide up to 10 lb. (4.5 kg) or more. It is highly recommended to start with commercial, certified disease-free seed potatoes, but having just said this, I grew some great russets using

Fingerling potatoes.

Above: Potatoes appreciate mulches.

Top left: Volunteer russet potatoes.

Left: Have you ever wondered what to do with stored potatoes that sprout in January? Remove all but the two strongest sprouts. Cover with damp coir (coco peat) or sawdust, and the potatoes continue to grow! TIP: Potatoes need to be hardened off to get them used to cooler temperatures outdoors before planting them.

certified organic potatoes from the produce section, and they volunteered again this year!

Ideally, small tubers—the size of a hen's egg—are planted uncut. Larger tubers should be cut in pieces with at least two, but no more than three, eyes. Leave cut pieces overnight to form a callous, which helps prevent them from rotting in cool soils. Minimum soil temperature at time of planting should be 45°F (7°C) but potato tubers should be planted no later than the end of May.

Planting Tips

- Dig a shallow trench running north/south to provide plants with the maximum exposure to sun. Line the trench with uncontaminated wood ash and granular seaweed, which provide potash for good yields.

- Plant seed potatoes 3 in. (8 cm) deep and 12 in. (30 cm) apart in the trench.
- Cover with a layer of compost or topsoil.
- Although potatoes appreciate rich, manured soil, don't over-manure, as this leads to scab.
- Do not lime soil where potatoes are to grow; they prefer acidic pH 6.0 to 6.5.
- Keep potato tubers dark to prevent exposure to sunlight, which turns them green, bitter and mildly toxic, but do not bury the tubers too deep, as potatoes naturally grow close to the surface.
- Keep developing tubers covered by earthing up against stems when plants are 6 in. (15 cm) tall, avoiding the leaves. Repeat every 6 in. (15 cm) of growth. Applying protective mulches also locks in moisture, which benefits growth.

- To get the longest harvest, plant one early variety ('Epicure', 'Caribe'), one mid-season variety ('Yukon Gold', 'Red Pontiac') and one late variety ('Russet', 'Yellow Banana').

You can enjoy an early harvest of new potatoes just two months after planting by "grabbling" with your hands under plants, without disturbing them. Cutting the stem cleanly with a knife, just above ground, speeds up ripening. Leave the tubers in the ground for two weeks before lifting, so the skin has a chance to harden. Store potatoes (protected from rats) in burlap bags or paper sacks in a cool dark frost-free place. Stored tubers need ventilation or they may sweat and rot; check periodically for spoilage.

PROBLEMS WITH POTATOES

Earwigs turn potato leaves into lace, but don't affect growth below ground.

Late blight (*Phytophthera infestans*) can affect potatoes, particularly in cool summers. Tops blacken and the potatoes perish. To prevent blight follow crop rotations, avoiding sites where Solanaceae (potatoes, tomatoes, peppers and eggplants) have grown before.

Wireworms are lured by potatoes. They especially cause problems in newly established gardens where sod has been removed. Nematodes are an effective biological control.

Colorado potato beetle can be a pest. Companion planting with marigolds and garlic is said to repel this beetle. Try side-dressing with neem seed cake as a systemic insecticide.

Scab (*Streptomycetes scabies*) adversely affects cooking quality, though not yield or storage. It shows up as brown rough "corky" spots on tubers. Avoid fresh manure.

The Garden Path Potato Salad

2 lb. (907 g) new potatoes, cooked 'til just tender, cooled and chopped
1 sweet onion, minced
1 small cucumber, chopped
2 dill pickles, sliced, or 1 tsp. (5 mL) capers
2 hard-boiled eggs, chopped
2 tsp. (10 mL) dill
1 tsp. (5 mL) salt
½ tsp. (2.5 mL) black pepper
3 Tbsp. (45 mL) mayonnaise
Toss all together and chill in refrigerator.

RADICCHIO

Chicory has been eaten and used as a medicinal in Europe from time immemorial, but the North American pallet is just starting to make its acquaintance. *Chicorium intybus* has two distinct cultivated species—one grown for witloof roots; the other for radicchio leaves and considerably easier to grow. Witloof has to be lifted in fall and stored to produce tender edible shoots ("chicons") that appear on root crowns. Witloof root is delicious eaten raw or steamed with sauces or dips. The roots can also be roasted to make a fine coffee substitute.

Radicchio is a hardy perennial suited to cool climates. Start transplants six weeks before setting them out, after all danger of frost. Direct sown in June you should be harvesting mature heads in September. Radicchio is best eaten at maturity, when the plants have formed heads and the leaves have developed their best flavour. Harvest by cutting the head off at the base, leaving a lower rosette of leaves. I love the impact of radicchio in the fall garden when their colours are the richest and most varied. TIP: Plant different cultivars 6 in. (15 cm) apart in all directions to fill a square. Enjoy the show in your garden and in your salad bowl!

'Rossa di Treviso' radicchio.

Palla Rossa radicchio.

Radicchio can be left in the ground in areas where the soil does not freeze in winter, but will fare best protected from heavy winter rains. See "Tips for Crop Protection" in August.

Mature heads cut in fall and stored in a plastic bag will keep in the fridge for a few weeks. The bitterness in the leaves decreases during storage.

'**Palla Rossa**' is an Italian favourite, a Chiogga-type radicchio with firm round heads 4 in. (10 cm) across.

'**Rossa di Treviso**' is showy as a leaf chicory. Long, pointy leaves in deep red and white offer tangy greens for salads, sandwiches and garnishes all winter.

Seed Saving

Chicory is biennial—establishing in the first year, setting seed in the second. The flowers are perfect, but are self-incompatible, so they need pollination from insects. Radicchio crosses with other species of chicory and endives that are flowering within ¼ mi. (400 m). (That includes the prolific wild blue chicory that grows along the roadside.)

Plants produce stalks covered in bright-blue flowers, a very pretty sight. The seeds are beige and tubular and adhere to the stalk, which makes it a little tricky to collect them. When the stalks are dry, thresh them against a wheelbarrow, so that the seeds fall out and to the bottom. A light hammering may be needed to release the remainder of seeds from the stalk. Usual seed life: 8 years.

RADISH

Radishes (*Raphanus sativus*) are one of the easiest crops to grow and vary in colour, so are fun to grow in children's gardens. The smaller annual radishes are best planted in spring, and act as good markers when grown with onions and carrots, seed that takes longer to germinate. Radishes grow best in cool temperatures, so seeds can be sown in early spring for fast harvests within 28 to 45 days. Seeds sown every 2 weeks will ensure continuous harvests.

The secret to large, mild, crispy radishes (the way they are best eaten!) is lots of moisture and fertile soil for fast growth.

The big winter and Asian radishes are biennials. Japanese daikon is a long white radish, which is the top-selling vegetable in Japan. 'Rat's Tail' radish (*Raphanus caudatus*) bolts to seed fast, but that's okay because it's grown for its long seed pods that have a pleasant flavour.

'Easter Egg' radishes are perfect for children's gardens.

Seed Saving

Radishes are in the Brassicaceae cabbage family. Select the largest roots to save seeds from, and choose the last plants to bolt. Smaller radishes are usually annuals, but larger winter radishes are biennials that take two seasons to set seed. Flowers are insect-pollinated, so leave several plants to go to seed. Radishes do not cross with other brassicas, nevertheless ½ mi. (800 m) separation is recommended between related cultivars flowering at the same time.

Flowers develop into attractive seed pods, swollen with light-brown round seeds. Huge quantities of seed can be collected from a short row of radishes. Cut stalks when seed pods change colour, but before they are fully mature, and ripen them in paper bags or buckets. Pods will not shatter, so they need to be crushed with a hammer to release the seeds. Screen to clean. Usual seed life: 4 years.

SALSIFY

Salsify (*Tragopogon porrifolius*), also known as vegetable oyster root, is actually a biennial with slender, white fleshy taproots with a delicate oyster-like flavour. The 3-ft. (90-cm) plants are eye-catching with long silvery leaves and feathery purple flowers. They self-seed readily. Roots are harvested as required from October through winter, and are prepared by boiling until tender. The youngest leaves can also be added to salads. Usual seed life: 4 years.

Salsify or oyster root.

SEA KALE

Sea kale (*Crambe maritima*) is a brassica that thrives wild in maritime conditions. It is not that well known now, but the Victorians once appreciated sea kale as a gourmet delicacy. The plants were forced

107

Sea kale in flower.

'Summer Perfection' spinach.

under special terra-cotta pots in January, which spurs the plants on to grow delicate shoots that taste like asparagus crossed with hazelnuts. The pure-white flowers are highly decorative, as are the light-brown seed pods that follow. The pea-sized seeds can be sown undercover in fall, where they will germinate in spring. It's also easy to propagate sea kale from root division.

SPINACH

Spinach (*Spinacia oleracea*) is a broad-leaved, cold-hardy annual, with either smooth or savoy leaves. These cool-weather plants should be sown in early spring or fall, because spinach is very sensitive to lengthening days and warmer weather, which cause it to bolt; even fluctuating temperatures can trigger spinach to bolt. The secret to success is starting early, growing fast and harvesting often! Spinach is short season, only 45 to 50 days from seed to harvest. It grows best sown in cool weather in March/April or September/October—sow every 3 weeks for continuing harvests. Seed germinates between 32 to 60°F (0 to 16°C) and grows best at temperatures between 55 to 60°F (13 to 16°C).

Spinach is one of the richest sources of beta carotene (only carrots and parsley contain more). It is also an excellent source of vitamins A, B_2, B_6, C and K, manganese, folate, magnesium, iron, calcium and potassium, and a good low-calorie source of dietary fibre. Take note that the oxalates in spinach block the uptake of calcium and iron when eaten raw.

Spinach is best seeded in blocks rather than rows. Make several shallow furrows 12 to 18 in. (30 to 46 cm) apart with a hoe. If soil fertility is in question line the furrow with granular organic fertilizer before seeding. Sow spinach seeds 1 in. (2.5 cm) apart and ½ in. (1 cm) deep. If seeds are viable they should germinate within 2 weeks. For "cut and come again" baby greens thin plants to 3 in. (8 cm) apart, but for large leaves space plants 6 in. (15 cm) apart. For bunch spinach cut leaves off at ground level, leaving the dirty roots in place. Washed spinach will store refrigerated for 10 to 14 days.

Leaf miner can be a problem. To remedy this, harvest the older leaves on a regular basis or use floating row cover if it is a serious problem. Crop rotations will break this pest's life cycle. (See "Insect Pests" in April.)

Spinach Varieties for Seed Saving

'Bloomsdale Longstanding' (1908): Thick succulent dark-green crumpled leaves with good cold-soil emergence. Savoy spinach is slower growing and resists bolting better than some varieties.

'Norfolk' (1880): An heirloom variety of spinach from Quebec hardy to -22°F (-30°C). Dark-green savoyed leaves with good bolt resistance.

'Summer Perfection': This Dutch variety is sweet and longstanding, with flat upright leaves easy for harvesting.

'Giant Winter': Large savoy leaves developed for cold hardiness. Recommended for a fall crop and greenhouse production over winter.

Other Types of Spinach

Perpetual spinach: *Beta vulgaris* is not a true spinach, but a cross between beet greens and Swiss chard; it does not bolt to seed readily and provides smooth, tasty, spinach-like greens year round.

Mountain spinach or orach: *Atriplex hortensis* can be used in place of spinach or chard in any recipe. Mountain spinach offers pickings of colourful leaves, and makes a good accent plant in the garden as well as in the salad bowl. Harvest by pinching the tips out to create bushy plants. This annual is easy to grow in full sun or part shade. TIP: If grown in part sun it does not bolt to seed as fast.

My favourite is purple orach, which is often grown as an ornamental edible. Flowers are tiny because it is wind pollinated, but different varieties of orach cross, so for seed saving either grow only one variety or cage plants with spun polyester to keep the variety pure. Tiny black seeds are enclosed in bracts that are easily stripped off the stalk when dried. Usual seed life: 5 years.

New Zealand spinach: *Tetragonia expansa* dates back to 1770. Spreading leafy plants have pointy pale-green leaves with delicious spinach taste. This is not a true spinach, but similar in texture and flavour. Unlike spinach it thrives in hot weather and does not

L to r: Perpetual spinach; purple orach goes to seed with 'Red Express' cabbage; New Zealand spinach; and strawberry spinach.

Spinach Salad

Serves 4 to 6

4 bunches spinach, washed and torn into
small pieces

½ lb. (227 g) brown mushrooms, sliced

1 medium mild white or red onion, diced

3 hard-boiled free-range eggs, chopped

½ cup (125 mL) goat's cheese, crumbled

Honey Mustard Dressing

Shake vigorously in a screw-top glass jar:

½ cup (125 mL) extra virgin olive oil

½ cup (125 mL) lemon juice

2 Tbsp. (30 mL) Dijon mustard

6 cloves garlic minced

3 Tbsp. (45 mL) liquid honey

Keep refrigerated.

bolt or get bitter. Some people prefer the smoother taste of New Zealand spinach.

Grown as an annual, it is started indoors, or direct seeded after danger of frost. Soak the hard seeds overnight before sowing, and be patient—these seeds are slow to germinate. It is best harvested when 4 in. (10 cm) long by pinching the tips out, and the more you pick the more it grows. New Zealand spinach needs heat to germinate and warm soils to thrive, yet it prefers partial shade. And watch out! In sandy, well-drained soils this plant self-seeds rampantly. Usual seed life: 5 years.

Strawberry spinach: *Chenopodium capitatum* is an eye-catching sixteenth-century plant still grown today. The ½-in. (1-cm) edible strawberry-like fruits grow on compact 18-in. (46-cm) annual plants. The foliage of young plants can be eaten as spinach, raw in salads or steamed. The berries are decorative and always inspire interesting conversations around the dinner table. Strawberry spinach does not cross with spinach as they are not related. Lots of tiny black seeds are produced on the fruits and can be collected by rubbing the seeds off the surface. Lay on plates to thoroughly dry and store in an airtight tub. (Word of caution: strawberry spinach self-seeds readily!) Usual seed life: 3 years.

Seed Saving

Spinach is a unique annual because it is dioecious, which means that a plant bears either entirely male or female flowers. Some plants produce seed and others only pollen. For best pollination, a ratio with double the number of male to female plants is required.

Spinach depends on wind for pollination, so tiny flowers are inconspicuous because they don't need to attract insects. Even though pollen can be carried large distances by wind, it's unlikely that small amounts from a home garden will carry farther than the garden. To insure varietal purity, an isolation distance of ½ mi. (800 m) is recommended. If you are concerned about crossing, cage blocks of spinach plants with Reemay™, because pollen cannot penetrate spun polyester.

Seeds stalks are harvested when they are still green and the seeds are light brown. The seeds will need to dry further, either in paper bags in a warm place, or for large quantities, laid out on a tarp in the sun. Strip the seeds off the stalks and screen them to remove large particles, and winnow them to clean before storage. Usual seed life: 3 years.

SQUASH

Squashes and pumpkins are what I refer to as "heat lovers," needing warm soil for germination and warm outdoor temperatures to thrive. This means that there's no rush to get seeds started, so I start squash plants mid May, when germination is fast, and seedlings will still be ready to go out in June when the weather is settled.

The fragile roots of squash and artichoke seedlings

Roasted Squash

Simply cut into sections and drizzle with olive oil and bake for 30 minutes. A delicious side vegetable with any dish, and great makings for wonderful soups and lasagnas.

Above: Squash seedlings grow fast in warm conditions.

Top right: Winter squash—hubbard, sugar pumpkin, buttercup, delicata, and spaghetti.

resent disturbance, so it's a good idea to plant each seed in its own pot. The best way to grow squash, which are heavy feeders, is to dig a pit 12 in. (30 cm) square and 12 in. (30 cm) deep and fill it with Super-Duper compost and/or aged manure. Using the excavated soil, build a mound 6 in. (15 cm) high and sow 4 seeds ½ in. (1 cm) deep on top of the mound. Thin to the best 2 plants.

Saving Space in a Small Garden

Vining squash can be planted at the edge of the garden so they run out over the lawn, but here's a great space-saving idea. Grow squash, spaced 18 in. (46 cm) apart, in a bed running parallel to a fence, wall or side of a shed. Use the same preparation method as above for amazing results! Lean 8-ft. (2.4-m) bamboo stakes up against the vertical support and attach the vines to them. This also makes it easy to

harvest the squash, which now grow hanging down. In the case of "whoppers," bag them in netting tied onto the bamboo canes for extra support.

The most common problem for squash is powdery mildew, which appears as white spots on both sides of the leaves, and affects yield and fruit size. Mildews are often symptomatic of lack of aeration or overcrowding. Space plants 12 in. (30 cm) apart for the bush varieties, and 18 to 24 in. (46 to 61 cm) apart for vining types.

Winter Squash

I consider winter squash a vital part of our diet. When left to mature on the vine before they are brought inside, they will store through winter. (I just line them up on the dresser, and we eat them as we need them.) TIP: They store best at 55°F (13°C) in low humidity.

To harvest winter squash or pumpkin, cut them off with a 1-in. (2.5-cm) length of stem attached and wash off any dirt. TIP: Wipe the skin with a 10:1 water: hydrogen peroxide solution to destroy bacteria and prevent rot from setting in during storage.

Summer squash has a higher water content, and winter squash a higher nutrient content, particularly in beta carotene in the orange flesh. All squash are an excellent source of fibre and low in calories. Spaghetti squash is a great low-calorie substitute for pasta, delicious served with homemade tomato sauce.

Seed Saving

Squash are in the Cucurbitaceae family and have separate male and female flowers, so they require insects for pollination. Crossing occurs only within relatives of the same species, which means you can grow one of each of the following (as long as none of your neighbours grow squash within ½ mi. (800 m).

Cucurbita maxima: Hubbards, turban, pumpkins, banana, buttercup. The most vigorous squash with long vines and rounded hairy, leaves. Seeds are thick and yellow in colour.

C. pepo: Acorn, crooknecks, cocozelle, pattypan (scallops), marrow, zucchini, baby pumpkins, spaghetti squash and decorative gourds. There are both vining and bush types with prickly leaves and vines. The leaves are more serrated than *C. maxima*. Seeds are small, flat and white.

C. moschata: Butternuts, trombocini, cheese.

Male flower with anther and pollen.

These have large hairy leaves and creeping hairy vines. Seeds are beige in colour, small, long and thin.

C. argyrosperma (C. mixta): Japanese pumpkins, cushaw squashes. These squash have spreading vines and leaves same as *C. moschata*. Seeds are grey in colour.

Squash Rings with Honey Glaze

Preheat oven to 375°F (190°C)

Cut squash into thick rings and scoop out the seeds.

Place rings in a single layer on an oiled baking sheet.

Bake in preheated oven for 15 minutes or until squash begins to soften.

In a small bowl whisk:

3 Tbsp. (45 mL) honey

1 Tbsp. (15 mL) soy sauce

2 tsp. (10 mL) apple cider vinegar

1½ tsp. (7.5 mL) fresh ginger, minced

2 garlic cloves, minced

Brush half of the glaze over the squash. Sprinkle with salt and pepper. Bake uncovered for 15 minutes. Brush the remaining glaze over the squash and continue to bake another 15 minutes or until tender.

Hand Pollination of Squash

The flowers of cucurbits are so attractive to pollinating insects, especially bees, that the best way to ensure you are maintaining varietal purity is by hand pollinating. Male flowers are borne on long stems and appear before the female flowers. Female flowers are on short stems, with a swelling (ovary) at the base. Saving seed from a minimum of 6 plants is recommended to ensure genetic diversity.

How to Hand Pollinate Squash

TIP: The first flowers on the vine are the most likely to take.

1. In the evening, choose a male and a female flower due to open.

2. Close each flower by using a piece of masking tape to seal the top together.

3. Cut the male flower off with a 6-in. (15-cm) stalk attached, and remove the petals to expose the anthers and pollen (see photo).

4. Pry open the female flower, but do not remove any petals.

5. Rub the pollen inside the female flower, brushing the stigma attached to the ovary.

6. After pollen transfer, to insure varietal purity, shut the female flower with masking tape so no insects can enter.

7. Wait until the flower withers (one or two days) and mark the developing fruit with the name of the variety.

Seed Saving

Squash fruits should be left on the vine as long as possible to allow the seeds to mature inside. In case of frost, take the fruit indoors where the seeds will carry on ripening. Scoop the seeds out and put them in a bowl of water. The good seed will sink to the bottom and the dud seed float to the top. Pour the duds off, and strain the rest. Leave seeds to ferment for a few days so that the jelly around them dissolves. This fermentation destroys seed-borne pathogens. Crumble apart any seeds that stick together with your fingers, and dry them again. Store dry seeds in an airtight tub in a dark cool place. Usual seed life: 3 to 5 years.

SUNCHOKE (JERUSALEM ARTICHOKE)

Sunchokes are an easy-to-grow source of carbohydrates, and should be harvested as needed from the winter garden, as they shrivel quickly in storage. They are often referred to as Jerusalem artichokes, but this is confusing, because they are not from Jerusalem nor are they artichokes. They are hardy perennial tubers, *Helianthus tuberosus*, related to sunflowers, hence their common name sunchokes. The tubers multiply like mad, and even if you dig all the roots up, they will come back. Generally once you plant sunchokes you'll always have them.

Sunchokes thrive in any garden soil but the best tubers are grown in well-drained soil in full sun. Tubers should be planted early in spring, and can be left until harvested in fall, once the tops have died down. They are sweetest if left in the ground until after hard frosts.

These knobby light-brown or red tubers are generally neglected as vegetables. In addition to being a versatile food, sunchokes are a natural source of insulin, which makes them good for diabetics. They are low-calorie alternatives to potatoes, with the same nutritional value. They can be french-fried, steamed, boiled, mashed or roasted just like potatoes. The taste is nutty, similar to water chestnuts, so they are also good raw with veggie dips.

Sunchokes are usually propagated by tubers that have been stored in the ground over winter and dug up in early spring. Plant tubers 12 in. (30 cm) apart

Blender Sunchoke Soup

4 cups (1 L) sunchokes, chopped

2 cups (475 mL) carrots or parsnips,
   chopped (optional)

12 cups (2.8 L) soup stock or water

2 bay leaves

   Boil sunchokes until soft. Remove bay leaves.
   Sauté:

1 cup (250 mL) chopped onions

3 cloves garlic, minced

1 tsp. (5 mL) ground coriander

2 Tbsp. (30 mL) olive oil

   *Add 3 Tbsp. (45 mL) flour and whisk with
enough cooking water to make a gravy. Add
salt and pepper to taste and combine gravy,
sunchokes and cooking water in a blender.
Blend until smooth. Garnish with a dollop
of sour cream and a dash of fresh, chopped
parsley.*

Sunchokes make good windbreaks and sunscreens.

in a corner where you will not mind them spreading. These fast-growing perennials grow to 6 ft. (1.8 m) tall by summer, so chose the site carefully to avoid overshadowing other plants.

I grow two varieties: one with prolific red tubers but no flowers, another with large knobby white tubers and showy yellow sunflowers in October. TIP: Choose the least knobby tubers for replanting, as these are easier to clean.

SWEET CORN

Corn shares a common ancestry with teosinte, a perennial Mexican grass, and was traded by ancient Incas, Aztecs and American First Peoples. Because it was adaptable to a wide range of conditions, it quickly spread around the world. In many indigenous languages the word maize and life are the same. Beans and corn have a symbiotic relationship in which their amino acids complement each another. Corn lacks amino acids lysine and tryptophan, but beans contain both of these, so when eaten together they provide a complete set of proteins in the diet.

5 TYPES OF CORN

Dent: The endosperm shrinks, creating a depression in the kernel. Long kernels are cracked for livestock feed.

Flint: The hardest-of-all corn is used for rolling into cornflakes and grinding into corn meal.

Flour: The endosperm is composed entirely of starch, and thin fragile kernels are easy to mill into flour.

Pop: Small cobs produce small kernels with air bubbles inside; they pop when heated.

Sweet Corn: (*Zea mays*) is the result of a natural recessive gene mutation that controls sugar conversion in the endosperm of the kernel. Sweet corn is picked immature (at the milk stage) and eaten as a vegetable rather than a grain.

'Golden Bantam' Corn (1902)

Open-pollinated (non-hybrid) corn has been replaced commercially by hybrids, which maintain their sweet flavour longer. 'Golden Bantam' is an heirloom open-pollinated variety introduced by Burpee in 1902—to this day it remains a popular choice for home gardeners, and is sweet and flavourful when consumed (or frozen) the day it is picked.

Optimal soil temperature for 'Golden Bantam' corn is 60°F (16°C), so plant corn between mid May and mid June. Corn is a heavy feeder that benefits from aged manure or Super-Duper compost, plus an application of organic fertilizer to the area before planting.

For optimal wind pollination, corn should be grown in blocks 8 ft. (2.4 m) square (minimum) rather than single rows. A minimum of 4 rows is recommended, spaced 2 ft. (60 cm) apart. Sow 2 seeds 2 in. (5 cm) deep every 12 in. (30 cm) along the rows (germination is only 75 percent). For a head start, seed corn indoors in April for transplanting out when the weather warms up.

THE THREE SISTERS

Traditionally corn was planted with pole beans and squash, using the corn stalk to support climbing beans, and the squash leaves to trap moisture in soil and suppress weeds (and deter raccoons with prickly hairs!). Nitrogen-fixing beans also nourish the high nitrogen needs of corn. TIP: Plant corn first. When corn seedlings are 6 in. (15 cm) tall, plant beans alternating with squash around it. Otherwise, the corn will be smothered before it emerges.

The main problem growing corn is raccoons—families of them magically appear as soon as the sweet corn ripens! Fishnetting over the corn patch (stretched tightly) is the only thing that worked for me! Keep an eye out for corn loopers, olive-green caterpillars that bore into young corncobs. Handpick them off. Practising four-year crop rotation for corn breaks the life cycle of this pest, and also protects the soil from getting tired.

THREE SISTERS SOUP

2 cups (500 mL) black beans, cooked

2 lb. (1 kg) squash—butternut, hubbard, pumpkin, acorn or kuri—peeled and steamed until tender

2 cups (475 mL) corn kernels

1 large onion, chopped

2 Tbsp. (30 mL) minced garlic

4 Tbsp. (60 mL) of butter (or ghee)

1½ tsp. (7.5 mL) cumin

1 tsp. (5 mL) ground coriander

1 tsp. (5 mL) chili powder (optional)

½ tsp. (2.5 mL) cayenne pepper

2 tsp. (10 mL) salt

1 bay leaf

4 cups (1 L) water or soup stock

In a large saucepan sauté the onion, garlic and bay leaf in the butter (or ghee) until soft. Chop the steamed squash into small chunks and add to the pan; while stirring blend in all the spices and salt. Cover the squash with water (or stock) and cook until just tender (15 minutes). Remove the bay leaf. Purée half the soup mixture in a blender until smooth. Add this to the remaining soup together with the corn kernels and the black beans. Bring to a boil gently, while stirring, and simmer over a low heat for 10 minutes.

No more blanching! Cobs of corn freeze beautifully left wrapped inside their inner husk leaves. Throw still frozen cobs into boiling water for exactly 10 minutes for crunchy "good-as-the-day-picked" flavour.

Seed Saving

Corn belongs to the Poaceae (Gramineae) family. Being wind pollinated it readily crosses with other corns. For small-scale corn production, isolation distances of 500 ft. (150 m) are required to prevent cross-pollination between different corn varieties. Tassels form on cobs, producing pollen, which is shed from anthers that hang down (emerging before the silks). Silks protrude from female "ears" on the cob. Each silk is attached to an individual kernel (seed) and requires more than one pollen grain for successful pollination. Pollen must reach all silks for the full development of a corncob.

Saving corn seed is not always practical on a small scale. Corn depends on a high degree of cross-pollination to maintain genetic integrity, and a minimum of 100 plants to avoid inbreeding depression. Apart from growing two varieties of corn that "flower" at different times, the only way to guarantee that corn maintains varietal purity is by hand pollination. Usual seed life: 2 years.

How To Hand Pollinate Corn

Day 1: Choose 100 "true to type" corn plants from which to collect seed.

Earmark the best 50 cobs, and remove their tassels before they shed any pollen. Cover them with a paper bag (special bags can be ordered online for this) and staple or tie the bag shut.

Day 2: Bag the remaining 50 earmarked cobs, covering the tassels to collect pollen when anthers emerge. Collect the pollen at midday by shaking the bag. Mix all the pollen collected into one bag. (It only remains viable for one day.) Pour the fine yellow pollen dust over the emerging silks of the 50 earmarked cobs, then bag immediately to protect them from any pollen floating in the air.

Days 3 to 7: Repeat to ensure thorough pollination, (the silks remain receptive for weeks). Leave pollinated ears covered until their silks turn brown, which indicates pollination has occurred. Leave the pollinated cobs on the plants until the husks dry (30 days), pull the husks back, and hang them in a warm, dry place for a few more weeks. Choose the largest kernels for seed saving. TIP: Freeze kernels for 2 days in an airtight container to kill any weevils that may be inside.

SWISS CHARD

Swiss chard (*Beta vulgaris*) is one of the easiest and most rewarding of the vegetable greens to grow. It is a cool-weather biennial, which produces copious amounts of nutritious greens year round from a spring sowing.

There are three different types of chard:
- Light green leaves and thin stalks with sweet flavour—e.g., 'Lucullus'
- Large leaves and thin stalks—e.g., 'Fordhook Giant'

Top: Silverbeet is two vegetables in one.

Bottom: 'Five-Colour Silverbeet' is an ornamental edible.

Top right: A 15-ft. (4.6-m) row of 'Five-Colour Silverbeet' produces masses of seeds!

- Large leaves with broad stalks—e.g., 'White Silverbeet' or 'Five-Colour Silverbeet' (also called rainbow chard).

Silverbeet has become my favourite type of chard because it is two vegetables in one. Mature leaves grow large, providing squeaky steamed greens, and succulent stalks can be used like celery and are crunchy in stir-fries! Offering multicoloured rainbow chard drizzled with a "sauce of the moment" always provokes admiring comments at the dinner table!

Seed Saving

Chard is in the Chenopodiaceae family and plants are self-incompatible; to preserve diversity collect

Swiss Chard Provençal

Preheat oven to 350°F (175°C)
Mix:
4 cups (1 L) of Swiss chard, chopped and
 lightly steamed
2 cups (475 mL) zucchini, grated
1 medium onion, chopped fine
2 cloves garlic, minced
2 cups (475 mL) cooked rice (you choose)
4 oz. (113 g) Gruyere or Swiss cheese
2 eggs, beaten
 Bake in an ovenproof dish, topped with
more cheese if desired.
 Serve accompanied by a homemade
tomato sauce from the garden.
 Delicious and nutritious!

from a minimum of 12 plants. Plants are wind- and insect-pollinated and will cross with other members of the family (beets, spinach and sugar beets) unless isolated by ½ mi. (800 m).

A flattish stem emerges from the centre of the leaves, which bears seed clusters called glomerules, which ripen to brown. Chard produces tall stalks with large volumes of seed; I spread them out on tarps to dry, out of full sun, in the garage where a warm breeze drifts through. Each glomerule contains 2 to 5 seeds. When dry, strip the glomerules off by hand (wearing gloves) and run a rolling pin lightly over them to break the seeds up. Sieve the seeds, discarding the smaller ones that produce inferior plants. Winnow to clean, and store in airtight containers in a cool place. Usual seed life: 4 to 6 years.

TOMATILLO (AND CAPE GOOSEBERRY)

The tomatillo (*Physalis ixocarpa*) is in the Solanaceae family and is a relative of the tomato, but it is there that any resemblance ends. Tomatillos (tomate verde) are a key ingredient in Mexican and Latin American cuisine. Light-green papery husks cover sticky fruits, 2 in. (5 cm) across, and as the fruit matures it fills the husks and splits them open. When mature the fruit changes colour from lime-green to yellow (or purple), and the husk turns brown. TIP: Roast for 5 to 10 minutes for the best flavour.

Grown in full sun and moist soil, tomatillos need more warmth than tomatoes. For best production I grow them in the greenhouse, one plant in a 5-gal. (23-L) pot (as for tomatoes), twining the lateral vines up strings for support. Maturity ranges from 80 to 120 days from transplanted seedlings. Vigorous tomatillo vines either need a support framework for the loads of fruit, or can be planted outdoors and left to sprawl where the fruits will drop off as they ripen.

Varieties to grow

'Toma verde': Early variety with uniform-sized fruits and high yields.

'Purple': Heirloom tomatillos said to be sweeter than green types.

'Purple de Milpa': Smaller variety that grows wild. Its 1-in. (2.5-cm) fruits have sharper flavour and do not burst through husks when ripe.

Cape Gooseberry

Although the Cape gooseberry (*Physalis peruviana*) was being grown in England as early as 1774, it has only been recently that the fruit has received attention in North America. The Cape gooseberry grows as an annual in temperate regions and as a perennial in the tropics. The plants are frost tender and will die off at temperatures of 30°F (-1°C). They can be overwintered under glass. Easily grown in pots, the plants adapt well to greenhouse culture, but they can also be grown outdoors once the soil has warmed up, where they produce well in hot summers.

They are easy to grow from seed (with a source of bottom heat like peppers), and plants can be propagated from one-year stem cuttings. The Cape gooseberry is a softwood perennial reaching 3 ft. (90 cm) in height. The heart-shaped leaves are velvety to the touch, and the cup-shaped flowers are yellow with purple-brown throats. The fruit is a golden-orange berry that drops to the ground as it ripens. The unique flavour of the fruit makes it an interesting addition to salads and cooked dishes, while its high pectin content makes it good for preserves and fruity sauces for desserts.

SALSA VERDE

Makes 6 cups (1.4 L)

4 cups (1 L) tomatillos, husked and halved

½ cup (125 mL) cilantro

4 cloves garlic

1 cup (250 mL) onion, chopped

1½ tsp. (7.5 mL) salt

1 cup (250 mL) water

½ cup (125 mL) oil

Combine all ingredients except 2 Tbsp. (30 mL) of the oil in a blender and process until smooth. Heat the oil and pour in the purée. Simmer over medium heat for 15 minutes. Cool the green sauce and freeze in batches. Thaw as needed for chip dips, tacos, enchiladas and tortillas.

Above: Cape gooseberries.

Left: 'Toma verde' green tomatillos produce lateral vines with huge yields.

Cape gooseberries and tomatillos are prone to root rot when grown in poorly drained soils, and do best in sandy gravelly loam. Choose a sunny location sheltered from the wind. They are susceptible to powdery mildew in high humidity, and whitefly and aphids may attack plants that are greenhouse grown.

Seed Saving

Tomatillo plants are self-incompatible, so isolated plants will rarely set fruit. Grow several plants together to ensure pollination and good fruit set. I grow six tomatillo plants side by side in the greenhouse, and as you can see from the photo, pollination is not a problem.

Cape gooseberries are self-pollinated but for greenhouse-grown plants pollination should be enhanced by gently shaking the flowering stems to move the pollen around. To save seed the recommended isolation between related species is 160 ft. (50 m).

The easiest way to collect seeds is to remove husks and put the ripe tomatillos (or ground cherries) into a blender with 1 cup (250 mL) of water. Give it a few whirls to macerate the flesh and free the seeds from the pulp. Put all this into a bowl and fill with water. Good seeds sink to the bottom—strain them off, sieve them and spread out on plates to dry. Crumble seeds apart with fingers before storing in airtight tubs. Usual seed life: 3 years.

TOMATO

Tomatoes (*Lycopersicon esculentum*) come in all colours from red, pink, orange, black and purple to yellow, and they even come splashed and striped! Sizes range from tiny currants to whopping beefsteaks, shapes from round to pear-shaped, and flavour from sweet to smoky. They are delicious fresh in salads, sandwiches and salsas, added to sauces and soups, roasted, and sun-dried.

Of all the vegetables gardeners look forward to harvesting, homegrown tomatoes "take the biscuit." Today's gardeners are favouring exotic heirloom varieties again, reputed to have the best flavour. These come with great descriptive names, in all colours and weird shapes, and they range in size from a few grams to a kilogram!

Indeterminate or Determinate?

Indeterminate and semi-determinate tomatoes are vining plants that grow 4 to 20 ft. (1.2 to 6 m) long, and represent about 75 percent of all tomato cultivars. They produce more flowers and fewer leaves as they grow, yielding tomatoes through to the end of the season.

Top-20 Tomato Tips

1. Start with high-quality seed in a sterilized growing medium.
2. Seeds need 75 to 85°F (24 to 29°C) for germination.
3. Seedlings need 60°F (16°C) daytime and at least 40°F (4°C) at night.
4. Tomatoes grow best in full sun.
5. At the first set of true leaves, transplant seedlings into their own 4-in. (10-cm) pots.
6. Fertilize seedlings weekly with liquid fish fertilizer.
7. Tomatoes fruit earlier if grown-on in 1-gal. (4.5-L) pots. Flowers indicate that roots are well enough established to support fruiting.
8. Make sure the ground has warmed up before setting indoor-grown seedlings out.
9. A soil pH of 6.0 to 6.5 is ideal.
10. Harden off before moving outdoors.
11. Add a handful of granular organic fertilizer to feed the plant throughout the season. Dig 1 tsp. (5 mL) Epsom salts into the planting hole at time of transplanting to prevent magnesium deficiency (which causes yellowing of leaves).
12. Use cloches, bell jars or landscape fabric as ways of warming soil and trapping heat in at night.
13. Fertilize plants regularly with liquid seaweed to boost fruit production.
14. Provide good support for vining tomatoes—a sturdy cedar stake 5 ft. (1.5 m) tall and 2 in. (5 cm) wide works best. There's nothing worse than finding loaded tomato plants flopped over because the stake broke! Staking exposes leaves to sunlight and results in increased fruit production.
15. In the fall, dig seaweed into the garden to increase crops the following year. Granular kelp meal is also good for feeding tomatoes.
16. Towards the end of August, prune the top off the main stem to stop growth and encourage fruit to ripen.
17. Erratic watering causes fruit splitting and blossom end rot. Deep soaking is better than light watering.
18. A mulch of seaweed makes a huge difference to yields.
19. Some varieties don't produce well under greenhouse conditions, because pollen becomes sterile in extreme heat. Choose varieties recommended for greenhouse growing.
20. Green tomatoes? Defoliate plants leaving clusters of tomatoes fully exposed to sun. Even though this may seem dramatic, it doesn't affect the health of plants. It does make a difference to how tomatoes ripen though! (Also, see "10 Great Ideas for Green Tomatoes" in October.)

Above: 'Green Zebra' tomatoes ripen to gold with green stripes and are incredibly sweet.

Left: Sturdy stakes are recommended for tall tomato plants.

Determinate tomatoes are "bush" varieties, where the main stem and suckers produce a limited number of flower clusters, which means a shorter period of production. Flowers bloom for less time, so tomatoes tend to ripen earlier. Bushy plants need support from a short stake or tomato cage.

Pruning Tomatoes

Indeterminate and semi-determinate tomatoes: Pinch off "suckers" growing between the main stem and the leaf axil. Keep vining tomatoes to one or two main stems by pinching out suckers, and keep energy directed at fruit production.

Determinate tomatoes: Beware of taking suckers off determinate bushy plants, as this cuts back on yield.

PLANTING TIP TO GET 10 TIMES MORE! When transplanting, strip all leaves off the stem except for the top truss. Bury as deep as the top truss. Tomatoes will develop roots along all parts of the stem buried underground. You can also lay the stem on its side to bury it by gently flexing it into an L-shape.

Container Growing

Compact growth habit makes determinate varieties better choices for container growing. TIP: If you grow tomatoes in containers, as soon as the roots fill the pot be sure to start feeding liquid seaweed weekly for the next four weeks to prolong fruit set. Good container-grown varieties are 'Silvery Fir', 'Sophie's Choice', 'Flamme', 'Gold Nugget', and 'Principe Borghese'.

Problems with Tomatoes?

Leaf Curl: In early summer, viral diseases, spread by aphids or by sap on fingers and tools, can cause leaf curl. Practice good hygiene, and keep aphids under control.

Above: 'Ardwyna Paste', a one-kilogram tomato!

Right: Growing tomatoes in 5-gal. (23-L) pots.

Tomato Blight: *Phytophthora infestans* is a serious disease, especially after periods of wet weather in August or September. Tomato blight first shows up as brown blotches on leaves, followed by olive-green spots on fruit. Later, a web of white fungal growth covers the whole fruit. *Phytophthora infestans* can wipe out a whole crop of tomatoes in a matter of days. To minimize risk of blight, remove infected plant debris from the garden immediately, and practise crop rotation diligently. If blight threatens, cover tomato plants with plastic to prevent the foliage from getting wet, which stops the spread of fungal spores.

Q The leaves on the 'Silvery Fir' tomato are tightly curled. Only the bottom leaves look normal. Now it's starting on top of the 'Black Cherry' tomato too. I cannot find an insect or trace thereof. What is causing this and what might be the remedy? Overnight and on rainy days the tomatoes live under a plastic hood.

A Members of Solanaceae are heat lovers that thrive in warm conditions. When the weather cools and soil temperature drops, the plants get stressed because they cannot access nutrients from cold soil. When nutrients are suddenly not available to plants that have been growing fast in warm conditions, it results in a condition called leaf roll. Other members of Solanaceae (eggplants, peppers, potatoes and tobacco plants) are also subject to this problem.

122

HERE ARE FOUR SOLUTIONS:

Solution 1: Keep plants under cover, using plastic or cold frames, until the weather settles, or place pots of tomatoes with leaf roll back in the greenhouse, where they gradually warm up. They should fully recover.

Solution 2: Tomatoes prefer slightly acidic soil, and they may need a pH adjustment to enable them to access nutrients. Adjust pH with a drench of diluted Epsom salts (magnesium sulphate).

Solution 3: It may be due to boron deficiency. Provide boron by watering ½ tsp. (2.5 mL) natural borax dissolved in 1 gal. (4.5 L) of tepid water.

Solution 4: Remediate nutrient uptake problems by spraying foliage or feeding roots with liquid seaweed or compost tea.

RECOMMENDED TOMATO VARIETIES

Red cherry: 'Chadwick's Cherry', 'Gardener's Delight', 'Peacevine'

Yellow cherry: 'Galina', 'Gold Nugget'

Salad: 'Alicante', 'Graham's Goodkeeper', 'Harbinger', 'Moneymaker', 'Yellow Perfection', 'Best of All'

Beefsteak: 'Costoluto Fiorentino', 'Cuor di Bue', 'Marmande'

Novelty: 'Green Zebra', 'Tigerella', 'Yellow Pear', 'Red Grape', 'Black Cherry'

Paste: 'Ardwyna', 'Roma', 'Big Ruby'

Greenhouse: 'Moneymaker', 'Harbinger', 'Alicante', 'Red Grape', 'Chadwick's Cherry', 'Gardener's Delight', 'Black Cherry', 'Silvery Fir'

Hanging baskets: 'Hawaiian Currant' and 'Coyote Yellow Currant'

TURNIPS AND RUTABAGAS (SWEDES)

Turnips (*Brassica rapa*) are annuals grown for their mild-flavoured crunchy roots and leafy greens. The shape of turnip roots varies considerably from flat-topped to globular, and the skin colour ranges from yellow to white, purple to red. They grow half in and half out of the soil, and are best harvested either as baby turnips at 3 to 4 in. (8 to 10 cm) in size, or full sized at 6 in. (15 cm). Turnips are an underrated vegetable, perhaps because in the past they were considered peasant food. Steamed turnips are surprisingly delicious, and young turnip greens also make fine steamed greens or greens for salads.

Rutabagas (*Brassica rapa* var. *napobrassica*) are close relatives to turnips that are grown as cool-season biennials, producing larger roots with more dense flesh. They are best eaten before they get woody and fibrous; the flavour is sweeter after a few hard frosts.

Seed turnips and rutabagas ¾ in. (2 cm) deep, 8 seeds per 1 ft. (30 cm), rows 18 in. (46 cm) apart, with plants spaced 6 in. (15 cm) apart. Seeds will germinate in a wide temperature range from 50 to 80°F (10 to 27°C). Turnips are fast-growing (55 days) but rutabagas need to be seeded in early summer in time to mature by fall (90 to 100 days).

Keep an eye out for flea beetles, detected by the appearance of small holes in the leaves (see "Pests of Brassicas").

Smashed Swedes

Peel the skin. Chop into 1-in. (2.5-cm) cubes. Boil for 20 minutes, until soft. Purée.

Season with butter, salt and pepper, or herbs such as parsley and thyme. Optional: Cook and smash together with potatoes or carrots. Yum!

those exhibiting the best characteristics in spring, setting the crowns 20 in. (51 cm) apart at the soil surface.

Turnips: Some turnips behave as annuals, setting seed in the first year; others grow as biennials. In cold winters they need to be harvested before a heavy freeze and stored. Trim the tops to 2 in. (5 cm) and store in boxes of damp sawdust or coarse washed sand. Turnips do not keep as well as rutabagas, survival is often as low as 50 percent. Select those that survive storage, and replant in spring, setting them 6 in. (15 cm) apart. Turnips may keep up to 4 months if stored at 40°F (4°C) in high humidity.

Once replanted, 3-ft. (90-cm) flower stalks will appear, the colour of the flowers often correlating with that of the roots. Flowers fade to form seed pods, which turn brown as the seeds inside mature. TIP: When pods form, pinch off the tips so that lower pods develop larger seeds. When the greatest number of pods has matured, cut the stalk down and finish ripening seeds in paper bags or buckets. Thresh dried stalks against a wheelbarrow, screen and winnow to clean seeds before storage. TIP: Watch out for marauding birds as the small, round black seeds mature. Usual seed life: 5 years.

'Marian' rutabagas are often called winter turnips or Swedes.

Seed Saving

Turnips and rutabagas are close relatives in the Brassicaceae family. The flowers are self-incompatible and so need insects for pollination. They cross-pollinate with other members of *Brassica rapa*—Asian mustards, Chinese cabbages and broccoli raab, unless isolated by 1 mi. (1.6 km).

Rutabagas: These cool-season biennials set seed in the second year, and should survive winter to set seed the following summer. In colder climates, roots need to be harvested and stored for the winter. Replant

April

LASAGNA GARDENING

Last year I was inspired to try a new method of growing food called "Lasagna Gardening," introduced by gardener Patricia Lanza, which supports the theory that the secret to success is growing the soil before growing the food. It all starts from the ground up, by adding of layers of organic materials (like making a lasagna) to create a planting bed. The finished bed should be no less than 12 in. (30 cm) in height, with the top layer prepared for seeds or transplants.

Lasagna gardening produces prolific harvests in no time, and does not require digging, tilling, sod removal or weeding. It recycles free organic waste, feeds plants and cuts down on watering. It's up to you as to whether you border the garden with boards or rocks—it's not necessary to contain it at all, but you can be as creative as you wish!

Site a lasagna garden where it receives 11 hours or more of sun a day for heat-loving plants such as tomatoes, squash, zucchini, beans and carrots. Seven hours may be adequate for cool-weather crops such as lettuce, chicory, leeks, onions, endive, parsley, peas, spinach, Swiss chard, kale, broccoli, cabbage, cauliflower, Brussels sprouts, kohlrabi, rutabaga and celeriac. Less than four hours of sunlight is insufficient for any food plant.

The first step is to plan ahead and stockpile lots of ingredients to build the lasagna garden. Gather any organic matter that is uncontaminated and biodegradable. The size of the bed is only limited by the amount of material required to build it. It takes one cycle of production for a bed to decompose by 6 in. (15 cm), as the layers of organic matter break down and release nutrients to plants. The high fertility of the growing medium results in huge healthy plants, which can be placed close together for increased productivity. Before planting another crop, simply renew the bed with fresh layers of organic matter, which also smothers any weeds that may have appeared. Organic matter also locks moisture in, which means less watering. How can you beat all this?

I just love the simplicity of lasagna gardening. It's possible for anyone to do, even if they don't own the land, because lasagna gardens can be temporary—when beds are no longer needed all that's left is quality compost! We could grow lots more food by creating lasagna beds on vacant lots and in unused spaces, and we would solve many of our waste-disposal problems at the same time.

BUILDING A LASAGNA GARDEN

1. Put down a 2-in. (5-cm) layer of manure and rake level. You can use fresh manure only in the bottom layer, where microbes will have broken it down before plant roots can access it. This manure will provide a nitrogen kick to plants later in the season. Cover the manure with overlapping sections of plain cardboard (no colour inks).

2. Build the bed up by adding layers of no more than 2 in. (5 cm) of any of the following:

- Manure (See "Know Your Manure!" in January)
- Leaves (TIP: store in circular wire cages in fall)
- Spoiled hay
- Grass clippings
- Wood ash (uncontaminated)
- Sawdust and fine woodchips (not cedar and always from untreated wood)
- Dolomite lime (neutralizes pH, adds calcium and magnesium)
- Seaweed
- Compost
- Topsoil

3. Finish with a top layer of screened compost or topsoil (photo 3). The finished bed should be 12 in. (30 cm) in height. Water well and now you are ready to sow seeds or tuck in transplants.

4. Three weeks after planting, this garden is chock-a-block with lettuces, spinach, chicory, peas, carrots and broccoli. TIP: Harvest baby greens by picking off leaves rather than pulling the plant out of the ground. Early crops of spinach, radishes, peas and lettuce are replaced by plantings of tomatoes, carrots, squash and beans. Garlic, winter leaf and root crops can follow in the fall.

TIPS FOR CROP PROTECTION

Raised beds provide extra drainage and warm the soil faster. A plastic cloche cover improves harvests in winter, and gives a head start for spring seedlings. TIP: Position against a south-facing wall for extra winter heat.

Heavy row covers act like blankets and keep warmth locked in. Black landscape fabric absorbs the sun's rays during the day and prevents the heat from escaping at night.

Q What is the difference between using straw and hay as a mulch?

A Hay comes from a mowed field of wild grasses or other herbaceous plants, and the grade of hay will depend on what was growing in the field. Hay makes a good mulch—especially when it's spoiled (mouldy) and free of charge from a horse owner—but beware of weeds! TIP: When you bury hay underneath a blanket of leaves and manure you can prevent the weed seeds from germinating.

Straw is the material left behind once grains have been harvested for threshing, then dried and compacted into bales. You'll pay more for a bale of straw because it comes without any seeds.

Top: Plastic cloche on raised bed.

Middle: Black landscape fabric.

Bottom: Protect your winter pickings.

SELF-SEEDING VEGETABLES

Can you imagine harvesting bunches of nutritious greens you didn't even plant? You can do this simply by growing kale, chard, spinach, salad greens, mustard greens, parsley and coriander—all of which are prolific self-seeding vegetables. Simply let some of the best plants go to seed and you will have a steady supply of food all year long. Talk about the Garden of Eden!

Arugula

Arugula (or rocket salad) provides patches of volunteers in spring and fall. I relish the nutty, slightly peppery flavour of young leaves in sandwiches and salads and lightly sautéed in pasta dishes. As the plant matures it develops a pungent mustard bite relished by some. The annual variety of arugula is very ornamental, going to seed with white flowers rather than the typical bright-yellow flowers of the mustard family.

Mache

Mache (or corn salad) produces leafy rosettes of juicy greens with a mild but refreshing taste for winter salads and sandwiches. It sets seed as soon as the weather warms up in spring. Small round light-brown seeds lie dormant in the soil until weather cools down in October, ensuring corn-salad greens are available all winter.

Purple Orach

Purple orach (or mountain spinach) offers pickings of deep-purple leaves, which make colourful accents in the salad bowl, as well as in the garden. Make it even more attractive by pinching out leaf tips, which cause it to bush out and produce more leaves. TIP: Grow in part sun/part shade, where it does not bolt to seed as fast and lasts longer.

Perpetual Spinach

Perpetual spinach is not true spinach, although it is used in the same way, but is a cross between chard and beet, with finer-textured leaves tender enough to tear into salads. It is also "squeaky sweet" served as a side dish of lightly steamed greens. I frequently use it as a base for vegetarian lasagnas. Perpetual spinach will grow year round without going to seed, and tastes even sweeter after hard frosts. TIP: Cut it back severely if it attempts to go to seed before the year is out!

Silverbeet

Silverbeet is a chard I originally encountered on a visit to the UK. It thrives in cooler conditions, is very winter hardy, and produces superior dark-green leaves with succulent white midribs so that you actually get two vegetables in one. It is always plentiful for steamed greens, and can be used as a replacement for cabbage in roll-up recipes. The juicy white stalks are crunchy and sweet when steamed or stir fried, and hard to distinguish from celery when covered with a sauce.

Five-colour Silverbeet

Five-colour silverbeet is a much more decorative version of chard that seeds around the garden and also looks great in containers. When it goes to seed you can select the colours you like best and create your own custom-tinted mix. Serving up a platter of these vibrant-looking vegetables, steamed or stir-fried, always leads to enlivened conversation!

Kale

Kale leaves are the most freely available greens volunteering around the garden. I choose 'Russian Red' or 'Green Curled', which are tender enough for salads year round. The flower heads can be eaten in lieu of broccoli spears, raw or lightly steamed. This is best done while still in bud, before flowers open.

Radicchio 'Palla Rossa'.

Radicchio

Radicchio (or chicory) seedlings pop up all over the garden, which is just fine with me because these plants are very appealing. 'Rossa di Treviso' and 'Palla Rossa' become an intense red as they develop into substantial tasty hearts. These edible ornamentals look good for most of the year and work very well along the edge of borders.

Parcel

A variety of parsley with a pronounced celery flavour, parcel can be chopped and used in generous handfuls as a seasoning. Toss it freely into omelettes, pasta, casseroles, salads and dressings, and you will be helping your family to keep up their intake of vitamin C. It has become my herb of choice in the kitchen.

Winter salads are more abundant when protected under glass. I use recycled metal-framed windows on top of recycled-wood frames to make effective cold frames. Simply place these over established salad patches planted in early fall. Providing protection from winter frosts means plentiful pickings of lettuce, mustards, endive, arugula, coriander, parsley, chard, spinach and kale throughout the cold season.

Q I'm a vegan and am trying to grow a steady supply of organic greens for myself in a Vancouver community garden. What is the easiest, fastest-growing and most reliable green for someone who wants big results from little work?

A I would grow kale, chard, spinach, Oriental greens, mustard greens, coriander, and parsley or parcel, because these greens grow year round and are prolific self-seeders. Choose open-pollinated varieties (not F1 hybrids) to start with and let some flower and go to seed. TIP: Keep named varieties pure by growing only one variety of each species. If you have a proliferation of seeds, trade a few at your local Seedy Saturday. A few seeds are all it takes!

CONTAINER GARDENING

When you know how many vegetables thrive in containers, you'll realize that you don't need a garden to grow food. Try lettuce, radishes, green onions, zucchini, tomatoes, and bush or pole beans in planters. Edibles need a maximum of 12 in. (30 cm) of soil to grow in, those that are shallow-rooted require only 6 in. (15 cm). Herbs, being mostly Mediterranean, are perfectly suited to planters in full sun. Imagine being able to pick sprigs of fresh mint, parsley, chives, oregano or basil from pots just outside your kitchen door.

I get the best results from basil and pepper plants when I grow them in 2-gal. (9-L) black plastic pots, because our summers are no longer reliably hot. I can harvest amazing yields of tomatoes, cucumbers, ground cherries and tomatillos from 5-gal. (23-L) pots. The secret is in the growing medium. I use a 50:50 blend of screened Super-Duper compost and coir (coconut fibre). This provides a nutrient-rich, biologically alive medium, with good aeration and moisture retention.

If you don't have any Super-Duper compost, you can incorporate granular organic fertilizer into a potting medium, or apply liquid fertilizer or compost tea throughout the season. Liquid seaweed boosts fruit and flower production, liquid fish fertilizer aids in the production of leafy greens, and both give plants extra resistance to the stress of being grown in confined conditions.

CONTAINER TIPS

- Plants in pots dry out quickly, especially in full sun. To be certain plants get enough water test the soil 2 in. (5 cm) below the surface.
- Water daily in hot weather and apply until water runs from the drainage holes below.
- When you are planning to be away, place vulnerable plants on top of pebbles in shallow saucers, and position in shaded places. Fill the saucers with water before you go.
- Clay pots allow faster water loss; plants in terra-cotta pots need more watering than those in plastic.
- Choose containers large enough to prevent plants from getting rootbound or they will dry out too fast.
- Top-dress established planters with screened compost every year to provide nutrients throughout the season.

Salad in a box.

Fill a planter box with high-quality compost and plant salad ingredients of your choice. From this box I harvested two varieties of kale, three varieties of lettuce, cilantro, parsley and radicchio. You can grow mesclun mixes of mustards, endive, lettuce, spinach, coriander, cress, kale and chard. Sprinkle a mix of seeds into a 4-qt. (4-L) bucket of sieved compost or coarse washed sand, and spread evenly over the top layer of the salad box. Using scissors, harvest with the "cut-and-come again" method for baby salad greens.

Garden Path Perennial Mix for Containers

In a wheelbarrow mix well:
- One-third screened topsoil
- One-third screened compost
- One-third aged horse manure

Add 10 percent of the above volume of perlite for drainage and aeration

Add a 1-gal. (4-L) ice-cream pail of a balanced granular organic fertilizer 5:2:4 (with such ingredients as alfalfa meal, gypsum, rock phosphate, sul-po-mag, greensand, zeolite and kelp meal). TIP: It's best not to use garden soil unless blended with organic matter because on its own it dries out quickly, compacts and deprives young plant roots of oxygen.

When plants are grown in containers their roots are subject to freezing because they are exposed to two extra zones of coldness. In other words, a zone-5 plant in the ground becomes a zone-7 plant in a pot. A combination of a heavy rain followed by a deep freeze will kill plants in containers by freezing their roots. Moving borderline plants under the eaves up against the house, or into a greenhouse or garage, prevents this from happening. Another way to protect roots is to place a pot inside a larger one, and stuff the space in-between with insulating material such as burlap or landscape fabric.

GARDENING WITH WILDLIFE

In an English Country Garden

How many insects come here and go in an English country garden?
We'll tell you now of some that we know, those we miss you'll surely pardon
Fire flies, moths and bees, spiders climbing in the trees
Butterflies drift in the gentle breeze
There are snakes, ants that sting and other creeping things
In an English country garden.
How many songbirds fly to and fro in an English country garden?
We'll tell you now of some that we know, those we miss you'll surely pardon
Bobolink, cuckoo and quail, tanager and cardinal
Bluebird, lark, thrush and nightingale
There is joy in the spring, when the birds begin to sing
In an English country garden.

It's sad to think how often gardeners overlook the crucial role of wildlife in the garden. By simply cooperating with nature, countless hours of toil and worry could be saved. In summer the garden buzzes with the sound and activity of bees, parasitic wasps and myriad other beneficials. They play a crucial role in controlling pest populations in the garden and increasing the harvest of fruits, vegetables and flowers through pollination. Of the thousands of wildlife species you will see in the garden, most are allies, very few foes. Over time, I have become familiar with these allies in all stages of their life cycles, as I don't want to inadvertently destroy them or upset the delicate balance of insect populations in my garden. Keeping a good identification book handy really helps!

To attract wildlife to the garden, three essential things are needed—habitat, food and water. If you pile up rocks where they will warm in the sun, you have built a haven for snakes. When you grow grasses, you are providing material for nesting birds. When you offer a source of water, wildlife will survive dry summers in your garden. This is a situation where if you build it they really do come!

Small ponds attract frogs and dragonflies, and feed thirsty wildlife.

Garter snakes gobble up slug eggs.

What You Can Do to Attract Wildlife:

- Put up nesting boxes, bat houses and bee boxes.
- Position bird-nesting boxes facing north or east, out of the reach of cats, and tilted slightly forward to reduce rain splash. Old nesting boxes should be emptied, cleaned with boiling water, and replaced in November.
- Leave dead wood of branches and tree trunks so that wood-dwelling bees can nest.
- Ensure there is a patch of undisturbed ground in the yard for the use of such bees as bumblebees to make underground nests.
- Stop using chemical pesticides that harm wildlife. Learn about less destructive methods of pest control.
- Grow plants that attract and feed wildlife.
- Create backyard "corridors" with neighbours to provide more accessible habitat for wildlife.
- Once a feeding regimen is established, try to avoid changing it. Keep feeders replenished and use rat- and squirrel-proof feeders.
- Plants that bear berries or hips are good food sources for birds.

- Add a pond or water feature to your garden to provide a source of drinking water. Your pond will also attract dragonflies and provide a habitat for frogs.
- Place shallow dishes around the garden to fill up when it rains or when the garden is watered.
- Log piles with some added turf attract a wide range of fungi and insects as they biodegrade.
- Plant ornamental grasses to provide summer shelter for ground beetles, ladybugs and other beneficials. The seed heads are a winter habitat for insects, and grasses provide nesting materials for birds.
- Add stone walls to provide habitat for a range of cavity-nesting creatures such as snakes and mason bees.
- Remember that bees and butterflies prefer the simple blooms of old-fashioned flowers, especially if they are strongly perfumed, rather than those of more fussy hybrids. Wildflower meadows fit this bill perfectly.
- Keep a birdbath topped up with clean water. Birds like to bathe.

Swallowtail butterfly.

Anise Swallowtails

The anise swallowtail butterfly (*Papilio zelicaon*) is native to western North America. This stunning caterpillar's major food plants are all members of the Umbelliferae family: angelica, dill, fennel and lovage. If disturbed, the caterpillar will display bright-orange "stinkhorns" or osmeteria from its head. Used for defence, these glandular structures give off foul odour.

The caterpillar grows to around 2 in. (5 cm) in length before forming a brown chrysalis about 1.2 in. (3 cm) long. The chrysalis hibernates through the winter before beginning the life cycle of an anise swallowtail butterfly. Learn to identify this beautiful and helpful pollinator and welcome it to your garden.

Top: Bird feeders in winter means birds stay in the garden.
Bottom: Clematis montana *var.* rubens *and swallow box.*

Birds in Winter

Winter is the harshest season for birds, with protection from cold and access to food imperative for survival. Nesting boxes and evergreen trees and shrubs provide shelter during these months. Feeders are also helpful, as are plants that bear berries or hips—cherries, cotoneaster, crabapples, hawthorns, saskatoon berry, serviceberry, currants and roses are all good foods for our feathered friends.

Swallow Boxes

The house or English sparrow, like many pesky birds, was introduced to North America in the mid 1800s. Since then, the house sparrow (not a true sparrow but a European finch), has become one of the most widespread and adaptive birds on this continent. They are very aggressive in establishing territory and soon dominate over other bird species in the garden.

I have seen sparrows throw swallow eggs out of the nest in their determination to take over. The helpful swallows gobble up mosquitoes, flies and other pesky insects, so I want to encourage them to return to my garden, and the only way to do this is to exclude the sparrows from the box. To do this we have attached a piece of wood to all our birdhouses, with an opening that keeps sparrows out and only allows swallows and smaller birds to enter.

Pacific tree frog.

look like six-legged crocodiles, dark brown in colour with bright-orange spots on the back of their lumpy bodies. A mature larva can eat as many as 50 aphids a day, and between 200 to 500 aphids in its three-week lifespan. Ladybugs produce up to six generations a year, which eliminates a lot of aphids!

INSECT PESTS

Aphids

Aphids are tiny pear-shaped insects that are most often green, but also come in grey and black. Aphids cluster together in colonies, making them easy to spot, and they grow and multiply quickly in the right conditions. One aphid can produce an entire colony! They are generally most active in spring, because they tend to die off in hot weather. Blasting them off the plant with water from a hose is generally all that is needed to get rid of them, because wingless adults predominate, making re-establishing colonies difficult. If you are brave like me, you can use your fingers to rub them off the tender tips of roses.

Aphids use needle-like mouthparts to suck juice out of plants (they do not chew). They are known as sapsuckers, and can cause leaves, buds, flowers or fruit to deform. Leaves curling up are a sign that aphids are present, and they also secrete a sticky substance (that ants love!) called honeydew, which attracts black and sooty mould, but does not damage plants. Sooty mould can be washed off using soapy water—this is a rather tedious job, so before you start I advise pruning the plant back as hard as you can!

When natural predators such as ladybugs, aphid midges and syrphid flies become established in the garden, colonies of aphids quickly disappear. Check for populations of beneficial insects before you take action against aphids. If they are present and you wait just a bit longer your problem may just disappear! Over the years I have observed nasturtiums, pepper seedlings, favas, cardoons and roses as the favourites of aphids in my garden. Knowing this reminds me to keep an eye open for aphid outbreaks on these plants when the weather warms up in spring.

Pacific Tree Frogs

Pacific tree frogs thrive in our surrounding Douglas fir ecosystem and are adorable peeping out from decorative dahlias or hanging out on gaillardia blooms. We look forward to the noisy springtime chorus from the marshlands below, which heralds the approach of warmer days (and more frogs!). These cute little critters need a source of clean, fresh water for tadpoles to develop. They spend the rest of the season in the garden gorging on insects before returning to water to lay their eggs for a new cycle of life.

Ladybird, Ladybird

One of the best natural predators for aphids is our native ladybug or ladybird (*Hippodamia convergens*). Ladybugs eat aphids in both their adult and larval stage; adults consume up to 5,000 aphids during their lifetime. It's important to recognize the larval stage of the ladybug, so it is not mistaken for a pest. Larvae

CONTROL:

- Attract predator insects—ladybugs and lacewings.
- Dislodge aphid colonies with a jet stream of water.
- Wash plants with soapy water or insecticidal soap.

Sowbugs and Pillbugs

Sowbugs and pillbugs are similar-looking, more akin to crayfish than insects. They are distinguished as the only crustaceans adapted to living on land. With gills that require constant moisture, they only thrive in damp conditions, and are primarily nocturnal. Their armadillo-like bodies are convex above and concave underneath. The way to tell a sowbug from a pillbug is that pillbugs roll up into tight balls when disturbed. Sowbugs and pillbugs carry eggs in a pouch for about three weeks until they hatch, then continue to carry the young for a few months.

They eat decaying wood and leaves, and burrow into vegetables and strawberries that come into contact with the ground. In the nursery business, I also discovered that they fed on tender seedlings, so I consider them pests. They are commonly found under boards, between rocks, and inside garden debris such as old flowerpots.

CONTROL:

- Cornmeal traps—sowbugs and pillbugs love cornmeal, but explode when they eat it.
- Remove damp or rotting wood and debris from around the garden.
- Dry out the area or expose it to light.

Leaf Miner

Leaf miners are tiny ⅛-in. (3-mm) black flies that lay eggs inside leaves so that their larvae tunnel within the leaf tissue. Before pupating they make semi-circular cuts into the leaf, and then drop to the soil.

Watch out for telltale tunnels in leaves of host plants such as aquilegia, beets, Swiss chard and spinach.

CONTROL:

- Remove infected plant material from the garden immediately. Bury it.
- Practise crop rotation to reduce populations.
- Companion plant to encourage diverse populations of beneficial insects.
- Spray with Safer's Trounce™ (contains pyrethrins). Note: Leaf miners are known to develop resistance to insecticides quickly.

Top: Sowbugs and pillbugs can have several broods a year!

Bottom: Severe damage from leaf miners reduces photosynthetic ability.

Cutworms

Cutworms are smooth, greasy-looking larvae of large grey or brown moths. They may be dull-grey, green or tan, with stripes or spots, and can be identified by the fact that they curl up when disturbed. Larvae cause the greatest damage between May and late June when feeding on garden vegetables, particularly young seedlings and transplants.

Cutworms hide in soil near plants by day, and feed at night, cutting off seedlings and transplants at the soil line. Young plants topple over or may disappear altogether. Some cutworms crawl up plants at night and chew large raggedy holes in leaves. If there is no accompanying slime, you know cutworms rather than slugs caused the damage. Thankfully, there is only one generation a year!

CONTROL:
- Turn soil over several weeks prior to planting to allow birds to find exposed worms.
- Make stiff plastic or metal "collars" around plants, press down into the soil. (Plastic bottles or drink cans with the bottom cut off are good for this.)

Tent caterpillars.

- Smear sticky molasses around the plant stem, to which cutworms stick and die.
- Sprinkle crushed eggshells around plants. Cutworms will avoid them.
- Plant tansy or marigolds to repel cutworms.
- Search with flashlight at night, near the plant stem at soil level.
- Apply parasitic nematodes as a non-toxic biological control around susceptible plants when the soil is warm.

Tent Caterpillars

Caterpillars generally chew large raggedy holes in leaves. Damage to trees is unsightly, but there is usually little long-term damage to plants.

CONTROL:
- Attract birds to the garden, as they will feed on some caterpillars and cocoons.
- Remove egg masses from branches when the tree is dormant.
- Prune out infested branches when the caterpillars are in the nest, then drown them in soapy water.
- Spray trees with dormant oil to kill overwintering egg masses.

Whitefly

Whiteflies are tiny insects with powdery-white wings. They colonize in large numbers on the undersides of leaves, feed on plant juices and excrete sticky honeydew. Infested leaves become pale or discoloured; plants may wilt and lose leaves.

CONTROL:
- Inspect seedlings and plants from nurseries before purchase to ensure they are free from whiteflies.

Above: Homemade sticky traps for whiteflies.

Top right: Weevil.

Right: Notches in leaves of peas or beans indicate weevils at work.

- Placing homemade sticky traps near plants to capture whiteflies is very effective.
- Apply insecticidal soaps to control as a last resort.

Weevils

Weevils are small, oval beetles recognized by their distinctive little snouts. The species to look out for in food gardens are the strawberry weevils and the pea and bean weevils. The adult weevils emerge from cocoons in late spring and chew semi-circular notches into leaves at night, hiding in the soil during the day. They feed for about four weeks, then lay their eggs on host plants. Larvae feed on roots (strawberry) as they burrow deeper to form cocoons for overwintering.

CONTROL:
- Smear stems with sticky substances to trap the weevils.
- Spray neem oil to stop the weevils from eating leaves, so that seedlings can outgrow the damage. TIP: Dilute neem oil in warm water, and spray while the water is still warm (to keep the oil in solution).
- Try neem seedcake, a by-product of the neem-oil industry, which has been discovered to be a fertilizer and systemic insecticide in one!
- Apply parasitic nematodes as a non-toxic biological control around the roots of susceptible plants when the soil is warm.

Earwigs

Earwigs are elongate bugs with prominent rear pinchers. Some say they do not bite, but I always feel a pinch! They are seldom more than a nuisance and generally don't require control—unless you operate a plant nursery with recycled wooden shelving. Then be prepared to wage battle with earwigs that hide under flats of seedlings during the day and demolish them at night along with the slugs! At one time at my nursery it got to the point where dramatic action was needed! As it turned out, the most effective solution was also the simplest. We had already put everything up off the ground on recycled pallets so we decided to add upturned flats underneath the flats of seedlings. That did it. By simply drying out the space underneath the starts, we were able to protect them from further damage.

CONTROL:
- Eliminate hiding places such as woodpiles and debris around the garden.
- Make traps from dampened rolled newspaper, or newspaper stuffed into pots. Place near plants being attacked. Check daily and shake earwigs into soapy water to drown them.

Stuffed with newspaper, these pots make funky and effective earwig traps.

Slugs

Slugs belong to the phylum Mollusca in a class of land-dwelling gastropods called Pulmonata, which use lungs instead of gills to draw oxygen from air. They can be found under plants, decaying leaves and boards and garden debris—anywhere dark and moist. At night and during wet, cloudy days, they feed on rotting plant material, fungi, lichen, green plants, worms, centipedes, animal feces, carrion and other slugs. They are prone to desiccation because they do not have shells, and are dependent on moisture for survival. Most slugs leave a slimy, silvery trail of mucus behind them.

Slugs mate between July and October and lay clusters of eggs between rocks, and under boards or decaying material. These pearly-white eggs are found in clumps of 40 to 100. Baby slugs can eat 30 to 40 times their weight in one day, and will live for 1 to 2 years. TIP: Check under pots and plants for slugs and eggs when damage first appears. Destroy egg masses if found.

Black Slug (*Arion ater*): This slug grows to 7 in. (18 cm) and can be black, brown, red-brown, green-brown or yellow-orange in colour with a red, orange, yellow or black foot fringe. When disturbed, it may sway from side to side and contract into a bell-shape.

Grey Slug (*Limax maximus*, *Deroceras reticulatum* and *Milax* species): These slugs are small, 2 to 4 in. (5 to 10 cm), with voracious appetites and causing serious damage in gardens and greenhouses.

Banana Slug (*Ariolimax columbianus*): As its name suggests, this slug is yellow or yellow with black splashes. Banana slugs prefer moist woodland habitats, and are not commonly found in city gardens. They grow to 8 in. (20 cm).

Slug Control

Barriers: Battery-powered low-voltage electrical barriers are effective in keeping slugs away from plants. Copper or zinc strips, available from garden centres, are also excellent barriers. Place strips around the plants, flowerbeds and pots you want

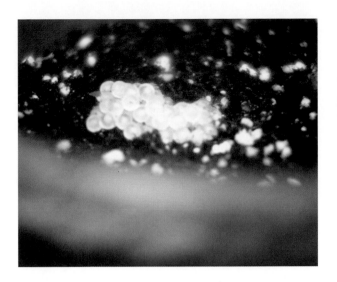

Above: Learn to recognize slug eggs.
Right: Banana slug.

protected. Other less expensive barriers include sharp gravel screenings, crushed eggshells, ground oyster shells or diatomaceous earth spread around your plants. Remember that these all need to be renewed periodically.

Beer: Slugs love beer! Make slug traps by filling yogurt containers with beer (or water and yeast mix) and push them into the ground. TIP: The edges of the containers should stick up ½ in. (1 cm) above the ground to prevent trapping beneficial creatures.

Biological: Nematodes that carry a bacterium fatal to slugs are now available and can be introduced using a watering can. This approach works best on moist, free-draining soils, at temperatures at or above 41°F (5°C). The treatment lasts about six weeks and is harmless to other wildlife and pets.

Handpick: Handpick slugs from the garden when they are actively feeding in the cool of dawn or dusk. Attract slugs by putting cabbage leaves or raw potatoes under boards or flowerpots. Turn over and destroy regularly, until the slug damage disappears. TIP: Reduce slug habitat by removing unwanted bricks, boards and debris from around the yard.

Wildlife: Ducks, geese, snakes, frogs, toads, other amphibians and ground beetles all eat slugs. Protect wildlife and work to encourage these natural predators to stay in the garden by providing habitat such as hedges and ponds.

Slug Bait: Thankfully, commercial low-toxicity slug-bait pellets are finally available! Non-toxic slug bait consists of pellets made of ferrous sulphate, which does not harm birds, pets or wildlife. Slugs eat them, then slither away and dehydrate.

WHAT'S IN THAT OTHER SLUG BAIT?
Unlike the low-toxicity options, metaldehyde is harmful if swallowed and must be kept out of reach of children and pets. All precautions should be taken to ensure that bait is not mistaken for food or feed. Contamination of edible plants should be avoided. Breathing of dust, skin, eye and clothing contact should be avoided. After handling, a thorough washing is recommended. All unprotected persons should stay out of the range of any drift. Protective clothing must be worn in treated areas until dusts settle, and prolonged storage should be avoided!

OH, RATS!

We used to own a home in an area referred to as "behind the tweed curtain," and it had a dark secret—rats! We grew food in raised beds in the backyard, and composted kitchen and garden waste using a wooden three-bin system. In spring, when it was time to dig compost out, we would always shudder, knowing we would find a rats' nest embedded in the warm compost pile. When we moved to the country, we made the decision to eliminate kitchen scraps from compost altogether to see if it would eliminate the rat problem—and it worked!

Kitchen waste goes into a rat-proof, recycled-plastic cone composter called an "Earthsaver." When it's warm in summer, I sprinkle layers of sawdust or leaves over the food waste to prevent odours. When the compost cone is full, we dig a trench 18 in. (46 cm) deep and bury the contents of the cone 9 in. (23 cm) deep. We plant on top right away if we need to, because trench composting means matter will have broken down by the time the roots get down to it.

BIRD FEEDERS
Put a large saucer under bird feeders to catch spillage and prevent it from falling where rats can reach it.

Discouraging rats also involves keeping poultry feed stored in rodent-proof bins with good-fitting lids, and sweeping up any spillage diligently. Rats are also drawn to chicken coops, so we keep the feeders inside the coop. We only feed kitchen scraps to the chickens and ducks during the day, so as not to attract these nocturnal pests.

Above: A rat of the decorative variety.
Left: Trench composting.

INTEGRATED PEST MANAGEMENT

By sticking to organic gardening practices, feeding the soil and working with nature, you will have fewer pest problems over time. When wildlife in the garden is in balance, this frees the gardener from needing to be "in charge." This more relaxed naturalistic approach to gardening means you spend minimal time dealing with pests and other nuisances, and maximum time enjoying the pleasures of being in the garden.

Integrated Pest Management (IPM) is an alternative approach to managing pest problems, where the key lies in prevention rather than cure. If you work with these four steps, you may find that preventative methods are enough to keep those unwanted pests at bay.

Step 1: Identify the problem

Sometimes what we think is the problem is actually the solution. The arrival of pests will invite predators to feast, so make sure you don't mistake any welcome guests for harmful pests. The beneficial insect destroying a pest is often larger and more noticeable than the pest itself, and often by the time the problem becomes apparent, the pest has gone. Also, many cases of damage are caused by salt, nutrient deficiency or fluctuations in temperature—so make sure insects are actually the problem.

Step 2: Monitor the problem

Once a problem has been identified, monitor it for clues about appropriate intervention.

Step 3: Is damage a problem?

Plants tolerate a degree of damage and can outgrow it. Monitor injury levels before taking action. Later in the season, predator populations will build up in the garden and take care of problems for you.

Step 4: Take appropriate action

Start with the least-toxic control first—sticky traps, spraying with water or hand removal may easily solve the problem. If not, try biological controls such as parasitic nematodes or bacterial sprays. Controls can be used alone or in combination for greater effect.

Prevention Tips

Where crops have finished, ensure that any debris is removed from the garden and composted. Left behind, it encourages pests and disease, causing problems for next year. Remember the mantra, "To prevent disease remove disease."

Ensure soil is healthy by feeding it regularly with organic amendments of compost, manure, seaweed and leaves. Plants take nutrients from soil as they grow, and these need to be replenished. Organic soil amendments decompose to create humus, which improves soil texture, water-retention and nutrient levels. Ensure soil has adequate drainage. Plants do not thrive in soggy, poorly aerated soils. Raised beds improve drainage. Watering deeply instead of frequently encourages and maintains strong root systems.

Site plants where they would thrive naturally. Dry soil or wet? Sunny location or shade?

Companion plant to attract beneficial species of wildlife, then keep them in the garden by providing habitat and water. Using a four-year cycle, rotate crops to prevent a build-up of soil-borne pests and diseases.

Biological Controls for Larvae Infestations

Nematodes are naturally occurring microscopic organisms that live in soil and prey on insect larvae. They carry bacteria in their intestines that are deadly to larvae. In cases of serious outbreaks (e.g., wireworms in new gardens where sod has been removed), apply when the soil has warmed up and keep moist for two weeks. In 10 to 14 days, cutworms, craneflies, leatherjackets, wireworms, and weevils will be gone. Nematodes are safe for non-target organisms such as earthworms.

COMPANION PLANTING

Over many years of gardening organically, I have discovered that the secret to keeping pest problems to a minimum in the vegetable garden is by growing a diversity of plants that attract wildlife. I dedicate two borders along the vegetable garden to flowers and herbs for this purpose, many of which either repel pests or attract beneficials.

PLANTS THAT LURE BENEFICIALS

Amaranth (*Amaranthus*): ladybugs, shield bugs (which gorge on mites), parasitic wasps and even slug-hungry ground beetles

Angelica (*Angelica sinensis*): lacewings

Anise Hyssop (*Agastache foeniculum*): butterflies and beneficial insects

Asteraceae family (such as asters, cosmos, goldenrod, sunflowers and zinnias): long season of bloom attracts a host of beneficials including parasitic wasps and predaceous beetles

Bachelor's Button (*Centaurea cyanus*): ladybugs, lacewings and beneficial wasps

Bee's Friend (*Phacelia tanacetifolia*): hoverflies and bees

Borage (*Borago officinalis*): green lacewings have a strong preference for laying eggs on borage

Candytuft (*Iberis*): hoverflies

Evening Primrose (*Oenothera*): ground beetles

Fennel (*Foeniculum vulgare*): beneficial parasitic wasps, lacewings and hoverflies

Golden Marguerite (*Anthemis tinctoria*): ladybugs, lacewings, flower flies, tachinid flies and mini-wasps

Sweet Alyssum (*Lobularia maritima*): syrphid flies, the larvae of which eat aphids

Umbelliferae family (such as dill, anise, coriander and parsley): members of this family have flower clusters that make it easy for beneficial insects to feed

Willow (*Salix*): produces pollen early in spring when beneficials are emerging

Plants That Repel Pests

Use strongly scented plants to repel pests, as it confuses them by masking their host plants. I plant a row of tall 'Taj Mahal' hedging marigolds to deter bugs from my garden. Cabbage pests and aphids dislike mint, so setting pots of this aromatic herb around the garden means you get to enjoy it while keeping bugs at bay. Sweet basil repels aphids, mosquitoes and mites. (It also enhances the growth of many food plants nearby.) Tansy fends off cucumber beetles, Japanese beetles, ants and squash bugs, but beware—it can be very invasive in gardens. (It does, however, have bright-green ferny foliage in spring and showy gold button-flowers in fall that might make up for this.) TIP: Tansy attracts cabbage worms, so keep it away from cabbages. Plant thyme with cabbage instead, as it controls flea beetles, cabbage root maggots and cabbage worms.

Anthemis *'Sauce Hollandaise'.*

142

Plants That Lure Pests

There are two ways of looking at nasturtiums infested with black aphids. One will cause you to curse, the other to be appreciative that the nasturtiums have drawn an annoying pest away from more valuable plants in the garden.

Plants That Act as Mini-Insectaries

When woolly grey aphids colonize lupines they also attract large numbers of parasitic wasps and predators. Having a strong presence of beneficials in the garden means pest problems are taken care of before they arise.

THE THREE MUSCOVIES

It all started with newly built lasagna beds that attracted banana slugs from the surrounding forest—monster pests that can devour a row of spinach overnight! This situation was followed by a chance conversation about ducks at a spring Seedy Saturday gathering where I learned that Muscovy ducks have a voracious appetite for slugs. Quicker than you can say "quack" I became the proud owner of two adorable baby ducklings, Amos and Abigail.

Unfortunately, a stealthy murderous mink massacred my A-generation. The B-generation, Benny, Betty and Blackie, arrived late in November. When "The Three Muscovies" first arrived, I bonded

Benny and the "Jets," Betty and Blackie.

them to the duck house before allowing them to free range. The duck house is simply a converted doghouse in a fenced yard, connected to the chicken run. The girls, Betty and Blackie, arrived with clipped wings and couldn't fly, but Benny's wings grew back quickly and he fast discovered the creek and pond on the property, returning to show his girls how to waddle down to the water.

I keep telling myself this "duck thing" is an experiment to see if Muscovies make a good fit for urban gardeners, perhaps even as children's pets. But in the meantime I have discovered that they lay large white eggs with huge rich yolks, excellent for sponge cakes, quiches and omelettes; plus, Benny is a 15-lb. (7-kg) meat bird, which may be a good thing to have around if there are food-security issues!

Although I have read it's a bad idea to get too friendly with a Muscovy drake, I enjoy Benny's company while he's plodding around the garden, usually with his girls in tow. Sometimes, there's a lot of tail quivering going on, and I am curious to know what this is all about. When their wings grow back, they enjoy spreading them to fly up to the roof of the house and off to the pond below. It's a good thing Muscovies stay close to home. At dusk when I call "Benny, Betty, Blackie!" they come running for a feed of mash, the same food the chickens eat. Sometimes they spend the night sleeping on the pond, where they are safe from predators, but it is important to keep them bonded to their house so from time to time I shut them in for the night.

As time passed, Benny took a fancy to Betty, and she was soon nestled into a pile of spoiled hay, turning 14 fragile eggs daily for 35 days, until 11 of them hatched out. Betty and the C-generation of 11 ducklings were too cute for words. I remember thinking, "Here I am, still in this experiment, and now I've got 14 ducks!" It worked out well in the end. By the time the ducklings were ready to leave Mama, I had found good homes for all but the two I'd selected to become the C-generation—Cocoa and Cecilia. (A donation of $10/duckling covered the cost of feed.)

Now I love watching the C-generation grow and adapt to life in part-captivity, and I am learning a lot about this breed of meaty quack-less ducks. They are the most land-based of the water birds, which makes them well suited to backyard runs with a small pond. A bathtub also works well, but needs to be refilled daily, as Muscovies "squat" a lot. They also need access to fresh drinking water at all times, especially when given dry mash. TIP: Baby ducklings can drown very easily in shallow water. It's important to allow them access to water, but they'll need a ramp to get out.

Although the verdict is still out on how perfectly suited ducks are to smaller gardens, I think a couple of Muscovies make a lot of sense in uncertain times such as these. Chickens and Muscovies get on fine free-ranging together, and once you are taking care of chickens it's easy to add the little extra care that ducks need. And they sure are cute, aren't they?

Cecilia is a real beauty!

A new generation of Muscovies.

144

May

PLANTING THE GARDEN

When establishing a new garden, rototilling or deep digging is needed initially to incorporate any organic soil amendments. Once the garden is established, there should be no need to cultivate deeply, as this destroys the soil food web, but if the earth becomes compacted it may be necessary to turn amendments under with a light forking. Future mulches of compost, leaves, seaweed and manure will generally break down readily in established beds and should not require turning under.

If soil fertility is in question, or when revitalizing soil, organic fertilizer blends are useful. Nutrients in natural-source fertilizers are released slowly to plants as they grow. Once good soil fertility has been established and is maintained, there should be no need to apply additional soil supplements.

After heavy winter rains, it's best to lime garden beds, except where acid-loving plants such as blueberries, strawberries and potatoes are growing. Dolomite lime adds calcium and magnesium and keeps soil in the neutral pH range favoured by most food plants.

If you are super-organized like me, you'll find sorting seeds into cool-weather vegetables, heat lovers and winter vegetables makes life much easier.

Cool-weather vegetables: Arugula, globe artichokes, beets, broccoli, Brussels sprouts, summer cabbage, cauliflower, chard, coriander, cress, kale,

Bean seedlings.

leeks, lettuces, summer mesclun mixes (baby salad greens), onions, orach, Oriental greens, peas, radishes and spinach.

Heat lovers: Amaranth, basil, beans, corn, dill, eggplant, quinoa, peppers, squash and tomatoes cannot go outdoors until the soil has warmed up.

Winter vegetables: Arugula, beets, broccoli, winter cabbage, cauliflower, chard, coriander, cress, favas, kale, lettuce, winter mesclun mixes, mustards, onions, orach, Oriental greens, radishes and spinach.

145

Root crops: Beets, carrots, celeriac, kohlrabi, parsnips and turnips can be direct seeded in spring, once soil begins to warm, but will not germinate until it has.

Heat-loving beans often rot if sown into cold soils. Either wait to seed them until mid June, or get a head start by seeding them into cell packs in the greenhouse—then you will have stout bean seedlings that establish very fast, instead of rotted bean seeds.

Hardening Off

When planting seedlings outdoors don't just throw your "green babies" from under cover out into the cold. They need to be hardened off to acclimatize gradually to cooler growing conditions to avoid shock. Harden young plants off for a period of seven to ten days by moving them outside during the day and back inside, or under frost protection, at night.

Hoe a Row in Five!

Established seedlings can be transplanted by a really fast method that I jokingly call "hoe a row in five." It all started when I began seeding into cell packs to get a head start on the season. By seeding sparingly, I wondered if I could plant the entire contents of the cell pack without having to tear seedlings apart. Following a straight line, I now make a shallow furrow using a hoe. TIP: If soil fertility is in question, line the furrow with granular organic fertilizer. Then remove the rooted seedlings from the cell pack, line them up end to end in the furrow, and use the hoe to fill the furrow in again with soil. Five minutes is all it takes!

Squash and artichoke seedlings resent being disturbed. Grow them in their own individual pots and wait until the soil has well and truly warmed up before transplanting the seedlings outdoors.

Planting the garden.

Crop Rotations

Crop rotations began with The Feudal System (in the Middle Ages), which stipulated a four-year cycle where every year the crops were rotated and one-quarter of the land under production was left fallow to rejuvenate. Crop rotation is a pillar of organic gardening because it significantly reduces the build-up of pest and disease problems that affect specific plant families. The concept is really very straightforward—don't plant related species of plants (in the same family) in the same place as the year before. TIP: Rotate plants that are heavy feeders, (e.g., cabbage, corn) with light feeders (e.g., peas, beans) to prevent depletion of soil nutrients.

Plant Families

Apiaceae: Carrots, celeriac, celery, parsley, parsnips
Asteraceae: Chicory, endive, lettuce, salsify
Chenopodiaceae: Beets, chard, spinach
Brassicaceae: Arugula, broccoli, Brussels sprouts, cabbage, cauliflower, kale, kohlrabi, radish, rutabagas, turnips
Cucurbitaceae: Cucumber, gourds, melons, squash
Fabaceae: Beans, chickpeas, favas, lentils, lima beans, peas, soybean
Lilliaceae: Garlic, leeks, onions, scallions, shallots
Solanaceae: Eggplants, peppers, potatoes, tomatoes
Poaceae: Corn

Mapping the Garden

I keep empty seed packets handy for reference when adding plants to a garden map, because referring to this makes crop rotation a snap! Creating a garden map is easy when you place markers at the end of every row of vegetables. TIP: Leave plant markers in place until you plant the following crop to make sure you have rotated.

Q I am planning to build a raised bed, but don't want wood that has been chemically treated so am unsure about what to use. I've heard that large rocks attract slugs. What do you suggest?

A For 10 years I grew vegetables in a backyard that was flooded with standing water in winter. I built five raised beds, 8 by 4 ft. (2.4 by 1.2 m), using untreated rough-cedar 2x12 planks. Oils in cedar naturally preserve the wood. TIP: Watch for sales at lumberyards! A 12-in. (30-cm) raised bed is deep enough to grow any vegetable. You can save money with 1x12 planks but 2x12s hold up much better. Top-dressing beds in spring with Super-Duper compost renews the soil and maintains good harvests. TIP: Screw galvanized hinges on the outside of the four corners to prevent the box splitting apart at the edges.

Gorgeous garlic in a raised bed.

PLANTING A SEED-SAVING GARDEN

As an avid seed saver, allowing many plants to complete the cycle of growth from seed to seed, I see my garden through different eyes. It takes a little knowledge, some planning and careful observation to save seeds successfully, but it's very satisfying and provides the best start a plant could wish for—fresh, organic seed.

Before starting to save seeds, I had no idea how stunning the purple balls of leek seeds were or how much they were loved by bees. Seed saving added a new dimension to gardening for me, providing a constant unfolding of exciting new discoveries.

Leeks in seed in a purple and silver border.

Many gardeners think saving seeds requires special skill and is best left to experts. This is not so! The main aim of seed saving is to collect seeds that come "true to type" in the next generation. It's not that complicated when you take the following into consideration.

Choose Open-pollinated Seeds

F1 hybrids are offspring of two different varieties of the same plant species. Seeds collected from F1 hybrids may revert back genetically to characteristics of one or the other parent, or may display an undesirable mix of both and will not "come true." Hybridization of seeds means that you have to buy seeds every year, but now more and more seed companies are offering open-pollinated (heritage) seeds, and you can find sources at www.seeds.ca.

Self-pollinating or Cross-pollinating?

To understand this, it helps to understand a bit about the sex life of plants. A plant with both male (anther/pollen) and female (style/stigma) on the same flower is called a "perfect" flower and is self-pollinating, requiring no intervention from insects or wind for pollination.

---

10 REASONS TO SAVE SEEDS

- Fresh seed has the highest vigour and germination rate.
- Seeds are regionally adapted to climate conditions.
- Seeds are not genetically modified while you're not looking!
- Fresh organic seeds are available in large quantities at a fraction of the cost.
- Plants that may not be available commercially can be grown.

- Seeds can be swapped and shared at clubs and local seed exchanges.
- Protects varieties from extinction and preserves our common plant heritage.
- Protects plant genetic diversity for the survival of future generations.
- You can select for the traits you most admire in a plant.
- Seed saving can also be plant breeding— which is great fun!

Plants that have separate male and female flowers ("imperfect" flowers) depend on carriers such as honeybees, insects or wind to transfer pollen from the male to the female flower. To prevent cross-pollination, it's important to plant using proper isolation distances between different varieties of the same species.

Isolation Distances

Self-pollinators: Plants that are self-pollinating can be grown in close proximity without jeopardizing the purity of the strain:

- A distance of 6 ft. (1.8 m) should separate varying varieties of tomatoes, peppers and eggplants.
- Tomatoes (potato-leaf varieties) should be separated by a distance of 30 ft. (9 m).
- Lettuces should be separated by a distance of 10 ft. (3 m).
- Bush beans should be separated by a distancc of 10 ft. (3 m).
- Pole beans should be separated by a distance of 30 ft. (9 m).

Biennial root crops: Beets, carrots, celeriac, leeks, onions, parsnips, radishes and turnips produce their edible crop in the first year and set seed the following season. These crops need isolation distances of ¼ mi. (400 m) to prevent cross-pollination.

- Carrots will cross with wild carrot 'Queen Anne's Lace' if grown within ¼ mi. (400 m).
- *Brassicas* (e.g., broccoli, Brussels sprouts, cauliflower, collards, kale and kohlrabi) must be separated by ¼ mi. (400 m).
- Squash family members need to be separated by ¼ mi. (400 m). If you've ever had a "USO" (unidentified squash object) volunteer in your garden, it was probably the result of pollen crossing between different varieties of squash the summer before.

There are ways to prevent cross-pollination if you plant two varieties of the same species that flower at the same time. Use lengths of PVC irrigation pipe to make a tent over one variety to prevent cross-pollination from happening. You can also choose one variety that goes to seed early and one that goes to seed late, so that they don't flower at the same time. Alternatively you can prevent one variety from flowering by deadheading it!

Seed tent made from Reemay™.

ORNAMENTAL EDIBLES

Q How do you eat sweet violets (*Viola odorata*)?

A Fresh or crystallized violet flowers decorate cakes in a special way, and young leaves and flowers of delicate perfume and mild flavour can be added to salads, a welcome decoration to the table in late winter. Flowers and leaves also make a soothing tea.

Recommended Edible Landscaping Plants

Amaranth: Purple or red amaranth for spires of ancient grain reaching 5 ft. (1.5 m) in height.

Artichokes, globe: Dramatic foliage, huge purple thistles and edible hearts.

Beans: 'Painted Lady' for red and white blooms, and runner beans, or 'Gramma Walters' for cranberry/cream bean pods and dry cranberry beans.

Blueberries: With red twigs in winter, pretty flowers in spring, blueberries in summer and red foliage through fall, these shrubs reward you all year long.

Blackberries (thornless): Flowers, berries and foliage that changes with the seasons—without thorns!

Chamomile: A lush groundcover with pretty yellow and white flowers for teas.

Chives: Edible purple or white blossoms and oniony leaves.

Crabapples: Beautiful apple blossoms in spring and edible fruit in fall.

Cherries: Pink or white blossoms and lots of fruit (watch out for birds!).

Elderberries: Attractive foliage, flowers and clusters of berries in fall.

Figs: Attractive foliage and lots of fresh figs in hot summers.

Garlic Chives: Edible oniony leaves and starry white or purple blossoms.

Left: Strawberries and sweet violets make great bedfellows.
Above: Purple amaranth.

Grapes: *Vitis vinifera* 'Purpurea' has dark-purple foliage and deep-purple grapes.

Hazelnuts: Shrubs for shade, with catkins in spring and edible nuts in fall.

Kale: 'Lacinato' has crinkly blue foliage, and 'Redbor' is gorgeous with dark-purple foliage all year long.

Lettuce: Try ornamental lettuces along garden borders, or on a boulevard!

Nasturtiums: Edible flowers, seeds and leaves.

Oca: Attractive foliage and edible tubers.

Peas: Flowers are pretty, with green yellow or purple pods.

Radicchio: Sumptuous heads of bright-red chicory.

Squash: Golden-yellow blossoms and showy squash in all colours.

Strawberries: Great foliage for groundcovers with lots of berries.

Strawberry spinach: Showy stems covered in edible "strawberry" berries.

Sunchokes: Yellow sunflowers in fall, edible tubers all winter.

Sunflowers: 'Taramara' seeds for sprouting, fresh eating and feeding birds!

Swiss chard: Colourful leaves from 'Rhubarb', 'Five-colour Silverbeet' and 'Bright Lights'.

Thyme: Low herbal groundcovers replace lawns and sprawl between patio stones.

Purple Amaranth

This heat-loving annual quickly grows to 5 ft. (1.5 m) in hot summers. It's best seeded indoors in late spring and transplanted outside once all danger of frost has passed. The tall purple bushy flower spikes eventually fade to light-brown grains. Amaranth grains are delicious popped or steamed, and nutritious added to cookies, cakes and cereals. Isn't it marvellous that an ancient high-protein grain once revered by the Aztec civilization can still be enjoyed as an ornamental edible in your garden today?

Strawberry Spinach

I first saw this sight in Anne Hathaway's garden in Stratford-upon-Avon, UK, many years ago. *Chenopodium capitatum* is an eye-catching sixteenth-century plant still grown today, with shiny-red edible fruits on compact 18-in. (46-cm) annual plants. These showy strawberry-like berries always start conversations in the garden and at the table. Leaves and shoots can be served in salads or steamed. Two words of caution about this plant—self-seeder!

Garlic Chives

These mauve-flowered perennial chives provide oniony leaves for recipes, and charming mauve starburst blossoms from summer to fall. This hardy *Allium* grows into generous clumps, so the show gets more dramatic over the years. Garlic chives make a good addition to window boxes, and attractive companion plants to keep bugs at bay.

Strawberry spinach. Kristin Ross photo

KEEPING ROSES ROSY ORGANICALLY

If you are going to add rose petals to beautify a salad you want to know that they had been grown organically. I adore the "Queen of Flowers" but she can be a fussy plant to care for, often tempting gardeners to reach for pesticides. Over years of adding roses to the garden I discovered several ways to make this completely unnecessary.

The worst plagues of roses are black spot, powdery mildew and rust, all fungal diseases spread by spores that are able to remain dormant on leaves and in soil for years. Organic cultivation provides the perfect remedy for this. Mulching the ground around the rose with aged manure, compost, seaweed or leaf mulch in fall smothers spores that may be in soil and prevents them from splashing back onto roses because of rainfall or watering.

In addition, rake fallen leaves from underneath roses and strip all remaining leaves off the plants every fall. This helps prevent spores from overwintering, and for good measure I suggest also smothering the plant with dormant oil/lime sulphur spray in early spring (See "Fruit Tree Care" in July for the recipe). Remember the mantra "To prevent disease, remove disease."

Pruning Roses

Remember that the 3Ds—dead, diseased and damaged canes—get removed first, then remove any spindly or crossing shoots. The aim is to maintain a framework of vigorous healthy canes. With hybrid teas and floribunda roses, cut back annually to the strongest canes and reduce these by two-thirds, removing one third in fall and one third in spring. Prune rambling and climbing roses to leave only the strongest canes from which vigorous shoots will grow.

What to Grow?

Ramblers: Ramblers are the best choice for growing on fences or for scrambling over trees or hedges.

Climbers: Climbers maintain a more manageable

Lynda's edible-flower salad was delicious served with a light vinaigrette dressing.

framework, and are a better choice for planting over arches and pergolas. Climbing roses flower more profusely when the main growth is tied down horizontally, encouraging the development of flowering laterals.

ORGANIC ROSE FERTILIZER
Before blooming:
> 1 cup (250 mL) alfalfa pellets
> ¼ cup (60 mL) rock phosphate
> 2 Tbsp. (30 mL) magnesium sulphate
> (Epsom salts)

Combine and mix well. Scatter around the drip line under rose bushes and work in gently.

After blooming:
> 1 cup (250 mL) alfalfa pellets
> 2 Tbsp. (30 mL) magnesium sulphate
> 2 gal. (9 L) water

Mix together, steep for 24 hours, and water root zone under each rose bush. TIP: Do not apply later than the end of August.
TIP: Roses also love banana peels! Bury cut-up banana peels around the bushes— they contain phosphorus (3.25 percent) and potash (41.76 percent), both of which stimulate rose blooms.

CULINARY FUN

How to Stuff Squash Blossoms

Enough for 12 male squash blossoms

Harvest only male flowers on long, slender stems. Store blossoms in cold water; they will last a day or two in the fridge.

1 cup (250 mL) mixed cheeses
2 Tbsp. (30 mL) fresh herbs, chopped
1 clove minced garlic
½ tsp. (2.5 mL) salt
½ tsp. (2.5 mL) black pepper
1 egg
⅓ cup (80 mL) flour
Olive oil for frying

Take 1 Tbsp. (15 mL) cheese mixture and stuff into the opening. Quickly but gently twist the ends of the petals closed. Dip in the slightly beaten egg, roll gingerly in flour and lay aside for frying. Pour ½ in. (1 cm) of olive oil into a skillet and heat until frying seals the blossom. Eat immediately or store in plastic containers for later. Good eaten cold as well.

Above: Male squash blossom.
Right: 'Glorious Gleam' trailing nasturtiums

Nasturtium Capers

2 Tbsp. (30 mL) salt
1 cup (250 mL) water
½ cup (125 mL) nasturtium seed pods (use young pods that are still green and soft)
¾ cup (180 mL) white wine vinegar
2 tsp. (10 mL) sugar
1 dried bay leaf
2 sprigs fresh thyme

Bring the salt and water to a boil in a small saucepan. Put the nasturtium seed pods in a half-pint glass jar and pour the boiling brine over them. Cover and let soak at room temperature for 3 days. Drain the seed pods. Bring the vinegar, sugar, bay leaf and thyme to a boil. Pour over the seed pods and let cool. Cover the jar and refrigerate for 3 days before using. Keeps 6 months refrigerated.

THE "BERRY WALK"

There's nothing healthier than organically grown, sun-ripened berries. Daily servings are critical to good health, fighting disease in the body. Five years after arriving at The Garden Path we started reaping abundant harvests of fruit from what became known as the "Berry Walk", a 50-ft. (15-m) border planted with raspberries, loganberries, blackcurrants, redcurrants, gooseberries and Jostaberries. The entire walk is underplanted with 'Totem' June-bearing strawberries as a groundcover. Luckily they grow very well together!

In the third year, a 50-ft. (15-m) arbour of forest logs was built alongside the "Berry Walk." The sunny side of the arbour supports kiwis, grapes and a host of different varieties of trailing berries, twisted around the upright posts. Marionberry, tayberry, boysenberry, cascade berry and thornless blackberries twine around the posts the length of the arbour, providing pretty flushes of flowers in spring, followed by amazing harvests of tasty sweet berries all summer and fall.

FEEDING BERRIES

Berries are hungry for potash. Mulch plants with comfrey leaves or wood ash (uncontaminated) when available. Covering beds with layers of compost, grass clippings or leaf mulch feeds fruit, represses weeds and helps soil retain moisture.

Raspberries

Raspberry canes are best planted in spring, in fertile well-drained soil. Choose everbearing varieties for fruit in summer (July/August) and again in fall (September/October). After harvest, cut brown canes that bore fruit down to the ground, leaving only green canes that will bear the following harvest.

Raspberries are an excellent source of fibre, manganese, vitamins C and B2, folate, niacin, magnesium, potassium, copper, and antioxidants that prevent cancer.

For easier picking install wire supports using 2x4 lumber and wires, and dig out any rooted canes that creep outside this framework.

The "Berry Walk."

154

Blueberries are very ornamental.

Top: 'Heritage' raspberries.
Bottom: Raspberry support system.

Blueberries

Blueberries are widely adapted and cold hardy, and once established will produce fruit with little care required. Ranging from a height of 3 ft. (90 cm) (low-bush) to 6 ft. (1.8 m) (high-bush), these hardy

shrubs are very ornamental. They provide year-round interest with bright-red twigs that sparkle in winter, peach-coloured flowers in spring, dark-blue berries in summer and foliage that deepens to red in fall. Six blueberry bushes will provide for a family once mature, but patience is required, as it takes a few years for the shrubs to get established.

Blueberries are low in calories—half a kilogram contains only 259 calories yet provides 64 grams of carbohydrate and 4 milligrams of vitamin C.

The two main problems growing blueberries are soil acidity and wildlife control. Wild blueberries are important sources of food for game and wild birds, which will swoop in as soon as berries ripen. Birds eat tops off tender growth in spring, (remedied immediately in my garden using tomato cages wrapped with chicken wire!). As soon as berries start to ripen, cover the bushes with loose netting to keep birds away. TIP: Plant blueberries in double rows so that a walk-in netted cage can be built over them.

To thrive, blueberries need moist acidic soil (pH 4.5 to 5.0). Rotted oak leaves, sawdust and pine needles lower soil pH, lock in moisture and keep weeds at bay. TIP: If you have chickens, use the wood shavings after cleaning out the coop to acidify the soil; the berries love the nitrogen from the manure. Set plants no closer than 8 by 8 ft. (2.4 by 2.4 m) apart, ideally in a location where they get full sun.

Growing more than one variety of blueberry results in better pollination with higher yields. Planting an early, mid-season and late variety extends the season of harvest.

It takes two years for plants to fruit and several years for them to mature. Wait two to three weeks after berries turn rich-blue for the ripest blueberries with the best flavour and the highest antioxidant content. The best berries are produced on wood two to three years old, so remove 20 percent of the oldest wood every year, reinvigorating the bushes to produce the highest yields.

Currants and Gooseberries

Blackcurrants tolerate shaded sites, but do best in full sun. They prefer heavy loam soils, enriched with well-rotted manure, and they are tolerant of wet ground. Blackcurrants produce fruit on one-year-old wood. In fall remove old wood and weak canes, but leave six to nine strong canes. They can give good yields for up to 15 years. Space bushes 5 ft. (1.5 m) apart in the row.

Redcurrants and gooseberries (genus *Ribes*) produce on two- and three-year-old wood. After the harvest, wood older than three years should be removed, leaving the eight or nine strongest canes on the bush. Shorten longer canes for side-branching and fruit-spur development. Rain in late spring and early summer will increase the size of fruit, but once fruit starts to ripen, excess water may cause it to split.

Top: 'Point Ellice House' heritage blackcurrants.

Bottom: Thornless blackberries produce surprisingly sweet fruit.

Currants and gooseberries are delicious and nutritious in fruit pies, cakes and desserts, jams and jellies, and for making wine and liqueurs.

The currant fruit fly can be a pest, noticed when larvae start to decimate the leaves. Control this problem immediately by applying a spray of *Bacillus thuringiensis* (Bt) on a calm day. The next time that worm eats this plant it dies, and within a week all recovers.

Thornless Blackberries

Blackberries have vigorous trailing canes, which are made more manageable in small gardens by tying them to supports with horizontal lines of wire, set 18 in. (46 cm) apart. Space plants 10 ft. (3 m) apart, gather the canes together in a "bunch" and have fun looping them either serpent fashion up and down, or spiraled into large circular swirls between the lower set of wires. Next year's canes then move onto higher wires. Once twisted into place, attach the canes to the wires using jute twine. Tying canes up prevents them from rooting around the garden and keeps fruit off the ground.

Right after harvest cut the old blackberry canes out, leaving only the most vigorous. Prune remaining canes to 4 ft. (1.2 m). The canes are now stimulated to produce laterals, which will now produce the biggest, juiciest berries.

Strawberries

"Doubtless God could have made a better berry, but doubtless God never did."
Dr. William Butler, seventeenth-century writer

Strawberries thrive being grown in oak half-barrels or in raised beds, ideally sited in full sun for the best flavour. Strawberries produce good fruit for three years, the best crop coming from second-year plants. After three years a strawberry patch will need to be renewed.

Renew a strawberry patch by pegging offsets (attached to the runners) down into the garden to root. This works best when done before the end of August. Space offsets 12 in. (30 cm) apart, and water them regularly to help them take root. TIP: Don't cover the strawberry crowns when planting; leave them at the soil surface.

June-bearing varieties provide bountiful harvests for four to six weeks starting in June. Grow these for jams and freezing. Day-neutral, everbearing varieties provide smaller occasional berries throughout summer, best for snacking. After harvest, rake straw or other debris from around the plants to get rid of any

'Totem' June-bearing strawberries.

diseased or damaged material. Cut the foliage right down to the ground. TIP: A weed whacker works well for this. Trust me, the new foliage comes back fast!

Do not start strawberry patches where potatoes, tomatoes, eggplant or peppers (Solanaceae family) were growing. This encourages verticillium wilt.

Strawberries are hungry for potash. Mulch plants with comfrey or wood ash (uncontaminated) when available. Covering beds with layers of compost, grass clippings or leaf mulch feeds the fruit, helps retain moisture and keeps weeds at bay.

Q Our strawberry patch has been in the same spot for a few years now. I noticed last year that we had powdery mildew, and it is back again this year. Is there an organic way to get rid of powdery mildew before more berries ripen?

A It sounds as if your strawberry patch is suffering from overcrowding! Lack of aeration and too much watering in heavy soils triggers powdery mildew. Being a fungal disease, spores persist and cause problems in following years, especially in cool wet springs.

157

Rootbound Plants

This happens frequently when plants have been left in their pots too long. Tightly coiled roots cannot establish, and will need freeing up before planting. Use a pruning knife or saw to score lightly into the rootball, and massage the outer and lower roots free.

Prepare a planting hole deep enough and wide enough to accommodate the roots when teased out. Plant at the same depth as the original soil level, whether pot grown or bare-root. Planting too deep is one of the most common reasons for plant death.

Tamp down soil around the roots when planting; air pockets can cause fungal problems.

Water thoroughly after planting. Drought stress commonly occurs until roots become established. Not enough water is a common cause of failure.

Rootbound salmonberry.

Flaky Pie Crust Recipe

Use this recipe to make the most amazing fruit pies in season:
Mixed berries (e.g., currants, raspberries and blueberries)
Blueberries with lemon zest
Rhubarb with orange zest
Strawberries and rhubarb
Sour cherry
Apple and blackberry
   Mix with hands until crumbly:
2½ cups (600 mL) unbleached flour (or 50:50 with whole wheat flour)
½ lb. (227 g) softened butter cut into small chunks
1 Tbsp. (15 mL) baking powder
Pinch of salt
   In a measuring cup, beat:
1 egg
1 Tbsp. (15 mL) apple-cider vinegar

Make up to ¾ cup (180 mL) using chilled buttermilk (sub. milk or water)

Pour liquid over the dry ingredients, and mix together using a fork, just until you can bring the pastry together into a smooth mound. TIP: Once this happens try to handle as little as possible. If too sticky add more flour; if too dry add a little more liquid. Cut in half.

Flour the counter, a rolling pin and the pastry lightly, and roll pastry into two large circles of ¼-in. (6-mm) even thickness. Lay one circle over a pie plate, trimming excess pastry off with a sharp knife. Fill the pie plate with the fruit filling. Lay the second circle over the top and crimp the two edges together, using your fingers and thumb to form a V-shape.

Brush the top with milk or cream to brown pastry, and sprinkle with cinnamon sugar (optional). Prick the top pastry using a sharp knife, and bake at 350°F (175°C) for 45 minutes.

GOING NUTS!

Hazelnut

The name hazelnut (or filbert) applies to the nuts of any species of the genus *Corylus*. Hazelnuts (*Corylus avellana*) grow as suckering shrubs or small trees, in full sun to part shade. Species range in hardiness from zones 4 to 8, but grow best in well-drained protected areas, in soils of neutral pH. Look for species that produce hazelnuts of a good size for eating.

I love the sight of the fuzzy yellow catkins that signal the start of another new spring! It's for these catkins that I tucked several groves of hazelnuts around the garden, but the hazelnuts are of the most value in these hedgerows.

Hazelnuts are not fussy and will thrive in abandoned gardens and shady laneways. Best of all, as wildlife continues to invade city space, hazelnuts are deer resistant. TIP: Hazelnuts require pollinators to produce nuts, so be sure to plant a qualified cross-pollinator.

The kernel of the seed is edible and can be used raw, roasted or ground into a paste. The seed has a thin brown skin, which has a bitter flavour, so this is sometimes removed. Hazelnuts are used in confectionery (especially good combined with chocolate). Oil pressed from hazelnuts is strongly flavoured and highly valued for gourmet cooking.

Hazelnuts are rich in protein and unsaturated fat, and contain significant amounts of thiamine and vitamin B6. A cup of hazelnut flour has 20 g of carbohydrates and 12 g of fibre.

Hazelnuts are harvested mid-autumn when the trees drop their nuts and leaves. Most commercial growers wait for the nuts to drop on their own, rather than use equipment to shake them from the tree. It's time to harvest when the nuts turn readily in their shells, which takes about six to eight months from pollination.

GOOD FERTILIZERS FOR NUT TREES
- Granular organic fertilizer—6:8:6 or 5:2:4
- Glacial rock dust
- Wood ashes, uncontaminated
- Seaweed mulch or granular kelp meal
- Super-Duper compost mulch annually (out to the drip line of the tree, avoiding contact with the trunk)

Almonds

If you can grow peaches successfully you can probably grow almonds; some are hardy to zone 6. Almonds (*Prunus dulcis*) belong to the genus *Prunus*, and are most closely related to peaches. Almonds do not like heavy clay soil, and are best planted in free-draining loam soils. The flowers are identical to other *Prunus* flowers, and are either pink or white in color—but they are also fragrant. Unlike the peach, its shorter-lived relative, almond trees can produce for up to 50 years! Fruiting begins 3 to 4 years after planting, with maximum production in 6 to 10 years. Almonds are ready to harvest when the casings split and release the nuts inside.

Almond trees are best not pruned regularly because lots of flowers are needed to set good harvests. TIP: Almonds bloom earlier than peaches, so planting under an overhang to prevent late-frost damage to blooms is a good idea.

Flowers are self-incompatible, so require cross-pollination. Because almonds are early-blooming and have a relatively short blooming period, honeybees have become essential pollinators in huge industrial almond orchards. On the home scale, cultivating solitary bees, such as the Blue Orchard Mason Bee, is a fun way to ensure good pollination of fruit trees in unseasonably cool spring weather. See the "Native Bees" in July.

Prunus blossoms in spring.

TREE GUARDS

Tree guards are spiraling plastic sheaths that protect saplings from animals and machinery, as well as provide support. In the second or third year, remove plastic guards, and if still necessary to protect trees, use wire mesh instead.

Sweet Chestnuts

Smaller yards can accommodate hazelnuts and almond trees, but sweet chestnut (*Castanea sativa*) is a large long-lived deciduous tree better suited to large gardens or acreage. Sweet chestnuts thrive in temperate climates, as they need adequate moisture for growth; under forest conditions they tolerate shade well. The most suitable soil is sandy loam, but chestnut trees grow in any soil that is well drained and of neutral-acidic pH (they are intolerant of lime).

Flowers in both sexes appear in late June to July. TIP: Plant two or more trees to ensure good cross-pollination for the best harvests. Female flowers develop into forbidding-looking spiny bur/cupules, which contain three to seven shiny-brown nuts. These are shed in October, when the spiny cases split open to reveal nuts inside. These nuts are wonderful roasted. I remember, as a student in London, often stopping to buy a bag from street vendors roasting them on open braziers.

The best kind of sweet chestnuts are called Marroni. They contain 15 percent sugar and yield thick sweet syrup that also yields a fine sugar. In France chestnuts candied in sugar syrup are enjoyed as a favourite sweetmeat, known as *marrons glacés*. Chefs today are rediscovering the delights of nutmeats in stuffings, and are puréeing sweet chestnuts for exotic sauces, soups and desserts.

Walnuts

Walnuts (*Juglans* spp.) are toxic to a number of plant species, emitting a chemical called juglone from roots, which leaches into the soil and causes nearby plants to turn yellow and die. The most potent of all is the black walnut, a fast-growing tree to 100 ft. (30 m)! Don't plant walnut trees anywhere near flower, shrub or vegetable gardens, as they affect plants within a range of 50 ft. (15 m).

June

HISTORY OF HERB GARDENS

Herbs date back to Roman times (physic garden at St. Gall, 816 to 820 AD), when they were considered essential for treating the sick and keeping food fresh and palatable. Herb gardens were laid out in simple grids of rectangular beds, each one planted with a single herb. The early apothecary gardens used the same simple plan, which made it easy to identify and harvest the plants. Herbs were a vital part of everyday life, forming the basis for cleansing products and beautifying cosmetics, medicines, insect repellants, strewing herbs and potpourris.

Formal knot gardens contained herbs growing within hedges of thyme, lavender, hyssop, wall germander or santolina (lavender cotton). By the late eighteenth century, herbs became less revered and were simply integrated into kitchen gardens amongst the vegetables. By 1760 to 1830 there were few herb gardens left—until a revival of interest occurred in the mid twentieth century with the traditional grid layout coming back into vogue.

Apothecary herbs used to ward off sickness in the sixteenth and seventeenth century were denoted by the Latin name *officinalis*, e.g., *Calendula officinalis, Melissa officinalis* (lemon balm) and *Digitalis officinalis* (foxglove).

HERBS

Harvest herbs on a sunny day, after the dew has dried and before the flowers have opened. This is when the aroma is at its peak. Pick stems and leaves about 6 in. (15 cm) long and tie them into small bunches. To capture the essential oils, put the bunches in a brown paper bag to dry. After a few days, the dried herbs will be ready to store in airtight jars in a dark place, which prevents deterioration from light. TIP: Herbs lose their aroma over time so replenish them annually.

Storing Herbs

Packaging is important. Plastic zip-lock bags allow aroma to escape. To prolong the flavour of herbs and spices, store them in sealed darkened glass jars, or line jars with brown paper before filling them with dried herbs.

Being Mediterranean plants, herbs love free drainage. The heat reflected off gravel pathways works well for edible landscaping a front yard in full sun. There's a constant drift of fragrance and colour from herb gardens as they develop their healing and aromatic properties.

Propagating Herbs

Annual herbs, such as basil, dill and chervil are easily grown from seed. Grow them under controlled

Hazelwood Herb Farm, Cedar, Vancouver Island.

conditions or wait and direct seed them into warm garden soil. Seeds of basil and dill need warmth and will germinate best when grown with bottom heat, on top of a heat pad or using heater cables.

Angelica, dill, parsley, sweet cicely, chervil, lovage and fennel are members of the Apiaceae (Umbelliferae) family. None have problems seeding around the garden, but growing them under controlled conditions is a different matter! I discovered the secret for success is using fresh seed and having patience, because these seeds are slow to germinate (21 to 28 days). When I collect Apiaceae seeds, I sow some right away to get the best germination results.

Growing perennial herbs such lavender, artemisia,

Soothing Herbal Bath

Makes 4 sachets

1 cup (250 mL) rolled oats finely ground in a coffee grinder or food processor
Add:

¼ cup (60 mL) baking soda

¼ cup (60 mL) of scented herbs such as lavender, mint, rose-scented geraniums, rose petals and lemon verbena

Mix and divide into four cotton or hemp bath bags, tied with cotton. Will store for three months in airtight containers.

162

germander, hyssop, rosemary, winter savory, thyme and sage from seed is slow—it takes a full year's growth to get a small plant. For this reason perennial herbs are mainly propagated vegetatively by plant division. A clump of chives or mint can be teased into many rooted sections.

Softwood herbs are short-lived herbaceous plants that can die off in harsh winters, and become leggy if left to their own devices. Prune them back after flowering each year. This is also an excellent time to root some tip cuttings! Last year I lost all the rosemary in the garden when the weather dipped to 15°F (-9°C), so was grateful for the cuttings rooting in the greenhouse.

PROPAGATION MIX FOR WOODY CUTTINGS
Mix equal parts by volume:
- Coarse washed sand
- Perlite
- Peat

Optional: add granular rock phosphate to aid rooting.

Tips for Rooting Cuttings

- Use a clean, sharp knife to prepare cuttings.
- The length of cuttings varies, but should be generally no more than 6 in. (15 cm) long.
- Trim the stem just below a node, ensuring that the growing tip is upright.
- Optional: soak the cuttings for 12 to 24 hours in Willow Water (see September for "Willow Water").
- Put in a plastic bag and keep out of sun (or in the fridge) if you don't have time to prepare the cuttings immediately.
- Prepare propagation mix, fill pots and moisten mix.
- Using a dibber to make a deep hole (a chopstick will do), place the cutting into the rooting mix, with any leaves above the mix.
- Place out of direct sun, but provide bright light— light stimulates rooting.

- Do not allow to dry out. Keep moist at all times. Misting is wonderful!
- New growth indicates that cuttings have rooted.
- Once cuttings have rooted, plant them into their own pots, ideally using screened compost. If not in screened compost then stimulate growth by feeding liquid fish fertilizer one week and liquid seaweed the next.
- In winter provide bottom heat to cuttings using a heat pad to achieve 85 percent rooting, compared to 55 percent without heat.

Culinary Herbs

Annual: Basil, chervil and dill
Biennial: Parsley
Perennial: Chives, winter savory, lovage, mint, oregano, sage, sweet marjoram, thyme

Cosmetic Herbs

Chamomile, calendula and rosemary are used in shampoos, skin creams and bath products.

Insect Repellants

Citronella deters mosquitoes; southernwood repels moths.

Potpourri Herbs

Fragrant myrtle, lavender, delphiniums, peonies and roses

Hazardous Herbs (health risk)

Datura (thornapple), rue, monkshood and foxglove are among herbs dangerous to your health. Always know your herbs before using.

Herbs for Lawns

Grow a creeping-thyme lawn.

BASIL

I feel sorry for basil (*Ocimum basilicum*) because often the first plantings do not survive. Gardeners are so keen to get fresh basil after a long winter, they forget what a tender plant it is, and that it needs warmth to survive. Seeds germinate between 75 to 90°F (24 to 32°C) and should emerge within 14 days. I don't bother seeding basil until May or June, when it grows like gangbusters in longer warmer days. Make sure to harden basil off before transplanting it out, and if there is any danger of frost at night be ready to cover it with a cloche or a floating row cover.

Annual basil is propagated from seed, and there are many different varieties to choose from in the pages of glossy seed catalogues. Over the years I've tried many for nursery stock, but in the end I always come back to Italian sweet basil, an aromatic large-leaf variety, because for me it's all about the pesto. TIP: Watering with compost tea or liquid fish fertilizer after harvesting makes basil grow back faster.

Seed Saving

Basil is in the Lamiaceae mint family. Plants are insect-pollinated, so provide separation of 55 yds. (50 m) between varieties, so that they do not cross. White flowers mature into light-brown seed capsules, harvested as they mature from the bottom to top of the flowers. Usual seed life: 5 years.

Hey Presto Pesto!

2 cups (475 mL) fresh basil

2 cloves garlic

½ cup (125 mL) chopped almonds, walnuts, cashews or pine nuts (your preference)

½ cup (125 mL) olive oil

½ cup (125 mL) fresh Parmesan cheese

¼ tsp (1 mL) salt to taste

Whirl basil, garlic, Parmesan and nuts in a processor until just blended. Add olive oil in a slow steady stream until a smooth paste is formed. Cover with a thin layer of olive oil to prevent discolouration and refrigerate in an airtight jar. Good for 2 to 3 weeks. Alternatively freeze in ice-cube trays and use cubes as needed.

Basil grows happily in one-gallon pots, as long as they are somewhere bright, warm and cosy.

Italian sweet basil seedlings.

BAY

Bay or sweet laurel (*Laurus nobilis*) is a perennial tree, native to the Mediterranean, and so needs a sunny warm location to thrive. Trees provide lots of oval aromatic leaves up to 3 in. (8 cm) long, which contribute a delicate flavour to many recipes. Bay leaves are added whole to soups, casseroles, marinades and bean dishes, and are an ingredient in bouquet garni and pickling spice. TIP: Whole leaves should be removed before serving.

When fresh, leaves are shiny and dark-green with lighter undersides; when dried they become matte olive-green. If they turn brown they have lost their flavour. When kept out of light, in an airtight container, whole leaves will retain flavour for a year.

When planting *Laurus nobilis*, be aware that the tree can grow 40 to 60 ft. (12 to 18 m) tall. Bay trees are suited to pruning, and can be kept to a controlled height and width if pruning is carried out regularly.

When bay leaves are dried, their flavour intensifies. Thin layers of bay leaves are dried in the shade, weighted down to prevent them from curling. Drying in the sun causes the leaves to turn brown and lose much of their essential oils.

Propagation

Propagation of bay is done from cuttings. They take time to root, but patience eventually rewards you with well-rooted cuttings. TIP: To ensure young bay laurel trees make it through winter, grow them for two years in a pot before planting out. (See September for "Propagation Mix for Softwood Cuttings.")

Bay laurel grows well in pots in a protected spot over winter.

A bay cutting.

Borage.

BORAGE

Borago officinalis is called the "herb of courage" because the ancient Greeks fed their warriors borage flowers before they went into battle. It's also a good companion plant, improving the growth and flavour of many plants in the garden. It makes great mulch if left to rot down. This is probably because borage is very high in potassium, a mineral that improves soil fertility and plant growth.

Borage is especially beneficial grown with tomatoes (deters tomato worm), squash and strawberries.

Borage is a rampant self-seeding annual, which is fortunate because the bright-blue flowers are edible (they taste like cucumber). The plants are easy to pull out if they go crazy on you, but wear gloves because the bristly leaves may cause skin irritation. Borage flowers look great with calendula petals in summer salads. TIP: Dried flowers of borage are great for potpourris.

FLORAL ICE CUBES
Pick borage flowers when fully open, place one in each compartment of an ice-cube tray, fill with water and freeze. Summer fruit punch will never be the same after enjoying it with sky-blue floral ice cubes!

Seed Saving

Borage seeds true to type (no separation between plants is needed), but collecting the seed is a little tricky because borage is always blooming and dry seeds are constantly falling out of the seed capsules. To collect the bulk of the seed from the plant, wait until all the blue flowers have faded and harvest the whole plant into a paper bag (cut the roots off first). Leave in the greenhouse to dry so that the rest of the seeds continue to ripen. With this approach most of the seeds will drop into the bag, rather than all over the garden. Usual seed life: 5 years.

CALENDULA

Calendula officinalis, also known as pot marigold, is in the Asteraceae family. It prefers full sun and well-drained soils, but will grow happily in part sun and any type of soil. It's a showy, hardy annual with yellow, gold or orange daisy-like flowers almost year round in mild winters. Single-flowered varieties are closest to their wild ancestors; the doubles produce an abundance of petals, but are often not as vigorous or hardy. Calendula also makes a good cut flower, height 18 to 24 in. (46 to 61 cm).

These cool-weather plants are easy to grow and will self-seed readily. They are good companions to many plants, deterring asparagus beetle, tomato worm and other garden pests. Calendula definitely belongs in the cook's garden; the flowers have delicate flavour

The Garden Path calendula mix.

Calendula Skin Treatments

INFUSION

8 oz. (227 g) dried calendula flowers
32 oz. (907 g) quality olive oil

In an old pot, place the calendula flowers and cover with olive oil. Using the double-boiler method, simmer for 1 hour. Repeat once a day for 3 days. Let cool completely and strain the infused oil through cheesecloth. Collect the infused oil and store in a dark bottle in a cool place. Store in the refrigerator for a longer shelf life.

OINTMENT

Makes about 12 oz. (340 g)

8 oz. (227 g) of infused calendula oil
3 oz. (85 g) of beeswax
2 oz. (57 g) cocoa butter
½ tsp. (2.5 mL) vitamin-E oil

Melt in a small pot on the stovetop on very low heat. Once the ingredients melt, carefully pour into dark-glass salve jars. Increase or decrease the beeswax depending on the consistency (firmness) wanted in the finished product. Infused oil can be used for skin creams, salves and soaps.

and add appealing colour to summer salads. They can also be used for colouring butter and decorating cakes and other dishes.

Seeds germinate in spring. Space 6 seeds per 1 ft. (30 cm) at a depth of ¼ in. (6 mm). If sowing indoors, transplant out after danger of frost. Keep deadheaded to encourage blooming.

Medicinal Uses

Calendula is best known for its soothing, healing properties for bug bites, stings, cuts and burns. It is invaluable as an ingredient in skin lotions and first-aid creams. Ointments are particularly effective when combined with St. John's wort (*Hypericum perforatum*). Faradiols are believed to be the efficacious ingredient that gives calendula its anti-inflammatory properties.

Seed Saving

Collect handfuls of dried brown seeds when deadheading the flowers. Lay out on plates to dry before storing. Usual seed life: Up to 10 years.

CHAMOMILE

German chamomile (*Matricaria recutita*) is an annual herb, and a very prolific producer of pretty yellow and white daisy-like flowers. It prefers full sun, and the feathery plants soon grow to 12 to 18 in. (30 to 46 cm) high. Chamomile can be tucked into food gardens as a charming companion to cabbages and onions, and as a major attractor of beneficial insects.

When starting indoors, barely cover the seed for germination (a general rule for tiny seeds). Chamomile is a prolific self-seeder and comes back so readily that you may not ever have to re-seed it.

The flowers last longer in cool summers, which means plentiful cups of fresh chamomile tea (an aid to digestion). TIP: When the tea goes cold, use it as a soothing and cleansing skin wash. Chamomile flowers are also used to make healing ointments.

Seed Saving

When flowers are fully open, harvest large bunches and leave to dry upside down in paper bags or buckets in a warm place. Shake the dried seeds off into a bowl, and use screens to remove the chaff and debris before storing.

CHIVES (See G for Garlic Chives)

Chives (*Allium schoenprasum*) belong to the Amaryllidaceae (onion) family.

They grow into thick clumps of thin tubular leaves and produce showy edible flowers. Chives are good companion plants, as they deter pests and attract bees for pollination.

Chive flowers come in different colours, so I chose some bright-pink chives for one border to contrast the purple-flowering chives in another border. Until they bloomed, I had no idea they would make such a beautiful display. The bees went nuts!

Chives improve the growth of carrots in the garden, and enhance the flavour of carrots in kitchen recipes. Chive greens promote digestion and stimulate appetite, and the unopened buds make great edible garnishes.

I feed Super-Duper compost to the borders every year, because fertile soil keeps chives growing well. If they stop flowering, the clumps are overcrowded, and should be divided. This is easily done by teasing smaller rooted clumps out and replanting them. TIP: Trim the roots and tops when dividing and replanting.

Chamomile Tea

Gather flowers before they fully open.
Use 1 Tbsp. (15 mL) of flowers per teapot.
Fill with boiling water and steep 5 minutes.
TIP: Great with lemon verbena leaves.

Harvesting German chamomile.

Chives make showy border plants.

Seed Saving

For seed-saving purposes, I allow one colour to set seed one year, and harvest from the other colour, and then switch the next year. The seed is good for two years, so I always have seeds of both chive colours handy.

If grown in fertile soil, chives re-grow after setting seeds early. After harvesting seeds, I cut clumps down to the ground, where they re-grow into new clumps that flower and set seed again (not as prolifically as the first time).

Chives are pollinated by bees, so you need more than one plant to collect a good quantity of seeds. A minimum of 12 onion plants is recommended for preservation of genetic variation. Large purple/pink globular flowers set huge quantities of hard black seeds. Chives do not cross with other species of onions, but (because they are pollinated by bees) will cross with chives of different colours flowering at the same time. Usual seed life: 2 years.

Herbed Carrots

6 medium carrots, cut into sticks and
　　steamed until tender
GLAZE
2 Tbsp. (30 mL) butter or oil
1 Tbsp. (15 mL) parsley, finely minced
1 Tbsp. (15 mL) chives, finely chopped
1 tsp. (5 mL) thyme, fresh or dried leaves
1 tsp. (5 mL) honey
½ tsp. (2.5 mL) salt

Prepare glaze in a small saucepan over medium heat.

Toss steamed carrot sticks in the glaze and serve hot.

Roasted Eggplant Cilantro Dip

Preheat oven to 350°F (175°C)
2 medium eggplants cut up into 1-in. (2.5-cm) cubes and tossed with:
1 Tbsp. (15 mL) coarse salt

Let stand until the eggplant starts to sweat. Rinse.

Place in a single layer in a baking pan drizzled with:
3 Tbsp. (15 mL) olive oil
3 cloves garlic

Bake 25 to 30 minutes in preheated oven until soft.

Process in a food processor (or mash with fork) until smooth.
1 cup (250 mL) fresh cilantro, chopped
2 lemons, juiced

Add half of the lemon juice and cilantro. Leave to stand 30 minutes. Taste. Adjust flavour with more lemon and cilantro (or salt) to taste.

CORIANDER

Coriander or Chinese cilantro (*Coriandrum sativum*) is an annual herb grown for its pungent leaves and aromatic seeds, essential ingredients in Asian, Latin and South American cuisine. For leaf production choose bolt-resistant strains; for aromatic-seed production choose varieties that bolt quickly.

Seedlings do not transplant well, so coriander is best grown from a direct seeding. Sow seeds 2 in. (5 cm) apart in spring and fall, and thin plants to 6 in. (15 cm) apart to allow room to grow. TIP: For continuous harvest sow seeds every 3 weeks. Coriander will overwinter in mild climates; otherwise it grows best protected under a cloche.

Seed Saving

Coriander is in the Apiaceae (Umbelliferae) carrot family. Flowers are self-pollinating, but will cross with different varieties of coriander in flower at the same time. As soon as weather conditions warm up, coriander bolts to seed, reaching 12 to 18 in. (30 to 46 cm) at maturity. The umbels of simple white flowers are very attractive to beneficial insects. Seeds mature at different times and drop to the ground. Watch for colour change to red/green and harvest the whole plant (remove roots and soil) into paper bags or buckets. Leave in a warm, dry place for the seeds to finish ripening. Screen to remove any chaff and debris, and make sure the seeds are dry before storage. Usual seed life: 3 years.

DILL

Dill (*Anethum graveolens*) is an attractive annual herb with finely divided foliage and umbels of yellow flowers, followed by aromatic seeds. 'Mammoth' dill grows to 40 in. (1 m), and is good for "dill weed" and seeds. 'Fernleaf' dill is a bushier, compact variety that grows to 18 in. (46 cm), and makes a better choice for container gardening. Dill is a good companion to brassicas because it deters cabbage worms. It also improves the growth and flavour of cabbages and broccoli. Tea made from dill seeds was used traditionally as baby gripe water. In

Coriander 'Santo' in seed.

Dill.

the cuisine of northern and central Europe, dill is commonly found combined with root vegetables, cucumbers and cabbage. Russians often use it in borsht, the classic beet soup. The leaves are delicious added to sauces, soups, fish dishes, egg dishes and potato salads.

Dill does not transplant well, so it is best to direct sow the seeds in early spring after all danger of frost. It's easy to grow, preferring well-drained, warm soil in full sun. Sow seeds ¼ in. (6 mm) deep, and thin plants to 6 to 8 in. (15 to 20 cm) apart. Continuous sowings will provide longer harvests. The seed is slow to germinate, requiring 2 to 4 weeks. Dill self-seeds readily, but in my garden with heavier clay soil it does not come back voluntarily.

Beets, Greens and Dill

Makes 4 servings
2 lbs. (907 g) beets, with leafy tops
Remove stems. Cut leaves into 2-in. (5-cm) pieces. Steam until tender. Drain.

Cook washed beets in boiling water until tender (25 to 30 minutes).

Drain. Cool. Peel. Julienne. Toss with the dressing.

DRESSING:
3 Tbsp. (45 mL) olive oil
1 Tbsp. (15 mL) lemon juice
2 Tbsp. (30 mL) fresh-chopped dill or
    1 Tbsp. (15 mL) dried dill
1 garlic clove, minced
Salt and pepper to taste

Seed Saving

Dill is in the Apiaceae (Umbelliferae) carrot family. Yellow flowers are produced in attractive umbels. Dill does not cross with other plants, so its seeds will be pure. To harvest, snip off umbels bearing light-brown seeds into paper bags or buckets to dry. Shake or bash the dried seeds off the stalks into a large container. Screen to remove chaff and debris before storage. Usual seed life: 3 years.

Bronze fennel.

FENNEL

"Above the lowly plants it towers,
The fennel, with its yellow flowers,
And in an earlier age than ours
Was gifted with the wondrous powers
Lost vision to restore."
Henry Wadsworth Longfellow

Fennel is grown as a perennial herb for its aromatic feathery leaves of green (*Foeniculum vulgare dulce*) or bronze (*F. vulgare dulce* 'Rubrum').

Florence fennel (*F. vulgare* var. *azoricus* from the Azore Islands) is grown for its large, fleshy, swollen base, sweet and crunchy with a light anise flavour. An annual in cold climates, Florence fennel is sautéed, stir-fried or braised, or thinly grated (using a mandoline) into salads. I love its crunchy aniseed addition to many dishes including pasta, soups, omelettes and salads. TIP: Florence fennel needs fertile soil and a long growing season to develop its large swollen base.

FENNEL SEEDS

- Anise-flavoured fennel seeds are used as breath fresheners.
- Fennel seeds make the tangiest tomato sauces.
- Seeds are used in baking, confections and for flavouring liqueurs.
- Tea made from fennel seeds is said to cure the hiccups, and is given to babies to calm them and cure flatulence.
- Keep seeds handy to munch on when you are dieting. They are known to ward off hunger pangs, and are prescribed as a remedy for obesity.

Bronze fennel is a host for swallowtail-butterfly larvae.

It's easy to grow fennel plants from seed; transplant them out after all danger of frost has passed. Keep in mind that fennel does not make a good companion to other plants, as many dislike growing alongside it. Never let *F. vulgare* go to seed. It has a deep taproot and is a real pain to weed out!

To make fennel a bushier and more effective accent plant, cut it back by 50 percent when 2 ft. (60 cm) tall.

Seed Saving

Fennel is in the Apiaceae (Umbelliferae) carrot family. Different species do not cross with each other (e.g., dill, coriander, chervil, fennel), but varieties of the same species can be cross-pollinated by insects. Yellow flowers produce attractive seed umbels that mature into prolific quantities of light-brown seeds. Thresh the seed from the stalks into a large bowl. Use screens to remove chaff and debris. Store in sealed containers. Usual seed life: 4 years.

FRENCH SORREL

French sorrel (*Rumex acetosa*) is a hardy perennial herb in the Polygonaceae family, a relative of rhubarb, dock and buckwheat. Plants grow into large clumps over the years, and will thrive for up to five years. Remove flower stalks to stop plants from going to seed, keeping tender leaves coming from March to November. Large succulent leaves, rich in vitamin C, add tangy zest to salads, soups and sauces.

Buckler-leafed sorrel (*Rumex scutatus*), is just 6 in. (15 cm) tall and is also cultivated for edible leaves. It grows best in full sun in dry sandy soils, and produces very acidic leaves that add tang to salads, soups and sauces.

Sorrel contains high levels of oxalic acid, which gives leaves their lemony flavour. The sunnier the site the more acidic the leaves will be. Leaves should not be eaten in large amounts, and oxalic-acid content is reduced when the sorrel is cooked. French sorrel is not recommended for people with rheumatism, arthritis, gout, kidney stones or hyperacidity.

Propagation by seed is surprisingly fast. You should have a good-sized 4-in. (10-cm) plant by the end of the first season. Space transplants 12 in. (30 cm) apart. The easiest way to propagate is by root division when plants are dormant. Divide clumps into separate sections for replanting with a sharp shovel.

French Sorrel Soup

1 bunch French sorrel leaves, stalks
   removed, roughly chopped
2 large (4 medium) potatoes, cubed
4 cups (1 L) vegetable broth
   Bring to a boil, reduce heat and cook until
the potatoes are tender. Purée in a blender
in batches, and place back into the soup pot.
   Sauté until translucent:
3 Tbsp. (45 mL) olive oil
1 onion, diced
2 cloves garlic, minced
   Add:
2 Tbsp. (30 mL) flour
2 cups (475 mL) soymilk or milk
   Stirring constantly make a smooth roux,
and blend with the puréed soup. Heat slowly
over a medium heat without boiling. Season
to taste with salt and pepper. Serve.

Seed Saving

   Seeds should not be left to stand in the garden
long. Harvest whole stalks when the seeds are still
light brown and before they turn dark brown. Place
stalks in a paper bag to dry, and then thresh them into
a large bowl. Use screens to remove chaff and debris.
Usual seed life: 2 years.

GARLIC CHIVES

Garlic chives (*Allium tuberosum*) originate from
Southeast Asia, and differ from chives in that
their leaves are flat and aromatic with garlic flavour.
The flowers also vary from chives in that they are
starburst in form. Bees love the pretty white or mauve
flowers and visit often. Garlic chives make great
ornamental edibles, and growing them as border
plants in food gardens provides the extra benefits of
keeping pests at bay and attracting beneficial insects.

Mauve-flowered garlic chives are very ornamental.

These hardy perennials grow into large clumps that need dividing every three years, which is a good time to propagate them from small rooted sections. From seed it takes more time; by the second year there should be enough leaves to start harvesting some. TIP: Make sure seeds are fresh, as they are only viable for one year.

Garlic chives are used anywhere you use chives, and with this plant you get the added benefit of garlic flavour and much prettier flowers.

Seed Saving

After harvesting seeds, cut clumps down to the ground, from where they will regrow. A minimum of 12 onion plants is recommended for preserving genetic variation. Pretty white or mauve starburst flowers set large quantities of hard black seeds. Garlic chives do not cross with other species of onions, but because of pollinating by bees the white-flowered garlic chives and the mauve-flowered garlic chives would cross if they were flowering at the same time. Usual seed life: 1 to 2 years.

LAVENDER

Lavender is a short-lived shrub (eight to ten years) that tolerates many growing conditions and is extremely drought resistant once established. A native of the Mediterranean, it thrives in dry habitats in full sun. Alkaline and chalk soils enhance lavender's fragrance (and it does not thrive in acidic soil conditions).

Lavender is a member of the Lamiaceae mint family. Flowers and leaves can be used fresh, while flowers in bud and stems can be dried. This versatile herb is making a comeback in upscale bakeries and restaurants. Lavender flowers taste especially good with chocolate, and for flavouring sorbets and ice cream. Fragrant flowers are dried for use in sachets and potpourris, and lavender oil is often added to soaps, cosmetics and perfumes.

TIP: The potency of lavender flowers increases with drying, so use one-third the quantity of dried to

White Spanish lavender.

fresh in recipes. Adding too much lavender can make the flavour bitter.

LAVENDER SUGAR
Grind lavender flowers with a mortar and pestle. Put the ground lavender in a jar with sugar and seal. Use for cookies, cakes, custards and sorbets.

English lavender (*Lavandula angustifolia*) (narrow-leaved) is also referred to as common lavender or true lavender. It is considered to have the sweetest fragrance of all the lavenders, and is the one commonly used for food preparation and drying.

Spanish lavender (*Lavandula stoechas*) has butterfly flowers that are showy and decorative but not as useful as English lavender. Even though they are not reliably winter hardy, I love *L. stoechas* for blooming early (May to July), which keeps me in purple heaven for longer!

French lavender (*Lavandula dentata*) has attractive, silvery-blue leaves with showy china-blue

Sacred Mountain Lavender Farm, Salt Spring Island.

flowers, and makes a very striking container plant.

Spike lavender (*Lavandula latifolia*) (broad-leaved) are the oil-yielding varieties used in making soap.

To preserve lavender, cut the stems when the flowers are first showing colour, then hang in small bunches to dry.

Propagation

Everything about lavender is calming and fragrant; even the shiny-black seeds retain the heady scent. Bees pollinate lavender, so if growing from seed, there will be variation in size and flowering characteristics, and it may be necessary to grow plants out first to be certain of consistency (in the case of lavender hedges), or buy lavender from rooted cuttings. You can harvest and prune lavender at the same time, collecting bundles for drying while cutting bushes to keep them trim. TIP: Beware of cutting down to bare wood, which may be too harsh and can kill the plant. (See September for "Propagation Mix for Softwood Cuttings.")

Lavender Hazelnut Bread

Makes 1 loaf
(Can be made using a bread maker)
1¼ cups (300 mL) warm water 110°F (43°C)
1 Tbsp. (15 mL) active dry yeast
1 Tbsp. (15 mL) olive oil
1½ Tbsp. (22 mL) honey
Leave for 10 minutes in a warm place, until yeast starts bubbling
3¼ cups (775 mL) bread flour or unbleached all-purpose flour
2 Tbsp. (30 mL) lavender flowers or ¾ Tbsp. (11 mL) dried lavender
½ cup (125 mL) hazelnuts (or nuts of choice), coarsely chopped
1½ tsp. (7.5 mL) salt

Place dry ingredients in a large mixing bowl, and pour yeast into a well in the centre. Using a wooden spoon stir and form into an elastic dough. If the dough is too moist add more flour; if too dry add warm water 1 Tbsp. (15 mL) at a time.

Knead dough for 10 minutes on a lightly floured surface. Form into an oval, place in a lightly oiled bowl, leave in a warm spot to rise for 1 to 2 hours until the dough has doubled in bulk. Preheat oven to 400°F (205°C). Remove dough, and punch down on a lightly floured surface. Form dough into an oval and place in lightly oiled bread pan. Leave to rise double again. Bake 30 to 45 minutes, until the loaf sounds hollow when you tap it on the bottom.

LEMON BALM

Lemon balm (*Melissa officinalis*) is a leafy perennial herb that quickly grows to 24 in. (61 cm). Leaves have a pungent lemon flavour and are used for teas and to flavour jams, jellies, custards and fruit salads. The lemony leaves are also good for fish dishes, sauces and marinades.

Lemon balm is easily grown from seed or plant division. It grows in any soil, but really thrives and spreads in moist fertile soil in full sun. Harvest the leaves before flowering, from June to October, as the aroma and medicinal properties decrease once the plants set seed. I get three harvests a year, and the first harvest is best for drying, as these leaves are largest.

Melissa officinalis 'Variegata'—an attractive version of lemon balm.

Lemon Balm Calming Tea

Sprigs of fresh mint, or 1 tsp. (5 mL) dried

Sprigs of fresh lemon balm, or 1 tsp. (5 mL) dried

1 cup (250 mL) hot water

Steep 5 minutes for a soothing tea that aids relaxation, eases nervous stomachs and induces sleep.

Rhubarb Lemon Balm Bread

Preheat oven to 350°F (175°C)

Grease a loaf pan (5 by 9 in. or 13 by 23 cm). Line the bottom and sides with wax paper.

1½ cups (350 mL) brown sugar firmly packed

⅔ cup (160 mL) vegetable oil

In a large bowl combine brown sugar with oil and beat well.

1 cup (250 mL) buttermilk

1 egg

1 tsp. (5 mL) vanilla extract

In a small bowl beat the buttermilk with the egg and vanilla.

Add to brown-sugar mixture and blend thoroughly.

2½ (600 mL) cups unbleached white flour

1 tsp. (5 mL) baking soda

1 tsp. (5 mL) salt

Combine flour, baking soda and salt. Gradually stir into above mix.

1½ (350 mL) cups fresh rhubarb, chopped

Fold in rhubarb and transfer batter to prepared bread pan.

½ cup (125 mL) sugar

⅓ cup (80 mL) fresh lemon balm, finely chopped

1 tsp. (5 mL) grated lemon zest

1 Tbsp. (15 mL) unsalted butter at room temperature

In a small bowl, combine sugar, lemon balm, lemon zest and butter. Sprinkle mixture over the batter. Bake for 50 to 60 minutes until tester comes out clean. Leave to cool for 10 minutes, turn out onto rack. Remove wax paper when the cake has cooled.

Seed Saving

Tiny black seeds mature after flowers fade. Cut seed heads off into bags or buckets for drying before plants disperse thousands of their seeds into the garden. After drying, thresh the stalks against the side of the bucket to release the seeds. Screen and winnow to remove chaff and debris. Usual seed life: 1 year.

LEMON VERBENA

Lemon verbena (*Aloysia triphylla*) is a short-lived woody perennial herb with heavenly scented leaves, cherished for hot lemony teas and iced teas in summer. Leaves and flowers can be harvested any time during the active growing season, and are equally wonderful fresh or dried.

Lemon verbena must be wintered indoors because it is not reliably winter hardy. For this reason I grow plants in 5-gal. (23-L) pots, which are easily moved into the greenhouse for winter. When weather cools down in November, the plants go into dormancy and all their leaves drop off. Try to time the last harvest just before this happens! Usually I get two harvests from each plant in one season, and once they have dried I strip the leaves off the stalks and store them

A five-year-old lemon verbena.

in a tea caddy in the cupboard. TIP: Lemon verbena pairs well with mint.

Lemon verbena thrives in full sun when growing in soils rich in organic matter. Propagation is by cutting, not seed, which is why it is often difficult to find lemon verbena plants for sale. The best way to keep a plant growing well is to give it a heavy prune back at the end of each growing season (also the best time to take cuttings). Prune plants to remove spindly branches, and take them down about 50 percent. Never fear, they will sprout back vigorously as soon as the weather warms up in spring.

Pests can be an issue if growing lemon verbena indoors—watch for spider mites and white flies. As a precaution, rinse plants under flowing water once a month.

LOVAGE

Lovage (*Levisiticum officinale*) is a tall vigorous plant of 5 ft. (1.5 m), definitely not suitable for smaller gardens. It is one of the first herbs to come up in early spring, and young leaves make the best soup stock ever. It has a taste reminiscent of the famous Maggi bouillon cubes, and adds a special flavour to stews and casseroles. TIP: You don't need much, only a few leaves, as this is a very aromatic herb.

Aromatherapists use lovage oil to remove spots and freckles from skin.

Lovage is easy to grow from seed, or from root division, best done in early spring. It prefers sunny locations but will grow in part sun. Plants last several years if they are grown in well-drained soil, but they survive longest when overcrowded clumps are divided. Simple yellow flowers that appear in June or July will attract beneficials to the garden. Lovage is also a host plant for the swallowtail butterfly.

MINT

Mint prefers a rich, moist soil of pH 6.5 to 7.0 in full sun or part shade. It only took watching mint take over my garden once to learn never to plant it there again. Now I always grow mint in a pot to contain it. If you don't harvest regularly, mints go to flower. The flowers are pretty, and attract bees, but it's better to shear plants back mid season to renew growth.

Mints sometimes get rust that appears as small orange spots on the undersides of leaves. Get rid of any infected leaves by cutting plants back. Whitefly, spider mites and aphids may bother stressed plants, but I have rarely experienced problems growing mint, as long as it's kept under control!

Harvest mint in sunny weather when the flavour is at its peak. Pick lengths of mint of about 6 in. (15 cm) long and tie them together in bunches. To capture peak aroma put these bunches inside a brown paper bag, and hang in a warm place to dry. Store dried mint leaves in airtight jars, kept in a dark place.

Try a candy-store collection of mint flavours:

Fruity: Pineapple, grapefruit, ginger, apple mint

Fragrant: Lavender, chocolate, basil mint

Savoury: Peppermint (*Mentha × piperita*), spearmint (*Mentha spicata*)

Make delicious tea blends by combining varieties of mint such as chocolate and lavender or ginger and apple, fresh or dried. Mints lose their aroma over time, so replenish from the garden annually.

Mints are best propagated from short-rooted sections of trailing stems, which root anywhere they come in contact with soil. They are easy to propagate by repotting rooted sections into 4-in. (10-cm) pots of screened compost, where they quickly grow into bushy little plants. Every March large pots of mint are divided into rooted sections (sometimes hundreds), and I replant three sections back into the pot, which is filled with mint again by the end of summer.

> ### Fresh Meadow Mint Tea
>
> *Makes 1 gal. (4.5 L)*
>
> 2 cups (475 mL) sugar
>
> 4 cups (1 L) water
>
> 2 cups (475 mL) mint leaves
>
> 2 lemons, sliced
>
> *Bring to a boil, stirring. Leave brew to cool.*
>
> *Strain and pour liquid into 1-gal. (4-L) container. Fill with water and ice.*
>
> *Serve with fresh mint sprig.*

The mint collection.

Pots of mints are a great way to harvest mint tea.

OREGANO

In the wild, oregano (*Origanum vulgare*) grows in pastures and on rocky scrublands in sunny well-drained sites. There are many cultivated species of oregano, and ornamental flowers range in colour from pink to white. Oregano is a good companion plant to grow here and there around the garden, but beware that in sandy soils it may take over. It makes a good pot herb in containers, growing as a 12-in. tall (30-cm) perennial herb, best grown alone as it out-competes other herbs.

The Italians are especially fond of oregano as it tastes particularly good in tomato sauces and tomato-based soups and casseroles. Greek oregano (white flowers) is an indispensable herb for a "true" Greek salad.

Garden Tomato Sauce

3 Tbsp. (45 mL) olive oil
1 Tbsp. (15 mL) garlic, finely minced
2 bay leaves
Sauté garlic lightly in oil with bay leaves
Add:
5 lbs (2.3 kg) beefy tomatoes, coarsely chopped
½ cup (125 mL) fresh oregano, finely chopped, or 1 Tbsp. (15 mL) dried oregano
1 tsp. (5 mL) dried fennel seeds
½ tsp. (2.5 mL) chili pepper seeds (optional)
1 tsp. (5 mL) salt
1 tsp. (5 mL) pepper
2 Tbsp. (30 mL) parsley, fresh-chopped
Slowly bring to a boil while stirring.
Reduce heat and simmer approximately 2 hours. When the sauce has thickened, taste, adjust seasonings, add parsley, and leave to cool. Remove bay leaves. Refrigerate.

Greek oregano setting seed (dark-pink).

Oregano is particularly good in tomato sauce.

The easiest way to grow oregano is from rooted cuttings. It is also relatively easy to grow under controlled conditions from seed. TIP: The seeds are tiny, so sow them close to the surface without covering. They are slow to germinate and it is important to ensure the medium does not dry out.

HARVESTING OREGANO
- Gather whole stems by cutting off at the ground.
- Hang in bundles inside brown paper bags to dry.
- Strip leaves off the stalk.
- Store in darkened glass jars.

Seed Saving

Oregano is in the Labiatae mint family. Seeds don't ripen at the same time, so keep your eyes open as the flowers fade and go to seed. Cut flower stalks off, and invert into paper bags. Leave to dry, and shake the bag to release the tiny seeds. Fine-screen to clean off dust and debris. Usual seed life: 3 to 5 years.

PARSLEY

Parsley (*Petroselinum crispum*) is a hardy biennial represented by different varieties of cultivated parsley, some curly and some flat-leaved. For centuries, parsley has been a favourite culinary herb, perhaps because it's loaded with vitamin C, iron, iodine, and magnesium, and adds zest to everything. In the garden it's a good companion to tomatoes and asparagus, and in planters it works well growing with other herbs. I add parsley liberally to many culinary dishes and use it as a lively garnish. I even allow it to self-seed liberally around the garden, so there's always some handy! Fresh seed is needed for successful germination. Parsley seeds are slow to geminate—taking up to 21 days—so patience is required.

Seed Saving

Parsley is in the Apiaceae (Umbelliferae) carrot family, so it relies on insects for cross-pollination. It is biennial, which means the roots need to overwinter before it sets seed the following year. All these parsleys belong to the same species and will cross-pollinate:

English Parsley Sauce

Delicious with vegetables and fish dishes
1¾ cups (425 mL) milk
A few stalks of parsley
1 bay leaf
1 onion sliced thin
10 whole black peppercorns
Bring everything slowly to a simmer, then leave aside to cool. Strain and discard the seasonings.
1½ oz. (43 g) butter
¾ oz. (21 g) unbleached flour
4 heaped Tbsp. (60 mL) fresh parsley, finely chopped
1 tsp. (5 mL) lemon juice
Salt and black pepper
Heat the butter until it melts. Using a balloon whisk, add the flour to make a smooth roux. Turn the heat down lower, and slowly pour the strained milk, a little at a time, to the roux, stirring as it thickens. When the sauce has thickened to the desired consistency, add chopped parsley and lemon juice, and adjust the seasoning to taste.

Parsley has attractive flower umbels that attract beneficial insects.

- **Curly parsley** (*Petroselinum crispum* var. *crispum*)
- **Flat-leaved Italian parsley** (*Petroselinum crispum* var. *neapolitanum*)
- **Rooted Hamburg parsley** (*Petroselinum crispum* var. *tuberosum*)

Umbels of hard brown seeds need to be collected regularly, as the seeds do not ripen all at the same time. Check plants weekly, and bag brown umbels to catch the ripe seeds before they disperse naturally. Sieve to clean and follow with a winnowing to remove dust. Usual seed life: 1 to 2 years if stored correctly.

ROSEMARY

Rosmarinus officinalis is an attractive evergreen shrub with aromatic needle-like leaves. *Rosmarinus* means "dew of the sea" because rosemary relishes the ocean's salt spray and does very well in coastal gardens. It thrives in temperate climates with mild winters, making a great landscape plant year round.

Rosemary leaves work well added to soups, casseroles and vegetable dishes, and can also be used to flavour jellies, jams, focaccia bread and crackers.

Garlic and root vegetables are even more tasty when roasted with sprigs of rosemary and/or other strong herbs such as thyme, sage and oregano.

Rosmarinus officinalis 'Tuscan Blue' is an excellent variety with broad bright-green leaves and beautiful bright-blue flowers in early spring.

Rosemary is a fast-growing woody shrub, and benefits from pruning every year to keep it from getting leggy. While it's very difficult to grow rosemary from seed, it's surprisingly easy to get cuttings to root. Being a Mediterranean herb, rosemary does not reliably overwinter, in which case you may be glad you took cuttings in the fall.

Greek scholars wore garlands of rosemary while sitting through examinations. It was believed to strengthen the brain and memory.

Rosemary Hair Rinse

Put several handfuls of rosemary in a saucepan and fill with water. Bring to the boil and gently simmer for 15 minutes. Cool and strain. Pour rosemary rinse through hair just after shampooing. There's no need to rinse off! Rosemary is ideal for dark hair, giving it shine and bringing out the highlights.

Rosemary has showy blue flowers.

Rosemary Vinegar

Fill a clean bottle with clean and fresh rosemary sprigs. Pour high-quality apple cider vinegar (unheated) over rosemary completely. Seal and leave in a dark cupboard for two weeks to infuse, shaking the jar from time to time. Mix several tablespoons of rosemary vinegar with lukewarm water and pour over the scalp weekly to rejuvenate scalp and hair.

Rosemary Hair Oil

Wash and dry two fresh sprigs of rosemary. Rub them lightly between your clean palms to release flavour, then place in a clean bottle or jar. Pour good quality extra-virgin olive oil over rosemary sprigs and seal. Leave in a dark cupboard for two weeks. Massaging rosemary oil into the scalp, and leaving it overnight to penetrate hair follicles, is said to help shedding hair regain strength and vitality.

SAGE

Culinary sage (*Salvia officinalis*) is a perennial sub-shrub with grey leaves and beautiful blue or pink flowers. The tricolour, golden and purple sages are drought-tolerant ornamental shrubs that can be used for culinary purposes, but are less flavourful. In Mediterranean cuisine, sage blends well with cheese in gnocchi, pizza and pasta dishes. It also makes a great addition to corn bread, cheese biscuits and scones, and is good with eggplant, asparagus, squash, mushrooms and tomato dishes, and heavy bean or split pea soups. Sage pairs nicely with other strong herbs such as rosemary, thyme, savory and oregano. TIP: Sage has a strong flavour that can overwhelm, so use sparingly.

Sage is easily propagated from cuttings after the flowers are cut back. (See September for "Propagation Mix for Softwood Cuttings.") Cultivars are also grown from seed, but selection may be needed due to diversity when plants are seed-grown.

Salvia officinalis planted with cabbage and carrots deters cabbage moth and carrot fly.

Sage Tea for Sore Throats

Make an antiseptic and soothing tea from:

1 part sage

2 parts lemon balm

1 tsp. (5 mL) honey

Culinary sage.

Drying Sage

Hang bundles of sage in a warm, dry place. Store the leaves whole, after stripping them from the woody stalks. They are best crushed just before using, and the most effective way to do this is to rub them between your hands.

Seed Saving

Sage is a member of the Labiatae mint family. Sage plants flower early, and the flowers turn into sticky bell-shaped capsules, with several seeds in each.

Harvest seeds when capsules are dry and brittle before they disperse naturally. Clean using screens and a final winnowing. Usual seed life: 3 years.

SWEET CICELY

With sweet cicely (*Myrrhis odorata*), the entire plant—leaves, seeds and roots—is edible. Triangular leaves add anise-flavour to desserts, and sweet cicely combines well with rhubarb, because it cuts sugar use in half.

Umbels of tiny white flowers appear in May and June, attracting many beneficial insects, which prefer these simple open flowers. The root has a sweet aniseed smell and taste, and yields its properties to water or diluted alcohol. Sweet cicely grows best in part sun in moist soils. It self-seeds all over my garden, and often needs to be controlled. (Dig some up for propagation.)

Q I bought sweet cicely seeds, and I have been trying to get them started ever since! I tried damp paper towels, then jiffy peat pellets, first in the fridge and then over the heat register. I am out of ideas! Can you help me?

A Sweet cicely seeds are tricky to grow, belonging to a group of seeds that need to be fresh to germinate. Sowing sweet cicely seeds while still fresh (within 6 to 12 months) is imperative. This is probably why it's difficult to find this herb listed in seed catalogues.

To propagate sweet cicely sow fresh seed either directly into the garden or into pots of well-drained seeding mix in late summer. Leave seeds to overwinter (stratification) and by spring there should be signs of life!

Seed Saving

Seeds of sweet cicely are very ornamental as they mature from bright green to black. When they turn jet-black they are ready for harvesting. Usual seed life: 6 to 12 months if stored properly.

Young seed pods of sweet cicely taste great!

SWEET MARJORAM

Sweet marjoram (*Origanum marjorana*) is a creeping aromatic perennial herb, related to oregano but with more perfumed flavour. A good groundcover, sweet marjoram forms large clumps 6 to 12 in. (15 to 30 cm) tall, which spread readily. Leaves add strong flavour to soups, sauces, stuffing and stews, and are excellent in tomato dishes, on pizzas and used as a bouquet-garni herb. Hang in bundles to dry; strip leaves off stalks and store in darkened glass jars.

Propagation is easy from rooted cuttings or seed. TIP: Seeds are tiny, so sow them close to the surface without covering, and do not allow them to dry out.

Seed Saving

Sweet marjoram is in the Labiatae mint family. Seeds don't ripen at the same time, so keep your eyes open as the flowers fade and start to ripen to seed. Cut flower stalks off and invert into paper bags. Leave to dry, and shake the bag to release the tiny seeds. Fine-screen to clean off dust and debris. Usual seed life: 5 years.

THYME

Thyme (*Thymus vulgaris*) is a low-growing Mediterranean perennial, best suited to full sun and well-drained (preferably alkaline) soils. In very cold regions it needs protection in winter. Common thyme (*T. vulgaris*) is the most popular variety for culinary purposes. Purple or white flowers from May to October make thyme an attractive groundcover for full sun. Thyme works well grown as a perennial pot herb. In the garden it is a good companion to cabbages as it deters cabbage worm.

Leaves can be stripped off the woody stems by pulling them through the fingers, and are often chopped before use. As with other strong herbs (e.g., sage, bay, rosemary, marjoram), the flavour is released during the cooking process, so thyme is added at the beginning. Thyme can be added to roast vegetables, stuffing, soups and stews, and has a particular affinity

Thymus serphyllum *makes a good groundcover for patios.*

to tomato and egg dishes. Thyme blends well with other herbs and is used in bouquet garni and Herbes de Provence.

Harvest thyme when it is blooming and the most potent. Afterwards, prune the plants back hard to keep them from getting spindly. To multiply plants, take stem cuttings 3 in. (8 cm) long with a "heel" of older wood attached at the base, then root them in propagation mix.

Pick your thyme according to your need:

English thyme: Common grey leaved, aromatic, best for culinary purposes.

Lemon thyme: With a lemon kick, good for culinary purposes.

Creeping thyme: Lowest growing, good for walkways and patios.

Silver thyme: Drought tolerant and good for draping over walls.

Seed Saving

While thyme is in the Labiatae mint family and is self-pollinating, bees love the flowers, so thymes blooming at the same time may cross-pollinate.

Seeds should be harvested soon after the flowers turn brown. The tiny seeds will disperse if left on plants for too long. Usual seed life: 5 years.

WINTER VEGETABLES

Winter vegetables are food plants that can be harvested from October to May, a period when gardeners typically leave their garden beds empty. Allocate garden space specifically for winter crops, or follow earlier crops of broad beans (favas), peas, lettuce, potatoes, garlic or shallots. When following an early crop don't forget to feed the soil. Mixing compost or green manures into it helps to renew fertility levels for the follow-on crop.

If sowing directly into the garden, the best time is June to August, but don't forget the importance of extra watering during hot spells. Thin out seedlings to help others establish more quickly. Sowbugs, cabbage worms, pillbugs and earwigs can be the bane of juicy winter seedlings as they establish. Floating row covers can prevent damage from cabbage worms. Banana and black slugs have voracious appetites, so I am often found doing slug patrols at dusk, with a bucket and scoop in hand. TIP: Cleaning debris from the garden removes hiding places for slugs. (See "Insect Pests" in April for more on pest control.)

Winter vegetables may be sowed directly into the garden as early as June.

THE WINTER GARDEN HARVEST

Greens: Broccoli, cabbage, cauliflower, chard, collards, kale, mustards, Oriental greens, spinach

Carbohydrates: (Root vegetables): Beets, carrots, celeriac, endive, parsnips, sunchokes, turnips and rutabagas

Onions: Garlic, leeks, perennial bunching onions, shallots, 'Walla Walla' overwintering onions

Winter Salads: Arugula, beet greens, chard, cilantro/coriander, corn salad (mache), cress, endive, kale, lettuce, mustard greens, Oriental greens, parcel, parsley, radicchio, scallions, spinach

Herbs: Bay, calendula, coriander, chives, oregano, parsley, rosemary, sage, sweet marjoram, thyme

Seeding Schedule

March/April: Leeks

May/June: Sprouting broccoli, Brussels sprouts, winter cabbage, chard, cauliflower, collards, kale

June/July: Root vegetables: beets, carrots, celeriac, endive, kohlrabi, 'Walla Walla' onions, parsnips, scallions, turnips and rutabagas

August: Direct seed arugula, cress, chard, coriander, corn salad, kale, winter lettuces, mesclun, mustards, Oriental greens, radicchio, spinach, winter radish

HOMEMADE SEEDING MIX

- 1 part screened Super-Duper compost
- 1 part peat moss or coir (coconut fibre)
- 1 part perlite for drainage
- A dusting of dolomite lime, if using peat
- Mix well and pre-moisten before seeding.

Tips for Winter Vegetables

- Grow your family's favourite vegetables.
- Follow where earlier crops of peas, potatoes, lettuces or garlic have been harvested.
- Sow seeds directly into the garden from late June to early August.
- Start seed in pots for transplants from late June to mid July; grow outdoors in a cool location out of full sun—and watch out for bugs!
- Transplant into the garden no later than September; plants should be well established by winter.

- Add lime to soil to prevent clubroot in brassicas.
- Help transplants get established with feeds of liquid fish fertilizer.
- Remove older leaves to prevent build-up of flea beetle and cabbage worm.
- Harvest after hard frosts when the food is sweeter.
- Be patient with sprouting broccoli (white and purple). Leafy plants form large heads in spring, followed by weeks of tender sprout production.

SEEDING WINTER VEGETABLES

1. Fill cell packs with a commercial sterilized organic seeding mix, or make your own seeding mix (see recipe previous page). Pre-moisten using a hose with a fan spray attachment. Seed directly onto the surface of the cell pack, envisioning a few seedlings growing in each cell pack as you drop the seeds sparingly and evenly over the surface. Overseeding results in stressed seedlings.

2. Tamp the seeds using empty cell packs to ensure they make contact with the growing medium. Cover with seeding mix and water once more. It's rare to get 100-percent germination, so for 6 to 8 cabbage seedlings sow 12 to 15 seeds.

3. Label to identify each flat of cell packs with name, source and date sown. (This way you have a trace if no seeds germinate.)

4. The main problem encountered growing winter veggies is BUGS! Slugs, earwigs and sowbugs love tasty young vegetable seedlings, and it's amazing how much damage a big banana slug can do in one night! I eventually discovered that by placing flats of seedlings on top of upturned flats these pests could not gain access to seedlings from underneath; and because this space was no longer moist and dark they would not hang out there anymore. Simple—but effective!

5. In an outdoor location that is out of direct sun, you can grow thousands of winter vegetable starts like this—and all it takes is one watering a day.

6. Plants are moved into the garden without having their roots disturbed. Rooted seedlings are removed from their cell packs in a block, and these are laid end to end in shallow furrows and covered. (See May for "Hoe a Row in Five!")

Left: The winter vegetable sale at The Garden Path Nursery.

July

ESTABLISHING A SMALL FRUIT ORCHARD

In the second year at The Garden Path I planted my first fruit-tree orchard. I was thrilled at the idea of establishing a small orchard on the south-facing lawn. I chose trees on dwarf 8- to 10-ft. (2.4- to 3-m) or semi-dwarf 10- to 12-ft. (3- to 3.6-m) rootstock to make care and harvesting easy.

HOW TO PLANT A TREE
1. Fall is a good time to plant fruit trees; winter rain ensures the roots do not dry out.
2. Bare-root specimens are preferable to container-grown ones, as roots will be better established and less likely to be rootbound.
3. Planting the tree at the correct level is important. If it is too high, roots may dry out; too deep and the bark on the stem collar may rot—leading to death of the tree.
4. Dig a planting hole no deeper than the height of the rootball. Trees should be planted so that the point where the roots flare out is near the surface of the soil.

5. Dig the size of the hole three times the diameter of the rootball.
6. Tease the roots out of the container or spread the roots out of a bare rootball to establish them in the planting hole.
7. If roots are injured, cut back to healthy wood before planting, to prevent the spread of infection.

TIP: If container stock is rootbound it may be necessary to score around the rootball with a knife to help get new roots established.

Fruit trees do best planted in full sun in well-drained, fertile soil. They prefer a neutral soil pH, so are best planted away from stands of evergreens where soil is more acidic. November is a perfect time to plant dormant fruit trees; they will establish more successfully with winter rain than summer heat. New trees need irrigation in their first year until better established. Adding Super-Duper compost to the planting hole, and regularly as mulch, improves soil with organic matter, which means trees get more nutrients and produce more fruit.

Established orchard with hardy geraniums as living mulch.

Fruit trees also appreciate seaweed from the beach in winter and wood ash (uncontaminated) from the woodstove as sources of potash. You can apply granular seaweed as kelp meal if you do not live near the ocean.

SOLUTIONS TO PROBLEMS IN THE ORCHARD

Dormant Oil/Lime Sulphur Spray

Sunshine with no wind and no sign of rain ahead is the perfect weather condition to dormant spray your fruit trees. The oil dries faster when the sun is shining. Whatever the weather, you must do this before buds open, as dormant oil/lime sulphur spray burns tender young foliage. Spray trees on a dry day with no wind for drift. Cover trunk and limbs on all sides. The oil seeps into crevices in the bark and coats the overwintering egg masses, destroying them.

This combination is effective against a host of problems: rust mites, scale insects, pear scale, red mite eggs, aphid eggs, twig borer, plum black knot and peach leaf curl:

In a 3-qt. (3-L) pressure pump sprayer mix:

- 4 Tbsp. (60 mL) horticultural oil
- 8 Tbsp. (120 mL) lime/sulphur
- Add 3 qt. (3 L) water

TIP: The sulphur stains yellow, so cover foliage plants below your trees with a plastic sheet.

Spraying for Fungal Diseases

To protect fruit trees against fungal diseases, dormant spray all surfaces of the tree with 2 Tbsp. (30 mL) wettable copper to 1 gal. (4.5 L) of water. First application at leaf fall; repeated again in December/January.

Grease Bands

After spraying, band fruit trees using burlap sacks or strips of old towels, and then smear Tanglefoot™ sticky paste over the bands. This traps crawling insects that lay eggs that hatch into fruit-eating maggots, such as the wingless female winter moth that climbs up fruit trees to lay eggs on the branches. The resulting green caterpillars feed on foliage and blossoms the following spring. Tying grease bands around fruit tree trunks keeps the moths out of the tree.

Canker

Establishing my small orchard was more challenging than expected. I quickly learned that wet coastal conditions (where I live) leave fruit trees prone to canker, symptoms of which show up as damaged, oozing darkened areas of bark. Canker gradually spreads and girdles the entire branch, so once detected it's best to remove infected branches by cutting back to healthy wood. If a branch has to be retained, cut out the cankered part with a sharp knife to remove any diseased bark. In order to prevent canker, treat with a fixed copper spray when the leaves fall, and repeat once more later in the winter. TIP: Make sure you disinfect tools with a 10-percent rubbing-alcohol spray, so that canker does not spread to other trees.

CODLING MOTH

Q: What's worse than finding a worm in an apple?

A: Finding half the worm!

Codling moth (*Cydia pomonella*) is an all too familiar intruder on fruit trees, especially apples and pears. Codling-moth larvae overwinter on the ground and in the bark of trees. In spring when temperatures reach 60°F (16°C) the female lays her eggs on developing fruit and surrounding leaves. When larvae hatch they eat into the core of fruit, and hopefully eventually out the other side!

Cardboard Traps

In spring, wrap strips of corrugated cardboard 6 in. (15 cm) wide, with the corrugated side facing inward, around the trunk and main limbs of apple and pear trees. Check every week for any pupating larvae, which will be wrapped in white silk. Replace the cardboard and bury any infested strips. Keeping up with this through to September will reduce populations considerably.

Pheromone Traps

The insides of hanging triangular traps are coated with a sticky substance and sprayed with female pheromone, the aim being to attract and trap males. Traps are also frequently used to monitor moth activity around trees.

Regular Monitoring

You can also monitor signs of activity by searching for frass (excrement or debris) left on the skin of fruit by burrowing larvae. If you find any, remove the infected fruit and bury it. This helps to lower populations of codling-moth larvae.

Orchard Cleanup

In fall, rake away fallen leaves that may be hosting spores of fungal diseases, and remove any debris that could provide a home for overwintering larvae. Keeping things tidy in the orchard goes a long way toward preventing problems with insects and disease.

Fruit Thinning

Most apples are spur-bearing varieties, which fruit on spurs that develop on one-year-old wood. Early July is the time to thin apple and pear trees, which will drop fruit automatically but not enough to ensure adequate energy for good-sized fruit. Pull off small apples or pears, leaving only one (sometimes two) growing every 6 in. (15 cm) on the branch.

Q Our peach tree has bumps on its leaves that look like boils, and a lot of the leaves are curling up. Is there something I can do?

A This is peach leaf curl, a fungal problem that affects peaches and nectarines, and one of the reasons peach and nectarine trees are best planted under overhangs to prevent fungal spores from spreading. Peach leaf curl causes reddish blisters on leaves, causing them to eventually become curled and distorted. Fruit can become deformed and drop early. This condition is aggravated by cool wet spring weather. Remove affected leaves—do not compost them, bury them in the garden. Use a fixed copper spray in September after harvest. Reapply in November after all the leaves have dropped. Apply dormant oil/lime sulphur spray two weeks before leaf growth in January/February. TIP: To help it stick use dish soap or Safer's™ Insecticidal soap, at 1 tsp. (5 mL) of soap per 1 qt. (1 L) of water.

Q There are little green worms feasting on the leaves of our fruit trees. Will these worms eventually go away and will the leaves recover?

A These little green caterpillars may be leaf rollers, webworms, winter moth or codling moth larvae, all prevalent in spring, sometimes spreading from neighbouring trees. If you have a severe infestation, spray the whole tree with *Bacillus thuringiensis* (Bt), available from garden centres. When the worms ingest the leaves they will die within

Keep an eye out for green worms in spring.

the week. Your tree will soon recover, and you should have no more problems.

APPLES

Harvesting

Lift the apple in your palm and give it a slight twist. If ripe, it should come away easily from the spur. If the stalk and spur break, it is not ready. Look for signs of ripening such as a change of colour and the first windfalls. For all but a few early varieties, the pips will turn from a pale colour to brown. Apples on the sunniest side of the tree usually ripen first. Early apples can be eaten straight from the tree, whereas late-harvested apples improve from storage.

Storage

Select unblemished fruit with stalks attached for storage. Ensure fruits are not touching and inspect regularly, removing any that have degraded. Unlike apples, pears can be stored down to 32°F (0°C). Refrigerators may be suitable, if well ventilated.

Apple-box liners are perfect for storing the fruit.

CRABAPPLES

Crabapples (*Malus*) are grown either for showy springtime blossoms with typically inedible fruits, or for edible fruits produced in fall. Choose a variety such as 'Tradescant', 'Centennial' or 'Dolgo' (hardy to zone 3) if you want crops of tart little apples for crabapple jelly. Crabapples make beautiful specimen trees, and any fruit that doesn't get picked usually ends up as winter food for birds.

PEARS

Pears (*Pyrus*) are best picked before they are fully ripe. Early or mid-season varieties left to mature on the tree have a tendency to go brown in the centre and get nibbled by birds and insects, but they may also shrivel if picked too early. The key is to watch for a colour change—pick a green pear when it turns lighter green and a yellow pear as it starts to turn yellow (if deep golden it's too ripe!).

Crabapple and Geranium Jelly

2 lbs (907 g) crabapples (unpeeled)
2 cups (475 mL) water
5 fragrant lemon or rose geranium leaves
2 cups (475 mL) sugar (approximately)
Cheesecloth or jelly bag

 Set fruit and geranium leaves into water, in a pot on the stove. There's no need to peel or core the fruit. Simmer the fruit to a pulp. Pass this mix through thick cheesecloth or a jelly bag. Measure the juice and add 2 cups (475 mL) of sugar to 2 cups of juice. Place in a large pot and stir well until the sugar dissolves. Cook at a rapid boil to a temperature of 220°F (104°C), or until a small sample sets on a cool spoon. Store in sterilized glass jars with a fresh geranium leaf set in the jelly.

Crabapples in fall.

193

Pear tree with five varieties grafted on one rootstock!

Lift the pear in the palm of your hand. It is probably ready if it parts easily from the spur, but test by biting into the fruit. If it's hard and sweet, the crop is ready to harvest. Pears tend to ripen at the same time, so I bring in pears as soon as possible to spread out the process.

Early pears: 'Bon Chretien', 'Beth', 'Bartlett' and 'Onward'
Mid-season: 'Conference', 'Beurre Hardy' and 'Louise Bonne of Jersey'
Late varieties: 'Doyenne du Comice' and 'Concorde'

CHERRIES, PEACHES AND APRICOTS

Contrary to the late-winter and early-spring pruning for fruit trees, cherry trees and stone fruits such as peaches and apricots should be pruned in late summer to early fall, after fruit harvest. This is due to prevalence of bacterial canker. When the wood is drier, pruning cuts heal more quickly, making it less likely for bacterial canker to enter these openings. Annual pruning is not required other than to help keep a balanced canopy or restricted form.

Low in calories and high in fibre and antioxidants, cherries contain vitamins C, B and E, as well as potassium, zinc, calcium, iron, magnesium and phosphorous.

'Stella' sweet cherry.

'Morello' sour cherries.

Sour-Cherry Pie Filling

For one 10-in. (25-cm) deep-dish pie
2½ lbs (1.2 kg) sour cherries, pitted
¾ cup (180 mL) granulated sugar
¼ cup (60 mL) cornstarch
1 Tbsp. (15 mL) Triple Sec
1 tsp. (5 mL) almond extract
   Slowly bring to a boil, stirring all the time to prevent sticking and burning, just until mixture has thickened.

While cherry trees reach maximum production at 12 years, they begin to produce well after 4. A sweet cherry tree can live for 50 years, compared to 35 for a sour cherry tree.

FIGS

Native to the Middle East, the common fig (*Ficus carica*) was one of the first fruits ever to be cultivated. The best harvests come from trees grown in hot dry conditions where roots are confined, which is why they thrive beside pathways up against houses. Being softwood, figs are a delight to prune (and tip cuttings root easily!). Prune fig trees after danger of frost in early spring and be rewarded with more fruit and less foliage.

Figs are high in simple sugars, minerals and fibre and contain high levels of potassium, calcium, magnesium, iron, copper and manganese. Dried figs contain an impressive 250 mg of calcium per 100 g, compared to whole milk at only 118 mg.

How to Enjoy Fresh Figs

- Add chopped fresh figs to fruit salads.

Portuguese fig tree.

- Poach fresh figs in red wine and serve with yoghurt or ice cream.
- Add quartered figs to a salad of fennel, arugula and shaved Parmesan cheese.
- Fresh figs stuffed with cream cheese and chopped nuts make easy hors d'oeuvres.
   TIP: Ripe figs do not keep. They should not be washed until ready to eat, and should be refrigerated.

Eating a fresh fig is like tasting "nectar from the Gods" as far as I'm concerned.

Fresh Fig Salad

Makes 4 servings

16 oz (454 g) mixed salad greens

4 large fresh figs, cut into eighths

2 Tbsp. (30 mL) coarsely chopped walnuts

BLUE CHEESE DRESSING

2 oz. (57 g) soft blue cheese, such as
   Gorgonzola

2 Tbsp. (30 mL) light sour cream

1 Tbsp. (15 mL) walnut oil

1½ Tbsp. (22 mL) white wine vinegar

2 Tbsp. (30 mL) apple juice

Pinch sugar

Salt and freshly ground black pepper

Blue Cheese Dressing: In a bowl, mash the cheese with sour cream and gradually stir in the walnut oil, vinegar, apple juice and sugar until well combined. Add salt and pepper to taste. Salad: Arrange the salad greens onto four individual serving plates, and arrange the fresh figs on top of the greens. Spoon the dressing over the salad and sprinkle with walnuts.

GRAPES

The main thing to remember about grapes is that they are warm-climate fruits. Exposure to cold wind is not appreciated, while protected south-facing sunny corners are ideal. Grapevines are one of the last fruits to leaf out, which is fortunate because the leaves are frost-sensitive and late-spring frosts are known to happen on occasion. Grapes thrive in free-draining sandy soils (preferably slightly acidic at pH 6.0 to 6.5). The soil needs to warm up and stay that way all summer for grapes to set and ripen. Beware of applying heavy mulches, because cool wet soils are not conducive to grape production. Uncontaminated wood ash, dolomite lime, compost and seaweed are all good fertilizers for stimulating grape production.

Grapes are a good source of vitamin B6, thiamin, potassium and vitamin C, plus are high in antioxidants. Grapes and their juice— and wine— can reduce risk of heart disease and lower cholesterol and blood pressure. Cheers!

Proper pruning results in huge yields.

Pruning Grapes

Grapes need proper pruning to produce well; light pruning results in large yields of poor-quality fruit, while heavy pruning produces too much growth with little or no fruit. Fruit is produced on the current season's growth.

YEAR 1: The purpose of the first year is to establish roots. Prune while dormant in late winter, cutting back to 3 or 4 buds on each vine.

YEAR 2: The purpose of the second year of growth is to establish vines that are at least 5 ft. (1.5 m) long, and as thick as a pencil. Prune everything else out.

YEAR 3: Tie straight canes horizontally, at least 2 ft. (60 cm) off the ground, onto support frameworks (arbours, fences, pergolas). Leave 8 to 12 buds to form the strongest horizontal canes and prune everything else off. A moderately growing grapevine should have no more than 50 buds on it at once.

YEAR 4: In early spring, while still dormant, cut vertical shoots back to 4-in. (10-cm) spurs, which will produce 2 new shoots each. For wine grapes to develop maximum flavour with high sugar and low acid, never leave more than 40 grape clusters on a single vine.

YEAR 5: Cut these 2-spur canes down to a 1-spur cane so that the number of canes stays the same.

Problems with Grapes

The two main enemies of grapes are powdery mildew and *Botrytis cinerea*. Keeping grapevines well pruned improves ventilation around each plant and can prevent both forms of fungus. TIP: If powdery mildew does affect leaves, coat with spray of wettable sulphur, a natural fungicide.

Drying Grapes

The green grapes on the arbour at The Garden Path were plentiful enough to dry as raisins using the dehydrator. I was surprised that they dried in just a few hours and were incredibly sweet compared to store-bought raisins.

Top: Drying sweet raisins using a dehydrator.

Bottom: Vitis vinifera *'Purpurea.'*

Purple Grapes

Vitis vinifera 'Purpurea' is a highly ornamental grape that has leaves darkening to deep purple throughout the season. I grow one in a 10-gal. (45-L) pot in the greenhouse and another up an arbour outdoors. I get an early-summer crop of grapes from inside the greenhouse, and in fall the outdoor vine bursts forth with incredible yields of luscious purple grapes. I always leave a few bunches of grapes on vines for the red pileated woodpeckers that swoop into the garden in October.

KIWIS

Kiwis (*Actinidia deliciosa*) are ornamental vines with irresistible furry leaves and the prettiest satin flowers in early summer. They are vigorous, needing good support and regular pruning, but are notoriously slow to start fruiting—be prepared to wait anywhere from seven to nine years!

A kiwi, also known as a Chinese gooseberry, is a furry green fruit the size of a hen's egg, with hairy skin that some people eat although I prefer to peel it. Kiwis offer a bite of citrus, akin to pineapple, and are particularly good when combined with strawberries.

Kiwis are packed with more vitamin C than the equivalent amount of oranges. They are helpful in reducing the severity of such conditions as osteoarthritis, rheumatoid arthritis, asthma, cancer and heart disease, and are a good source of dietary fibre, reducing high cholesterol levels. A medium-size fruit contains only about 46 calories.

Kiwis are dioecious with male and female flowers on separate plants—you need one male for every six females. They bloom for 10 days starting mid June, which is when you hope for healthy populations of honeybees (*Apis mellifera*) and bumblebees (*Bombus terrestris*) for pollination. If the weather is cool, and bees are not flying, a paintbrush comes in handy to increase fruit set by hand pollination!

When carrying a full crop during the hottest part of summer, mature vines may use up to 5 gal. (23 L) of water a day, depending on soil type, so it's important to water kiwis consistently. Fruit should not be left on the vines to ripen. Check for ripeness in October by applying a gentle pressure test and then cutting slices off the top and bottom to check for juiciness. Store cooled fruits around 32°F (0°C) in the absence of ethylene gas from other fruits being stored, especially apples and pears.

Feeding Tips

In winter kiwis appreciate a mulch of seaweed from the beach and wood ash (uncontaminated) from the woodstove as sources of potash. (Granular kelp meal applied in summer works as a substitute for seaweed when there's no beach nearby.) Kiwis need readily available nitrogen for fast growth, which can be applied in April/May as manure or Super-Duper compost, or in summer by using organic granular seed meals (e.g., alfalfa). Apply lime to balance pH in early spring. as kiwis thrive in pH 6.0 to 7.0.

Beautiful flowers of kiwi.

Actinidia deliciosa 'Hayward.'

Pruning

Pruning is needed to keep vines in check and is best done December to February before the sap begins to flow. Some summer pruning may be required to control vines after fruit set, but to avoid winter damage don't prune later than August. TIP: If male vines are pruned just after flowering they generate lots of one-year-old wood, which carries more flowers in the next season.

Before you get too carried away with your pruning, keep in mind that the one-year wood produces the fruit. The pruned sections of vine can be rooted in propagation mix (under protection for winter), but make sure you remember which are the males and which the females!

NATIVE BEES

The honeybee (*Apis mellifera*), was brought to North America by European colonists in 1662 to pollinate their crops. Before European honeybees were imported to North America, generations of growers depended upon the more than 4,000 species of native bees. (In Canada there are 800 species of native bees.)

The solitary, non-aggressive blue orchard mason bee.

These bees do not live in communal hives; they are solitary, dwelling in little caves in the ground or in bark crevices in trees, where they raise their young.

Today more than 25 per cent of America's 2.4 million honeybee colonies have been lost to what has been named "colony collapse disorder." The bees are stressed by mites, viruses, toxic pesticides, long-distance trucking and poor nutrition. Hundreds of acres of monocultured crops do not provide the diversity of food they need to stay healthy. This has farmers worried about how they are going to get their crops pollinated in future.

The answer is right there in front of them! If we returned to the smaller-scale, diversified food production model of our forebears, one that protected habitat such as hedgerows and ponds for wildlife, we would not need to be concerned about the failures of "rent-a-bee" services!

There are 20,000 species of bees in the world, which means there are thousands of bees we know little about. In Victoria, BC, where I live, there are 30 species of native bees, which live in wild places such as salmonberry thickets, dead trees, decaying logs, riverbanks and abandoned railway corridors. The closer to a city, the more native bees are under threat, due to loss of habitat.

Bees belong to different tribes. Bumblebees belong to the *Bombini* tribe and live in colonies. The *Andrena* tribe burrow tunnels in the ground and often live in colonies. The *Ceratina* tribe are carpenter bees that excavate into woody stems of bushes. The *Halictid* tribe are tiny hovering bees that may be attracted to you in hot summers if you are sweating.

Here in Victoria, my friend, Rex Welland spent many years studying native bees as a result of his interest in heritage fruit trees. He noticed that apples typically produce 10 to 20 seeds, depending on the variety. When he noticed the seed numbers drop in his fruit he became concerned that bee populations were being negatively affected by mite infestations, so

A bee box (with stackable trays).

he decided to try attracting native species of bees to increase the rate of pollination.

Native bees forage close to home, within 300 ft. (90 m), so they are perfect pollinators for urban food growers. All it takes is putting up a bee box!

Rex perfected a wooden bee box, with slotted trays that could be taken apart at the end of the season to clean pollen mites off the cocoons. Hatching unencumbered by mites enhances the adult bee's survival rate. In no time, the native blue orchard mason bee (*Osmia lignaria*) found and moved into Rex's bee boxes. This non-aggressive solitary bee is shiny blue-black and slightly smaller than a honeybee, making it easily mistaken for a bluebottle fly. There are 35 different species of orchard mason bees in North America.

EDIBLE NATIVE PLANTS
Black elderberry (*Sambucus racemosa* ssp. *pubens* var. *melanocarpa*)
Saskatoon berry (*Amelanchier alnifolia*)
Tall Oregon grape (*Mahonia aquifolium*)
Flowering currant (*Ribes sanguineum*)
Nootka rose (*Rosa nutkana*)
Evergreen huckleberry (*Vaccinium ovatum*)
Indian plum (*Oemleria cerasiformis*)
Red elderberry (*Sambucus racemosa* ssp. *pubens* var. *arborescens*)

EDIBLE PLANTS THAT ATTRACT NATIVE BEES
Apple (*Malus*)
Cherry and plum (*Prunus*)
Blackberry and raspberry (*Rubus*)
Saskatoon berry (*Amelanchier alnifolia*)
Dandelion (*Taraxacum officinale*)
Mint (*Mentha*)
Marjoram (*Origanum*)
Nasturtium (*Tropaeolum*)
Red clover (*Trifolium pratense*)
Sunflower (*Helianthus*)

This wood-dwelling bee emerges in early spring, at the same time as the early-flowering fruit trees that they pollinate. They forage under overcast skies at temperatures as low as 54°F (12°C). They are effective pollinators, visiting up to 2,000 blossoms a day. Effective pollination by mason bees does not require large populations; 50 bees can adequately pollinate a small orchard of a dozen trees.

Studies have shown that they pollinate certain crops (e.g., apples, cherries, squash, watermelon, blueberries, sunflowers and cranberries) with greater efficiency than honeybees. In fact, only 250 female orchard mason bees were needed to pollinate an acre of apples, when it takes 15,000 honeybees to do the same job!

Females are the primary pollinators and the sole nest builders. Males also pollinate, but their foraging is done purely for nourishment. The female lays about 30 eggs in her lifetime, with activity ending in June. Within a week of laying the eggs the larvae hatch and start feeding on stored nectar and pollen reserves. After two weeks most of the food has been consumed, so the larva spins a cocoon and pupates. Later in the summer the pupa develops into the adult bee, which remains in the cocoon throughout winter, to emerge again the following spring.

TIP: Bees like to nest in a dry place protected from wind. Under the eave on the southeast side of the house or shed, somewhere that receives morning sun that warms them up is best. Orchard mason bees have a limited foraging range of 300 ft. (90 m), so place bee houses close to the area needing pollination.

(See: "How to clean a bee box" in November.)

'Taramahura White' sunflowers are great for attracting bees.

CANNING 101

Home canning is a great way to store the harvest, resulting in healthy homegrown food sometimes years down the road. In the freezer, food only stays good for one year before it loses flavour. Canning allows you to enjoy tasty homegrown fruits, vegetables, pickles, preserves, jams and jellies for longer. It's not hard to do and quite inexpensive to get started.

You will need a water canner, available from most hardware stores for about $20. These big blue metal pots come with lids and wire racks—you are probably already familiar with them. It's a good idea to pick up a pair of canning tongs at the same time. Canning jars don't have to be purchased new, although they are not expensive, and they are available from most grocery stores. They are also often on sale for a song at yard sales and once you have them can last generations.

Canning is safe for all high-acid foods including jams, jellies, preserves, nut meats, pickles, chili sauce, catsup, relish, tomatoes and tomato sauce (without mushrooms or meat), fruit and fruit products such as butters and conserves.

TIP: Don't double or alter recipes. Pick up a canning booklet with instructions on recommended processing times for different fruits and vegetables.

Canning Basics

1. Wash canning jars in warm soapy water, rinse, and put into a saucepan of boiling water to sterilize. Leave jars in hot water until they are needed so that they are still warm when hot syrup is poured into them. Place canning lids in a small saucepan of boiling water until they are required. Lids should be new, because rubber is only good for one use. A jar improperly sealed allows food to spoil, something that is not worth risking.

Franzi and the tools of the trade: Canning jars with metal rings and lids, long-handled tongs, a stainless-steel funnel, measuring jug, ladle and stainless-steel bowls, an apron and a good pair of oven mitts.

The preserved harvest.

Fill hot jars with hot syrup using a funnel.

Quart jars of peaches are processed for 25 minutes in a water canner.

Organic peach slices in a light honey syrup.

2. Using jars with chips or small cracks results in broken jars or incomplete seals. Before filling, check jars carefully for imperfections. Also, a combination of hot food and cold glass, or cold food and hot glass, results in cracking. Put hot food into hot jars and cold into cooled jars. Don't place hot jars onto cold surfaces, and keep them out of cool drafts.

3. It's easier to fill jars using a funnel. Fill up to within ½ in. (1 cm) of the rim. If syrup gets on the rim of the jar, wipe it with a clean, hot cloth to allow a good seal with the lid. I preserve fruit in light honey syrup, which accentuates the natural flavour without excess sweetness.

4. Fill a water canner three quarters full and bring to a boil. Use the wire rack to load jars in and out of the canner. Wire racks prevent the bottoms of the jars from cracking and stops jars from bumping each other. If boiling water does not cover the jars by at least 1 in. (2.5 cm), add more water and bring back to a boil. Processing is done at a steady rolling boil; too furious a boil may crack jars.

5. At the end of the recommended processing time, carefully lift jars out of the canner using long-handled tongs. Place jars on a wooden board (out of cool drafts). Leave them until they have sealed—usually you hear a satisfying ping when this happens! After the jars have cooled, remove the rings, wipe the jars and store in a cool dark place. Always check seals before you store jars—the lids should be indented in the middle, with no give. If not sealed, either reprocess using a new lid, or store in the fridge and eat soon. Label lids with the contents and the processing date to make rotation in storage possible. Bon appétit!

Light Honey Syrup

One part light honey to four parts water.

Fruit Liqueurs

1 lb. (454 g) berries or fruit (e.g.,
  blackberries, plums or cherries), cut
  into small pieces
3 cups (700 mL) 80-proof vodka
1¼ cups (300 mL) granulated sugar

*Rinse the fruit and place it in a glass
or ceramic container with a lid. Add the
vodka to the chopped fruit. TIP: Don't mix
different types of fruits in liqueurs, but you
can make a successful blend of a bitter
berry with a mild one, such as blueberries
and cranberries.*

*Store in a cool dark place, stirring
weekly for 4 weeks. Strain the fruit through
a cheesecloth-lined sieve. TIP: Use the
leftover fruit in desserts or with ice cream!*

*To each 3 cups (700 mL) of the liquid,
add 1¼ cups (300 mL) granulated sugar.
Pour carefully into a glass bottle with a cap.
Fruit and berry liqueurs should be stored
for at least 6 months for the best flavour.
The alcohol content of fruit liqueurs is
30-proof. Cheers!*

*Cherries (centre), grapes, yellow and red plums and
apples are easily dried using a dehydrator. They make
a delicious fruit compote by simply covering with
boiling water and leaving overnight to rehydrate.*

PRESERVING THE TOMATO HARVEST

To supply the needs of my small seed business, Seeds of Victoria, I grow 40 different varieties of tomatoes each year. After every weekly harvest and seed collection I am left with bowlfuls of colourful tomatoes. To preserve the tomato harvest, I divide the tomatoes into type—cherry, salad, beefsteak, paste and novelty—to decide what to do with them all. Here are some recipes that inspired me.

Tomato Paste

Throw big paste tomatoes into a large stainless-steel saucepan, and slowly cook down on low heat with no lid until the liquid has evaporated and all that's left is a thick tomato paste. Freeze in tubs. Use in sauces, casseroles or as a base for cream of tomato soup.

Tomato Sauce

Meaty paste tomatoes also make a scrumptious tomato sauce. Chop the tomatoes, add garlic, onions, squash or peppers from the garden, with a bay leaf, parsley, fennel seed or fresh basil. Slowly cook down on low heat with no lid until you get a sauce of thick consistency. Freeze in tubs. Thaw the sauce in the morning for "10-minute pasta" at night, famous for the taste of summer in mid winter.

Tomato paste.

Salsa fresca. Kristin Ross photo

Salsa Fresca

1 cup (250 mL) tomatoes (cherry or salad
   tomatoes are best)
¼ cup (60 mL) onion, finely chopped
1 garlic clove, minced
1 tsp. (5 mL) jalapeno, seeds removed and
   minced
3 Tbsp. (45 mL) fresh cilantro, finely
   chopped
1 lime, juiced
Salt and pepper to taste

*Whirl the tomatoes in a food processor
until coarsely chopped. Add the rest of the
ingredients and leave to marinate. Strain
off liquid and freeze as ice-cube-tray cubes
or in plastic tubs. Perfect for the winter
munchies!*

Bruschetta To Die For!

*The tomato flavour is accentuated by
slow roasting; try this for a real treat.*

*Prepare ahead. Makes approx. 2½ cups
(600 mL)*

Stir together:
4 to 6 tomatoes, seeded and chopped
2 green onions, minced
1 avocado, in small cubes
Whisk:
2 tsp. (10 mL) olive oil
2 tsp. (10 mL) lemon juice
1 clove garlic, crushed
1 tsp. (5 mL) salt
½ tsp (2.5 mL) pepper

Toss in:
2 Tbsp. (30 mL) fresh basil, finely chopped
2 Tbsp. (30 mL) freshly grated Parmesan
Serve on a warm toasted baguette.

Roasted Tomatoes

Roasted tomatoes have intense flavour. Add them to a multitude of recipes, or just eat them on crackers.

Preheat oven to 325°F (160°C)

2 lb. (907 g) whole tomatoes
2 Tbsp. (30 mL) extra virgin olive oil
2 tsp. (10 mL) coarse salt
1 tsp. (5 mL) freshly ground pepper
Italian dried herbs (optional)

Place tomatoes in a single layer into a large roasting pan lined with parchment paper. Drizzle with olive oil and season with salt and pepper and Fines Herbs as desired. Put uncovered pan into preheated 325°F (160°C) oven for 15 minutes. Turn the oven down to 250°F (120°C) and roast for 1 to 2 hours, until tomatoes are reduced in size and lightly browned on top. Let cool for 15 minutes.

The flavour intensifies when you roast tomatoes.

Freezing Tomatoes

If tomatoes are firm, simply cut them in half and fill up freezer bags. I add blocks of frozen tomatoes to soups, casseroles, sauces and pasta dishes. TIP: For the best results add them to the recipe while they are still frozen; if they thaw they become mushy and lose flavour.

Freezer bags of tomatoes for winter recipes.

August

SEVEN STEPS TO BUILDING A WINTER LASAGNA GARDEN

1. Decide on an area for the garden and cover it with a thick dusting of dolomite lime—which neutralizes pH, breaks down clay and adds calcium and magnesium to soil.

2. Put down a 2-in. (5-cm) layer of manure. It can be fresh or aged. Rake to level. Manure provides a nitrogen kick to plants and introduces worms that till soil. Microbes will break down fresh manure on the bottom of the pile before roots can access it. Some manures are mixed with straw or woodchips (e.g., horse and chicken), while some are pure pellets with no additives (e.g., llama and sheep).

3. Cover over the manure with sections of plain cardboard (no coloured ink), with edges overlapping. Wet down with a hose.

4. Add a layer of spoiled hay (or grass clippings) and a layer of leaves. Rake to level.

5. Add another layer of manure (aged this time) or a layer of garden soil. Rake to level. (Half a yard of topsoil costs just $15 if you can pick it up.)

THE WINTER GARDEN HARVEST

Greens: Broccoli, cabbage, cauliflower, chard, collards, kale, mustards, Oriental greens, spinach

Root vegetables: Beets, carrots, celeriac, endive, parsnips, sunchokes, turnips and rutabagas

Onions: Garlic, leeks, perennial bunching onions, shallots, 'Walla Walla' overwintering onions

Winter salads: Arugula, beet greens, chard, cilantro/coriander, corn salad (mache), cress, endive, kale, lettuce, mustard greens, Oriental greens, parcel, parsley, radicchio, scallions, spinach

Herbs: Bay, calendula, coriander, chives, oregano, parsley, rosemary, sage, sweet marjoram, thyme

SEEDING SCHEDULE

March/April: Leeks

May/June: Sprouting broccoli, Brussels sprouts, winter cabbage, chard, cauliflower, collards, kale

June/July: Root vegetables: beets, carrots, celeriac, endive, kohlrabi, 'Walla Walla' onions, parsnips, scallions, parsnips, turnips and rutabagas

August: Direct seed arugula, cress, chard, coriander, corn salad, kale, winter lettuces, mesclun, mustards, Oriental greens, radicchio, spinach, winter radish.

6. Ideally, the finished bed should be about 12 in. (30 cm) in height. Always finish building with a top layer of screened compost or topsoil. Water well. You are now ready to plant. You can direct seed or transplant into the top layer of the bed. The high fertility of the growing medium means it is possible to plant in close rows or blocks so that overlapping leaves keep weeds at bay and lock moisture in around the roots.

7. Layers of organic matter constantly break down, releasing nutrients to plants as they need them. This means faster, more natural growth, and fewer problems with pests and diseases that attack plants grown in poor soils. Organic matter locks in moisture, which means you can cut back on watering. If weeds appear, simply add another layer of mulch and smother them. Problem solved! Happy Lasagna Gardening!

SAVING SEEDS SUCCESSFULLY

"I have great faith in a seed. Convince me you have a seed there, and I am prepared to expect wonders."
Henry David Thoreau

Farmers and agriculturists have been growing food and selecting seeds for future harvests for ten thousand years. Fewer than six generations ago, our ancestors lived rural lifestyles, growing food and saving their own seeds, or acquiring them locally. Today the majority of farmers don't save seed, and most of the rest of us have forgotten how to. As passive consumers in a global economy, despite all the amazing technology at our fingertips, we have lost the ability to feed ourselves!

Modern seed production is directed towards agribusiness, which is geared towards making food production as low cost as possible. Plant breeders hybridize seeds for identical plants for uniformity in harvesting and processing. In this Biotech Age, seeds are genetically modified for resistance to the ever-increasing amounts of pesticides needed for "farming" based on unnatural monocultures. Today's consumers have become addicted to an abundance of cheap food from around the world, made possible by an era of plentiful fossil fuel. Unfortunately, the reality is that cheap food is costing the Earth, and killing us through poor nutrition in the process!

The Global Assessment of Human-Induced Soil Degradation (GLASOD) showed a decrease of between 20 to 30 percent of global topsoil in the 30 years from 1961 to 1991. Soil

The garden going to seed.

degradation is caused by overgrazing (35 percent), agricultural activities (28 percent), deforestation (30 percent), fuel wood (7 percent) and industrialization (4 percent). The bottom line on soil production is that it takes about 100 years to generate just a millimetre of soil.

The transition towards sustainable agriculture needs small-scale regional food production and naturally pollinated seeds—from which we can save seeds. Seeds that have been hybridized and genetically altered do not provide the solution to feeding ourselves.

"Of the Earth's quarter-million plant species, only two hundred are cultivated for food on any serious scale. The vast majority of the world's food comes from just twenty crops, in just eight plant families. Most of these monocultures are dangerously vulnerable to diseases (both old and new), pest infestations and a rapidly changing climate.

"The 'genetic pool' on which plant breeders might need to draw, to build resistance and adaptability, is being constantly eroded as older non-commercial varieties disappear. Seed banks can only do so much in this massive salvage operation. The seeds they store need to be regularly germinated, otherwise they too will die.

"The best way of maintaining an active and vibrant seed bank is to ensure that farmers (and gardeners) are planting out those 'land races' and rare varieties of plants that are now so endangered."
Jonathon Porritt, Forum for the Future

Trays of seeds ready for the final winnowing.

Seed Selection

As a seed saver you participate in selection, encouraging the qualities you most value in a plant. Flowers are chosen for qualities such as beauty, colour or fragrance. Vegetables are selected for traits such as early ripening, late bolting, disease resistance, high yields, size and good flavour. Select seeds from the healthiest, best-performing plants in the garden, displaying the most typical characteristics of the variety. These seeds will grow into plants of great vigour, and should carry forward a variety's reputation of being worth growing. If selection is not carefully maintained it's easy to lose the favourable traits of a named variety.

When creating something new, select and save seeds from plants most representative of your intended goal; it can take up to 10 generations of growing a plant to stabilize a new characteristic.

"Off Types"

It is a good idea to inspect the plants frequently to identify any "off types"—plants that show different traits from the other plants. In order to maintain the purity of the strain, these should be "rogued" out by removing them before they flower.

After collection, seeds are dried in a warm greenhouse.

Seed Collection

Timing for seed collection is critical, and observation is the key to success. Wait until seeds are ripe enough for collection, but don't wait until they have dispersed into the garden (or the finches have eaten them!). TIP: When collecting seeds be aware of weeds that hide among plants, and remove them before inadvertently collecting their seeds.

I collect most seeds in brown paper bags, on which I write the name and date of collection and any other pertinent information. If there's a large volume of seeds to collect, I line large plastic tubs with bags and put seeds into these. The bags stay in the greenhouse for two weeks to dry the seeds, and then are moved to a cooler, dry garage, where the seeds remain until they are cleaned in October.

Labelling Seeds

If you've ever found an envelope of seeds and wondered what they are or how old they are, you'll know how important labelling is. For everything you collect, record the name of the plant, date of collection and any other pertinent information.

SAMPLE SEED DATA FORM
Location: Street address and/or microclimatic zone
Species: Botanical name (and/or common name)
Variety: Common varietal name
Isolation: Distance between plants of same species, or method of isolation (e.g., cage)
Number of plants: Population of parent plants grown (insures genetic diversity)
History: Seed source
Characteristics: Disease resistance, early blooming, height, colour, etc.

Drying Seeds

Thorough drying is critical before storing seeds in sealed containers or envelopes. The larger the seed the longer it needs to dry. If possible, leave seeds to mature on the plant. Sometimes it's necessary to harvest seeds before they are quite ripe, birds being one reason for this, and ripening will finish off in the warm greenhouse as the seeds are drying. TIP: In some cases quantity necessitates drying seeds on tarps in the sun.

Seeds can be further dried using silica gel (available at local florist shops). Wrap the gel in cloth or a paper bag and place an amount equal to the seeds with the seeds in an airtight container. The seeds will finish drying after one week (no longer), and the silica gel should be removed for reuse. Coloured gel grains are the easiest to work with. When dry the particles are blue; as moisture is absorbed they turn pink. Dry for reuse by spreading on a tray and heating at 200°F (95°C) until particles are blue again.

Chard seeds dry on a tarp in the sun.

Cleaning Seeds

Chaff and other debris can be removed by sieving seeds through screens of different-sized mesh, then winnowing them in a light breeze to remove the very last traces of tiny particles or sand. I used to use a seamless kitchen baking pan and a medium-sized stainless-steel bowl to do this, waiting for the perfect weather condition—a light breeze. As I began collecting more and more seeds, I soon had to give that up. Now I use my hair dryer on a cold setting to do the final winnowing of seeds. It requires a bit of practice, but only takes a few times of the seeds blowing away before you get used to how far away the dryer needs to be from the bowl!

Tomatoes are cleaned using a wet process where they are fermented for a few days; this eliminates seed-borne pathogens. Melons, squashes, cucumbers and tomatillos are also cleaned using water, allowing dead seeds to float to the surface and good seeds to sink to the bottom of the container.

Storing Seeds

The ideal temperature for storage is 40°F (4°C) in a dark, cool humid area, away from fluctuations in temperature. Paper bags, envelopes or airtight containers (yoghurt tubs) work well for seed storage. Before storing seeds, winnow them to remove chaff and debris. Dating containers of seeds is important, because without dates the seeds cannot be rotated. Every year I clear out seeds that are no longer viable. Check "The A to Z of Vegetables" in March for usual seed life (or viability).

Seeds retain longer viability when refrigerated or frozen. Place dried seeds in small zip-lock plastic bags, pack these into a sealed glass jar, and place in the fridge. Viability lasts longest when the seeds are frozen in airtight plastic tubs. TIP: When you need seeds, keep them sealed in the tub, and allow it to reach room temperature before you open it. This prevents cold and moist air from condensing on seeds.

The Safe Seed Pledge

"Agriculture and seeds provide the basis upon which our lives depend. We must protect this foundation as a safe and genetically stable source for future generations. For the benefit of all farmers, gardeners and consumers who want an alternative, we pledge that we do not knowingly buy or sell genetically engineered seeds or plants. The mechanical transfer of genetic material outside of natural reproductive methods and between genera, families or kingdoms, poses great biological risks, as well as economic, political and cultural threats. We feel that genetically engineered varieties have been insufficiently tested prior to public release. More research and testing is necessary to further assess the potential risks of genetically engineered seeds. Further, we wish to support agricultural progress that leads to healthier soils, genetically diverse agricultural ecosystems and ultimately healthy people and communities."

Council for Responsible Genetics (CRG)

BENEFITS OF SEED SAVING

- You collect organic seeds from healthy plants adapted to local growing conditions, which display greater vigour as a result.
- Fresh seed has the highest germination rate.
- Plants become available to you that may not be commercially accessible.
- Seed saving safeguards food security.
- Seed saving protects genetic diversity, which increases the plant's ability to adapt to rapidly changing environmental conditions.

SAVING TOMATO SEEDS

It's fun and rewarding to collect seeds from your own tomatoes, because growing from these seeds means plants become adapted to your garden, and as a result will outperform other seeds. Tomatoes belong to the Solanaceae family and are self-pollinating. A few feet of separation between different varieties is all that is needed, so even if all you have is a small garden, you can grow many types of tomatoes. Save seeds of tomato plants that display desirable traits such as high yield, early ripening, disease resistance and excellent flavour.

When tomatoes are potato-leafed they have fully double flowers, which increase the chance of cross-pollination. Lots of heirlooms are potato-leafed so space these 30 ft. (9 m) apart from each other.

The weekly tomato collection.

How to Save Your Own Tomato Seeds

1. Cut tomatoes in half and squeeze the seeds into a bowl. Look close and you will see a protective gelatinous coating, which inhibits germination around each seed. Pour the seeds into plastic tubs and put plastic labels in each tub to keep track of the tomato variety.

2. Leave tubs for four days, during which time fermentation forms mould on the surface. This process dissolves the gelatinous coating, and destroys any seed-borne pathogens, preparing seeds for planting. TIP: Put a saucer over the tubs because fruit flies love this process!

3. On the fifth day pour the seeds into a large bowl and fill with water. Good viable seeds sink to the bottom and dud seeds and scum float to the top. Gently pour these off, and repeat rinsing until all that's left is a clump of clean seeds. Strain in a sieve and tap off excess moisture.

4. Tap sieve upside down onto plates, and spread the wet seeds out with the plastic label. Leave plates in a warm place to dry for a day or two. Scrape seeds off plates and crumble with fingers to separate any stuck together. Spread out on plates again to thoroughly dry before storage. Store seeds in labelled, airtight containers. The seed life is five to ten years when stored properly.

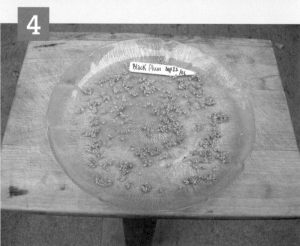

September

PRUNING STONE FRUIT TREES

Peaches, Nectarines, Cherries, Plums and Apricots

Contrary to the late-winter pruning recommended for pome fruits, the timing for stone fruits is after harvest in early fall. This is due to prevalence of bacterial canker in wet conditions, which the more tender stone fruits are prone to. In fall, pruning cuts heal much faster, making it less likely for canker infections to take hold. Prevention is worth a pound of peaches in this case!

Peaches, nectarines and sour cherries fruit on the previous season's growth. The trees need yearly pruning to stimulate new growth.

Plums, sweet cherries and apricots fruit at the base of the previous season's growth on older wood. Annual pruning is not required for these fruits, other than to keep a balanced canopy or a restricted form.

If pruning is done yearly it only needs to be light, removing crossing branches and the "3Ds"—dead, diseased and damaged wood. New growth can be cut back by as much as half, making cuts to two outward-facing buds. This helps control the size of trees. By pruning regularly, it's possible for cherries grafted on semi-dwarf rootstock to actually stabilize at 12 ft. (3.6 m)! Cherries have long-lived fruiting spurs, so the older branches maintain fruit production for up to 10 years, something worth considering when pruning!

Stone fruits benefit from summer pruning. The intention here is to allow good air circulation and sunlight to penetrate the tree. Thinning out the branches that shade maturing fruit in summer results in desirably coloured fruit because it redirects the tree's energy to ripening fruit. Pruning also stimulates new growth, which means development of fruit buds for next year's bumper crop.

For all branches on the tree, count four leaves beyond the last fruit, and remove the rest of the branch. Once pruned, extra sunlight stimulates the development of fruit buds for next year's fruit. Summer pruning is necessary for cordons and espaliers to restrict growth, maintain shape and promote development of fruit spurs.

PROPAGATION OF SMALL FRUITS AND BERRIES

Fill ½-gal. (2-L) square pots with propagation mix and moisten well. Using a dibber (chopstick), insert 9 cuttings into each pot, spaced as 3 rows of 3. In winter, providing bottom heat to cuttings, using a heat pad or heater cable, achieves 85 percent rooting compared to 55 percent without heat. When cuttings grow leaves, you know they have taken root.

Above: Lots of blackcurrant bushes from cuttings in fall.

Left: Rooted cuttings of blackcurrants.

PROPAGATION MIX FOR SOFTWOOD CUTTINGS

Needs to be sterilized, free draining and moisture retentive.

Mix equal parts by volume:

- Coarse washed sand
- Perlite
- Peat

Optional: add granular rock phosphate to aid rooting

Cuttings should be positioned out of direct sunlight, because until they form roots they are liable to wilt. Water evaporates from leaves, but there is no uptake from roots to make good the loss. Create a humid atmosphere (a propagation unit with misting is ideal), or cover cuttings with plastic bags.

High levels of filtered light are essential, because photosynthesis is necessary for cuttings to grow and produce roots. Try to maintain an even temperature around 68°F (20°C). Check cuttings daily; any attempt at flowering should be nipped in the bud.

Once rooted I plant cuttings into their own pots, using screened compost as a growing medium. Any well-drained medium will do, as long as nutrients are added. If not, stimulate growth by feeding with liquid fish fertilizer one week and liquid seaweed the next.

Taking a Tip Cutting

1. Use a clean sharp knife to prepare cuttings.
2. Choose vigorous and healthy sections of stem.
3. The length of cuttings varies, generally no more than 6 in. (15 cm) long.
4. Cuttings must possess at least 2 nodes (leaf-joints).
5. Trim just below a node, ensuring the growing tip is upright.
6. Cuttings should be green/yellow but not hardened into woody tissue.
7. Anything with flowers or buds is best avoided.
8. Take cuttings on wet days when plants are charged with water.
9. Keep them damp and sealed in a plastic bag until ready to insert.
10. Prepare propagation mix.
11. Insert the cutting into propagation mix so leaves remain above.
12. Water in well.

Willow Water

For rooting hormone I use willow water, which contains salicylic acid, a natural rooting agent. I simply soak the cuttings overnight (and they can even sit in the water at the same time the willow is soaking if you haven't pre-mixed the willow water).

1. Choose sections of young willow (*Salix*) the diameter of a fat pencil.
2. Strip off leaves, leaving only twigs.
3. Chop into 2-in. (5-cm) lengths and soak for 24 hours.
4. Strain out the willow sections; the water will keep for 7 days.
5. Soak cuttings for up to 24 hours before placing in the propagation mix.
6. Optional: water the cuttings in with willow water.

Figs and Elderberries

These fast-growing softwood shrubs can be pruned yearly to keep them in check. They root easily.

Currants and Gooseberries

These rapid-growing bushes root easily from cuttings taken in fall after fruit is harvested.

Blueberries

The best blueberries are produced on three-year-old wood. To prevent bushes petering out, remove 20 percent of the oldest wood every year at ground level. Blueberries are slower to take root.

Strawberries

You get three years of production from a strawberry patch; expect the second year to be the best. Take strawberry offsets in fall, overwinter in small pots with screened compost and plant in spring after danger of frost.

Raspberries

Raspberries are easily propagated from all those rooted canes that creep outside of the support framework. Early spring is the best time to dig creeping canes out to create a new raspberry patch or distribute them among friends.

Trailing Hybrid Berries

Layering canes, while still attached to the plant, is the easiest way to propagate blackberries. Peg a trailing cane down in fall, and cover nodes with soil. Leave all winter and in spring you will have several rooted sections to cut off. Short sections of cane will also take root in propagation mix.

Some popular trailing hybrid berries are:
- Boysenberry (blackberry x loganberry x raspberry)
- Loganberry (blackberry x raspberry)
- Jostaberry or Worcester berry (gooseberry x blackcurrant)

Kiwis

Kiwis need pruning to keep their vigorous vines in check, which is best done in spring while plants are dormant and before sap starts to flow. Kiwis are dioecious vines, which have male and female flowers on separate plants. When taking cuttings don't forget you only need one male plant for every six females!

Grapes

Grapes grow on the current season's growth, and pruning stimulates new growth. Pruning is key to good grape production. In spring while the grapes are dormant select straight canes approximately ¼ in (6 mm) in diameter, and prune back to a few two-bud spurs, leaving no more than 50 buds in total for a moderately vigorous plant. Cut short sections of grape canes to root in propagation mix.

10-MINUTE EGGS

One of the biggest thrills in my life was getting chickens. It started with a request to my husband, Guy, to build me a chicken house for Christmas. As this project neared completion I began feeling apprehensive as to how much time it would take to look after these birds.

Having a small flock of chickens turned out to be no big deal; the rewards more than compensate for the effort—chickens are layers, "de-buggers," cultivators and fertilizers all in one! As it turns out, we now enjoy "10-minute eggs," and I call them this for several reasons. It takes only 10 minutes to clean the chicken house weekly and 10 minutes to feed and water them daily, and on several occasions we have had the wonderful fortune to be eating eggs that have only been laid 10 minutes before!

I now have a gorgeous flock of heritage hens that come in all shapes and colours—light Brahma, Rhode Island Red, Barred Rock, Buff Orpington and black Australorp. A flock is considered to be a minimum of three birds. Our "girls" have the freedom of a large protected run in spring and summer and do an admirable job of keeping the weeds there under control. At the same time they turn all the weeds and kitchen scraps thrown into the run into chicken manure that can be added to the garden or left to grow the next year's crop, guaranteed to be AMAZING!

In winter, our chickens peck around the place, removing bugs and fertilizing as they go, becoming a feature of the landscape. Once the winter vegetable garden is going it can withstand the scuffling action of chickens' feet; if it's not established it will need protection. It's easy to get ranging chickens into their run by enticing them with hen scratch. At dusk their instinct for safety impels them to go back into the coop anyway, so our last task of the day is to simply shut the door of the coop to keep out such predators as raccoon and mink.

In fact, protecting poultry from predators needs to be a high priority. Ideally the run should be fenced all round, with a sturdy gate and roof overhead. Use mesh small enough to stop the mink from squeezing through. My experience with free-ranging birds has

Above: Eggs come in all colours.

Right: Happy free-ranging hens.

been very good in this respect; we have not lost any adult hens while they were gadding about the garden. (Watch out for eagles, hawks and chasing dogs, though.)

For the chicken house we chose a design from a 1940s British homesteading book. We reckoned this would give us a good workable prototype, as back then having chickens was commonplace. The house is raised 4 ft. (1.2 m) off the ground, providing shelter underneath from sun in summer and rain in winter, and making it easier to clean out. It takes 10 minutes to clean the coop because the floor is lined with tent awning, which is then covered with absorbent wood shavings. When the shavings need changing, I simply gather up the four corners of the awning, lift it out to the wheelbarrow and shake in the soiled shavings. These are added to the compost pile, and sometimes spread as a mulch for blueberry bushes, which respond well to the nitrogen of the manure and the acidity of the wood shavings.

Two large wire-screened windows, with shutters that slide up and down on the outside, provide adequate ventilation, as well as safety and insulation in winter. A wide central door provides easy access to the inside of the coop for cleaning. The three nesting boxes on the outside of the house make checking for eggs and cleaning very accessible. It's important not to overcrowd birds. This is where the term "henpecked" is derived from—too many birds in an allotted space means a pecking order kicks in. According to organic standards each bird needs two square feet of space (or five chickens to a square metre). De-feathered backsides and scrawny necks indicate distress to the chickens lowest in the order, so a decision needs to be made—fewer chickens or another coop!

The diet for our "girls" is comprised of organic layer mash (16 percent protein) and is supplemented with crushed oyster shells, which provide calcium for eggshells. Keeping the feeder inside the coop, suspended on a hook, is the way to keep rats away. Kitchen scraps are thrown into the run daily. The chickens also love a little bit of "Afternoon Delight," which encourages them to exercise by scratching around for it.

Above: Chicken coop.

Right: Good ventilation is important for healthy chickens.

Far right: Keeping the feeder inside the coop keeps rats away.

"AFTERNOON DELIGHT" CHICKEN SCRATCH
A blend of equal parts:

- Organic wheat kernels
- Organic barley kernels
- Organic triticale flakes
- Organic wheat flakes
- Organic oat flakes
- Organic flax seeds

(All are available as bulk food)

A dust bath provides the means for birds to clean their feathers. Mites can become a problem if dry sandy soil is not available for dust bathing. If mites become an irritation, mixing diatomaceous earth into established dust baths helps to control them. Another problem may be scale mites, that build scale around feet and legs, which in severe cases can lead to limping. Applying a greasy balm or mineral oil to the legs of infected birds suffocates the scale mites. The easiest time to treat birds is when you can catch them. The easiest way to catch them is at dusk or in the morning, when the birds are inside the coop.

If you are inclined towards self-sufficiency I heartily recommend a flock of feathery friends. Check your local bylaws in regards to backyard poultry. As long as you don't drive your neighbours mad with a rooster that crows at 4:00 every morning and you look after your "girls" properly, I think there's no reason for anyone to complain. If they do, just give them a dozen 10-minute eggs!

Many people clip the wings of birds to prevent them flying out of the run or to help settle them into a new home. The feathers will re-grow. Follow this diagram to do this correctly and without causing injury.

FLUFFY OMELETTES

Preheat grill in the oven. Check that the frying pan fits about 6 in. (15 cm) below the grill.

3 eggs
1 leek, chopped into fine rings
6 finely-sliced mushrooms (optional)
2 cloves garlic, minced
Butter or oil
Salt (if butter is unsalted)
½ tsp (2.5 mL) peppercorns
1 Tbsp. (15 mL) fresh garden herbs—your choice of dill, oregano, basil, chives, sweet marjoram, thyme
2 Tbsp. (30 mL) cold water
Cheese—your choice of Parmesan, cheddar, feta

Whisk eggs with water until well beaten. Add the salt, peppercorns and finely chopped herbs. Heat a cast-iron frying pan and melt butter or oil, sauté the leeks and garlic until they are soft and aromatic. Pour the just-beaten eggs over the leeks, and cook just until the base begins to set. Allowing the eggs to spread around to the side of the pan makes it even fluffier!

Sprinkle cheese over the eggs before putting the frying pan under the grill. Continue cooking until the cheese has melted and the top of the omelette has risen to a fluffy golden peak. Don't go away—it happens fast! Fold the omelette in half and serve proudly with a garden salad.

TIP: Get everyone to the table before the omelette goes under the grill!

October

GROWING GREAT GARLIC

October is the month for planting garlic, a sustainable crop that is easy and rewarding to grow. The best part is that you begin with one bulb that splits up into ten cloves, each of which matures into a new bulb—you see what I mean by sustainable! I plant enough cloves to keep plentiful garlic in the kitchen until the next harvest comes around the following summer.

Garlic has been revered for centuries for fighting infection, so the fresh garlic harvest in July comes in good time to boost the immune system in preparation for winter colds and flu. Garlic complements many culinary dishes, and I love the aroma when it sizzles in the frying pan. It also contains selenium, an essential trace element often lacking in our diets.

Softneck garlic (*Allium sativum*): With smaller cloves and no central stalk (as it does not flower), softneck garlic is highly suitable for braiding. It stores for a year and the flavour is generally spicier than hardnecks. Softneck garlics are planted in fall, with the exception of a few varieties (e.g., 'Silverskin'), which are best planted in spring.

Hardneck garlic (*Allium ophioscorodon*): Also known as Rocambole garlic, hardneck has larger easy-to-peel cloves, but the bulbs only store for up to eight months. Rocambole garlic is not suited to braiding, as about a month before harvest it develops a central flower stalk, a scape, which carries a seed head. I cut these scapes off when they appear, as the energy used to go to seed takes away from bulb development. I enjoy the boost in flavour that scapes provide to summer meals, especially salads and salad dressings.

Elephant garlic (*Allium ampeloprasum*): Not a true garlic but a perennial leek with much milder flavour, elephant garlic does not store well as the cloves tend to split up when drying.

Freshly-dug garlic bulbs prior to cleaning.

Above: Garlic scapes.

Right: Garlic is ready for harvest when two-thirds of the tops are yellowed.

Most garlic from the supermarket has been fumigated with methyl bromide, an anti-sprouting chemical, so it's best to start with bulbs of organic seed garlic from a reputable garlic grower. Make sure the garlic is free from white rot, a fungal disease that wipes out garlic harvests for years to come.

Garlic is usually ready for harvest between late June to mid July, or when two-thirds of the leaves have turned yellow. Stop watering three weeks before harvest to allow the garlic bulbs to cure. Don't wait until all the leaves have yellowed, as the cloves separate in over-matured bulbs and the garlic does not store well. Remove surface soil from bulbs, preserving the protective skin layer around them. Hang to dry in bunches of no more than eight in a warm airy place, where they take about six weeks to thoroughly dry and cure. For the final cleaning, cut the stalk 2 in. (5 cm) above the neck of the bulb, and snip off the roots to release any last soil traces. A cool, dark place with ventilation provides the longest storage life.

SLOW-BAKED GARLIC

6 bulbs garlic
⅔ cup (160 mL) olive oil
Salt and pepper
Sprigs of fresh thyme or rosemary

Preheat oven to 275°F (135°C). Chop ½ in. (1 cm) off the top of the bulbs to expose the tips of the individual cloves. Place the bulbs on a baking dish. Pour or brush the olive oil over the bulbs. Season with salt and pepper. Cover and bake with sprigs of thyme (or rosemary) for 25-30 minutes, baste and cook another 15 minutes or until soft.

Slow baking makes garlic sweet and nutty and takes the bite out of it.

Squeeze the paste from the cloves onto a warm baguette.

PICKLED GARLIC

For surprisingly sweet and crunchy pickles

½ lb. (227 g) garlic cloves, peeled and left whole

1 large sweet red pepper, seeded and cut into thin slivers

2 cups (475 mL) white or apple cider vinegar

⅔ cup (160 mL) granulated sugar

½ tsp. (2.5 mL) mustard seed

½ tsp. (2.5 mL) celery seed

Place mustard and celery seed in a cheesecloth bag, tied up with cotton. Put this bag with the vinegar and the sugar into a saucepan. On medium-high heat, stirring frequently, bring this to a boil and continue to boil for 5 minutes. Add the garlic and red pepper. Return to a boil. Boil 5 minutes more. Discard spice bag.

Fill hot sterilized jars with garlic and red peppers to within 1 in. (2.5 cm) of the top. Pour the hot brine over them to within ¼ in. (6 mm) of the top of the jar. Cool to seal lids. Let stand several weeks to marinate.

White Rot in Garlic

White rot first hit California in 1939. It is an aggressive fungus with fruiting bodies (*sclerotia*) that wake up in cold wet weather, activated by chemicals released by garlic. It only takes one *sclerotium* per 22 lb. (10 kg) of soil to set off the disease, which spreads rapidly through root systems. This fungal pathogen survives in soil for 8 to 15 years once established and is almost impossible to eradicate.

Prevention of White Rot

- Make sure any garlic you purchase is free of this deadly disease.
- Avoid spreading contamination by way of footwear or harvesting equipment.
- Destroy infected plants immediately and do not compost.
- Practise crop rotation yearly.

A basket of gorgeous garlic.

HOW TO PLANT GARLIC

Plant individual cloves about six weeks before the first hard frost. Garlic needs a month of near-freezing temperatures and 100 days of cold weather to mature. Choose a sunny site with fertile, well-drained soil. If your soil is poor, amend it with compost and aged manure, and sprinkle the planting area with rock dust and wood ash to aid bulb formation.

If your soil is fertile you can space the cloves 6 in. (15 cm) apart in the row, and the rows 6 in. (15 cm) apart, just enough that the root hairs don't get tangled up. Otherwise plant the rows 12 in. (30 cm) apart. If garlic is spaced too close it results in smaller bulbs.

1. At harvest in mid-July the bulbs are bundled together in bunches of no more than eight and are hung along the rafter in the garage where a warm breeze blows through. Here the bulbs are left to cure for at least six weeks to ensure they are thoroughly dry for storage and replanting.

2. The bulbs are cleaned by removing the soiled outer wrapper skin and cutting off the root hairs close to the bulb, shaking out any remaining soil. Then the bulbs are split into separate cloves. The largest cloves are selected for replanting because these grow the largest bulbs.

3. Choose a sunny, well-drained site. Practise crop rotation yearly to avoid problems with white rot. Sprinkling a mix of 50 percent wood ash (uncontaminated) and 50 percent rock dust re-mineralizes the soil and aids in bulb formation.

4. Spread a layer of well-rotted compost or aged manure over the site, as garlic does not thrive in soils lacking organic matter.

5. A dibber comes in handy. Moisten the site before poking holes 3 in. (8 cm) deep and 6 in. (15 cm) apart in rows. The rows are also 6 in. (15 cm) apart. Drop the cloves in, pointy end up, about 3 in.

(8 cm) deep below the soil surface. If garlic is spaced too close it results in the development of smaller bulbs.

6. After planting all the garlic cloves, rake over the surface to cover the holes.

7. Mulching the garlic patch with spoiled hay, straw or shredded leaves eliminates competition from weeds, which results in smaller bulbs. It also allows you to harvest the garlic by hand pulling rather than forking, which can injure the bulb. Signs of life often appear in January when green shoots appear above the mulch.

HOW TO BRAID GARLIC

1. Lay three clean dried stalks with good-sized garlic bulbs on a table, with the foliage facing towards you. Place one bulb down and then place two more bulbs side by side just above it. Place the stalks of bulbs two and three underneath the stalk of bulb one, and cross them over it. Tie the stalks together using string tied with a tight knot. If stalks are pliable enough you can tie the bulbs together without using string.

2. Place the fourth bulb between bulb two and three, aligning the stalk with the centre stalk. You are now holding three groups of stalks—one on the left, one on the right, and two in the middle. Fold the left stalk toward the middle, over the middle two stalks. Now pull the middle two stalks over to form the new left side.

3. Lay bulb five beside bulb four, aligning the stalk with the centre stalk again. Now fold the right-hand stalk over the two centre stalks to become the new centre. Pull the middle two stalks over to form the new left.

4. Repeat this sequence, alternating the side that you lay the bulbs on each time, and always aligning the stalk with the centre stalk. Note that the number of stalks you fold in the middle increases each time.

5. When you have braided the last garlic bulb in, carry on braiding the foliage until you are almost out of it. Tie the braid off above the last fold, leaving string to hang the braid with.

6. Make beautiful and decorative gifts by simply tucking bay, rosemary and lavender sprigs in with the garlic as you braid.

Kristin Ross photos

10 GREAT IDEAS FOR GREEN TOMATOES

GREEN TOMATO CAKE

Preheat oven to 350°F (175°C)

2¼ cups (525 mL) sugar

1 cup (250 mL) vegetable oil

3 eggs

2 tsp. (10 mL) vanilla

3 cups (700 mL) flour

1 tsp. (5 mL) salt

1 tsp. (5 mL) baking powder

1 tsp. (5 mL) cinnamon

½ tsp. (2.5 mL) nutmeg

1 cup (250 mL) pecans or walnuts

1 cup (250 mL) raisins

2½ cups (600 mL) diced green tomatoes

In a large mixing bowl beat the sugar, vegetable oil, eggs and vanilla until smooth and creamy. Sift together the flour, salt, baking powder, cinnamon and nutmeg; slowly beat into the egg mixture. Blend well. Stir in pecans, raisins and tomatoes. Pour into a greased 9-by-13 in. (23-by-33 cm) pan. Bake for 1 hour or until a wooden pick inserted in centre comes out clean.

GREEN TOMATO MINCEMEAT

Makes 6 cups (1.4 L)

8 cups (2 L) chopped tart apples (peeled)

8 cups (2 L) chopped green tomatoes

3 cups (700 mL) brown sugar

3 cups (700 mL) raisins

3 cups (700 mL) currants

2 tsp. (10 mL) cinnamon

½ tsp. (2.5 mL) ground cloves

½ tsp. (2.5 mL) ground allspice

½ tsp. (2.5 mL) mace

½ tsp. (2.5 mL) nutmeg

2 tsp. (10 mL) grated orange peel

1 lemon (grated peel and juice)

1 tsp. (5 mL) salt

1 cup (250 mL) apple cider vinegar

¾ cup (180 mL) butter (optional)

Mix apples with tomatoes and add remaining ingredients except butter. Bring gradually to the boil and simmer gently uncovered for approximately 2 hours to thicken. Stir occasionally to be sure it doesn't stick. Drain off excess liquid. Add butter and mix in. Pour hot into sterilized Mason jars and cover with lids (which seal as the jars cool).

GREEN TOMATO AND APPLE JAM

Makes 3 cups (700 mL)

3 large apples or 1 lb. (454 g), peeled and
  chopped
5 medium or 1 lb. (454 g) green tomatoes,
  chopped
1 cup (250 mL) water
½ tsp. (2.5 mL) ground ginger
½ tsp. (2.5 mL) ground nutmeg
1 cinnamon stick
2½ cups (600 mL) sugar, approximately

*Combine the apples and green tomatoes
in a large saucepan and add the water and
spices. Bring to a boil, and simmer covered
for 30 minutes or until the fruit has softened.
Remove the cinnamon stick.*

*Measure the fruit mixture and add 1 cup
(250 mL) sugar for each cup. Return to the
saucepan and stir over medium heat until the
sugar has dissolved, without allowing boiling.
Then bring to a boil, and boil uncovered for
about 15 minutes, or until a gel test shows that
the jam has set. Pour hot into sterilized Mason
jars and cover with lids (which seal as the jars
cool).*

MARTINE'S EASY FRENCH TOMATO JAM

2.2 lb. (1 kg) green tomatoes
3 cups (700 mL) sugar
1 lemon
Cut tomatoes into 4
Cut the lemon into 8

Mix with the sugar and leave for 24 hours.

*Cook until the jam begins to set and looks a
little brown.*

*Pour warm into hot sterilized glass jars, and
leave the lids to seal with a pop as the jam
cools.*

FRIED GREEN TOMATOES

3 medium firm green tomatoes, unpeeled
½ cup (125 mL) unbleached flour
¼ cup (60 mL) milk
2 beaten eggs
⅔ cup (160 mL) fine dry breadcrumbs or
  cornmeal
¼ cup (60 mL) olive oil
½ tsp. (2.5 mL) salt
½ tsp. (2.5 mL) pepper

*Cut tomatoes into ½-in. (1-cm) slices.
Sprinkle slices with salt and pepper. Let tomato
slices stand for 15 minutes. Place flour, milk,
eggs and breadcrumbs into separate shallow
dishes. Dip tomato slices in milk, then flour,
then eggs then breadcrumbs.*

*Heat 2 Tbsp. (30 mL) of olive oil in a skillet
on medium heat. Fry the tomato slices 4 to 6 at
a time on each side, or until brown. As you cook
the rest of the slices add olive oil as needed.
Season to taste with salt and pepper.*

'Alicante' tomatoes are very prolific.

GREEN TOMATO CHUTNEY

Makes 6 cups (1.4 L)

10 medium or 2.2 lb. (1 kg) green tomatoes,
  chopped
2 medium onions, chopped
3 large apples, chopped
4 cups (1 L) malt vinegar
2½ cups (600 mL) firmly packed demerara
  sugar
1½ cups (350 mL) raisins
1 tsp. (5 mL) mustard powder
1 tsp. (5 mL) cinnamon
½ tsp. (2.5 mL) ground allspice
¼ tsp. (1 mL) cayenne pepper
1 tsp. (5 mL) salt

*Combine all ingredients in a large saucepan.
Stir over medium heat until the sugar dissolves,
without boiling. Now bring to a boil, and
simmer uncovered, stirring occasionally,
for about 1½ hours, or until the mixture has
thickened. Pour warm into hot sterilized glass
jars, and leave the lids to seal with a pop as the
chutney cools.*

GREEN TOMATO PICCALILLI

Makes 4 cups (1 L)

4 cups (1 L) green tomatoes, chopped
1 red pepper, chopped
1 green pepper, chopped
2 cups (475 mL) onions, chopped
½ cup (125 mL) kosher or pickling salt
2 cups (475 mL) apple cider or white
  vinegar
1 cup (250 mL) sugar
1 oz. (28 g) pickling spices, tied in a
  cheesecloth bag

*Mix chopped tomatoes, peppers and onions
and cover with brine made of ½ cup (125 mL)
pickling or kosher salt to 4 cups (1 L) water. Let
sit overnight. Drain.*

*Heat vinegar and sugar in a saucepan until
the sugar dissolves, making sure it does not
boil. Pour over the vegetables, bring to a boil,
add the pickling spices in the bag, and simmer
gently for 30 minutes. Remove pickling spices
and ladle into hot sterilized Mason jars, leaving
¼ in. (6 mm) headroom. Cover with lids, which
will seal as the relish cools.*

GREEN TOMATO SAUCE

Makes 5 cups (1.2 L)

10 medium or 2.2 lb. (1 kg) green tomatoes
4 shallots, chopped
½ cup (125 mL) water
1 Tbsp. (15 mL) caraway seeds
2 tsp. (10 mL) turmeric
2 tsp. (10 mL) mixed spice
½ tsp. (2.5 mL) ground ginger
1 cup (250 mL) water extra
1½ cups (350 mL) sugar
1 cup (250 mL) apple cider vinegar

*Combine tomatoes, shallots and water in a
large saucepan and bring to a boil, simmer
uncovered for about 20 minutes or until
tomatoes are pulpy. Blend or process this
mixture smooth and return to the saucepan.
Add the remaining ingredients and stir over
medium heat until the sugar has dissolved,
without bringing to a boil. Then bring to a boil
and simmer uncovered, stirring occasionally
for about 45 minutes, or until the mixture has
thickened. Pour sauce into hot sterilized jars
and leave lids to seal as they cool.*

CURRIED GREEN TOMATO PICKLES

Makes 5 cups (1.2 L)

10 medium or 2.2 lb. (1 kg) green tomatoes, sliced

1 large onion, sliced

1 small green cucumber, sliced

1 stick celery, sliced

¼ cup (60 mL) coarse cooking salt

2 cups (475 mL) apple cider vinegar

1 cup (250 mL) brown sugar

½ tsp. (2.5 mL) cayenne pepper

2 tsp. (10 mL) curry powder

2 tsp. (10 mL) mustard powder

¼ cup (60 mL) corn flour

½ cup (125 mL) extra apple cider vinegar

Combine the tomatoes, onion, cucumber and celery in a bowl, sprinkle with coarse salt and cover. Let stand overnight. Drain. Rinse under cold water. Drain again.

Combine the vinegar and the sugar. Dissolve the sugar in the vinegar over heat, stirring, and without bringing to a boil. Add the vegetables and the spices. Dissolve the corn flour in the extra ½ cup (125 mL) vinegar to a smooth paste, and add to the mix. Bring to a boil, while stirring, and stir until the mixture thickens. Pour into hot sterilized jars and leave to seal as they cool.

PICKLED GREEN TOMATOES

Makes 4 cups (1 L)

2.2 lb. (1 kg) unripe tomatoes (about 4 the size of baseballs), cut into wedges

2 medium red onions, peeled and cut into rounds about ½ in. (1 cm) thick

2 Tbsp. (30 mL) coarse salt

Piece of fresh ginger, thumb-sized, peeled and cut into thin disks

1½ cups (350 mL) red wine vinegar

¾ cup (180 mL) sugar

4 tsp. (20 mL) coriander seeds, toasted and ground in spice mill or coffee grinder

In a medium non-reactive bowl, combine the tomatoes and onions with the salt and toss well. Cover, refrigerate for 4 hours or overnight. Drain and rinse twice to remove the salt, and then set aside.

Place the ginger in a fold of plastic wrap to catch the juices and crush with a mallet or other heavy object. In a non-reactive saucepan, combine the ginger with the remaining ingredients and bring to a boil over medium-high heat, stirring once or twice to dissolve the sugar. Reduce the heat to low and simmer for 5 minutes, stirring occasionally. Remove from heat, cooling for 5 minutes, then pour over the tomatoes and onions. Allow to cool to room temperature uncovered, then cover and refrigerate. These pickles will keep covered and refrigerated for 2 weeks.

THE FINAL SEED COLLECTION

Seed harvesting continues throughout the year with the grand finale in October, when there is a rush to beat the onset of rain and cooler weather. At this time, bags of seeds awaiting the final cleaning are organized. Patience is needed to see if the last rays of summer will ripen seeds still maturing in the garden. A common problem encountered is not drying seeds thoroughly before storing them, which leads to mould problems. After winnowing, allow the cleaned seeds to dry again before storage. Seeds are stored in airtight tubs in a dark unheated room with minimum fluctuations in temperature.

Another problem for novice seed savers seems to be harvesting the seeds before they have matured enough on the plant, so that they do not ripen. Many vegetable seeds continue to mature even after they have been removed from the plant, but in order for this to happen the seeds must have reached a certain stage of maturity. This is usually indicated by change in colour and texture, so wait until the seed pods turn light brown before harvesting. For larger seeds try a squeeze test for hardness with your fingers. If still soft, it's too soon.

The food garden going to seed in fall.

Lettuces

Lettuces (Asteraceae family) have "perfect" flowers that are both male and female, meaning they self-pollinate, and because of this you can grow many varieties in a small garden without worrying about them crossing up. Lettuces produce large quantities of seed and you will know they are ready when feathery parachutes appear. These seeds should be collected before strong winds disperse the parachutes with the seeds attached. Clean lettuce seeds by bashing the stalks into a wheelbarrow to release the seeds, and then pass the seeds through screens to remove all the chaff and debris. Blow any fine particles away using a hair dryer on the cold setting.

Top: Lettuce in seed.
Bottom: Leek seed heads.

Leeks and Onions

Onions and leeks (Liliaceae family) are biennial plants that set seed in the second year. They are cross-pollinated by tiny insects, so to maintain varietal purity it's important that no other alliums are flowering within 1 mile (1.6 km). Seeds develop in small inflorescences on large globular seed heads and require patience for ripening; they can take a long time. TIP: Do the squeeze test before harvesting—if they are squishy they are still maturing.

Leek seeds take the whole season to mature. The large seed heads develop in spring, but the seeds are not ready to remove from the plant until late September/October. Cut the seeds off with sharp scissors and rub them between gloved hands to remove the chaff. (The strong onion smell will make your eyes water.) Screen these seeds to remove debris, and lay out on plates to dry.

Beets, Chard and Spinach

Beets, chard and spinach (Chenopodiaceae family) are cross-pollinating biennials with fine pollen that can be carried great distances by wind. Beets, chard and spinach plants need an isolation distance of ¼ mile (400 m) from one another to insure seeds come true in the next generation. Seeds are produced in abundance along tall stalks, and are light brown when

Perpetual spinach seeds.

ready for harvest. Strip seeds off the stalk using gloved hands, and pass them through a series of screens to remove the chaff and debris. Blow any fine particles away using a hair dryer on the cold setting.

Peas and Beans

Legumes (Fabaceae family) are also self-pollinating, so you can grow different varieties for seed in a small garden. I leave a buffer zone of 30 ft. (9 m) between the pole beans, and plant another vegetable between the bush beans for extra caution. I take the first few harvests for the kitchen, because I know that the more you pick the more they produce, so that I will still have plenty for seed collection.

Usually seeds don't all ripen at the same time, so regular picking is needed.

If you spot white egg masses on pea seeds you've had pea weevils. To solve this problem, remove the infected seeds, and put the rest into an airtight container and freeze for one week. I shuck and inspect pea and bean seeds as soon as possible after collection due to this possibility.

Tomatoes, Peppers and Eggplants

Tomatoes, peppers and eggplants belong to the Solanaceae family and are self-pollinating. It's fun to grow a diversity of tomatoes and peppers and collect the seeds of your favourites, and a few feet of separation between varieties is all that is needed. If tomatoes are potato-leafed (and a lot of heirlooms are) they have fully double flowers, which increase the chance of cross-pollination, so it's best to space these 30 ft. (9 m) from each other. (See August for "Saving Tomato Seeds.")

Tomatillos, Cape Gooseberries and Ground Cherries

These exotic fruits are commonly encountered as edible garnishes on restaurant plates. The fruits develop inside papery husks and have a tangy fruity flavour when eaten. The tiny seeds are part of the

Brazilian snow peas in seed.

Top: A pepper collection.
Bottom: Aunt Molly's ground cherries.

233

flesh inside the fruit. The most efficient way to extract them is to put husked fruits into a food processor, add 1 cup (250 mL) of water, and give them a few whirls to macerate the flesh just enough to release the seeds. This pulpy mixture then has to be rinsed with lots of water in a large bowl so that the pulp floats up to the top and is removed. The seeds sink down to the bottom and can be captured with a kitchen sieve, tapped to release excess moisture, and spread onto a plate to dry. They stick together so need crumbling before storage.

Brassicas

Brussels sprouts, broccoli, cabbage, cauliflower, kale, collards, arugula, mustards, turnips, kohlrabi and rutabaga are all members of the cabbage family, Brassicaceae. Although brassicas have perfect flowers, with both male and female, most cultivars are self-incompatible and need insects for pollination to occur. Plants belonging to the same species will cross-pollinate; so to maintain genetic purity an isolation distance of 1 mile (1.6 km) is required. To maintain genetic variability it's best to collect seeds from a minimum of six plants of the same variety.

Sprouting broccoli in seed.

Copious amount of seed is produced in pods, which turn light brown when the seeds are ready. Sometimes little birds will tell you when the pods are ripe by eating them! Cut the seed stalks off and invert them into labelled paper bags, where the pods become brittle as they dry and burst to release the matured black seeds into the bag. Crush the bag lightly with a hammer or rolling pin to release the rest.

Squash and Cucumbers

Members of the squash family (Cucurbitaceae) have separate male and female flowers on the same plant and require insects for pollination. You sex the flowers by searching for the male for its long stem, with anthers and stamens bearing pollen, and the female for its short stem, with a swelling (ovary) at the base of the flower.

Female squash blossom.

Cucumbers, melons, gourds, watermelon and the four different species of squash do not cross-pollinate with each other, but squash plants of the same species do and need to be isolated by ½ mile (800 m) to maintain varietal purity. You can control parentage by hand pollinating, taking pollen from the male flower and applying it to the female flower before it opens, and taping closed the female flower afterwards. The seeds in the fruit that develops are now insured to have varietal purity.

Male squash blossom.

Squash fruits should be left on the vine as long as possible to allow the seeds to mature. In the case of cucumbers, leave the fruit until it turns yellow—allowing the seeds more time to mature inside the fruit will mean a higher rate of fertility. Remove seeds from squash as you eat them throughout the winter. This way nothing goes to waste.

CLEANING SEEDS

Seeds are produced freely by plants for the future viability of the strain. All you have to do is collect them before they are naturally dispersed by Nature. Over the year, collecting seeds is made easy by using recycled brown paper bags. When harvesting I invert the seed heads into the paper bags, and leave them to dry on the top shelf in the greenhouse for a couple of weeks. This is when the seeds finish maturing or disperse into the bag as they mature. Label bags of seeds using a permanent marker to record the variety, date collected and any other pertinent information you may need in the future.

Top: *Paper bags are perfect for seed collection and drying.*

Bottom: *A series of screens of different-sized meshes cleans seeds easily.*

Screening is the first step to removing seeds from chaff and debris. I use a series of screens with three different-sized meshes—fine, medium and large. Wire screening to make these is available at hardware stores. You can also use colanders, tea strainers and sieves from the kitchen if you do not have time to make screens. The finest of the chaff is removed with a hair blow-dryer!

Use a magnifying glass to identify the seeds you are collecting, and to inspect the cleaned seeds for weed seeds or contaminants.

HOW TO COLLECT AMARANTH SEEDS

1. You know the seed is maturing when the vivid colour of the amaranth starts to fade to brown.

2. Grab the amaranth like a big bunch of flowers and bash it against the steepest side of a wheelbarrow so that the grain falls into the wheelbarrow.

3. Put this through a fine screening so that the grain falls through but the chaff remains on top.

4. Removing the last of the chaff and debris requires a hair dryer!

5. Set the dryer to "cold," then turn it on. Hold it a fair distance away, and slowly approach the bowl until you get a sense of how close you need to be to blow off the chaff without blasting the seeds out of the bowl. The seeds are heavier than the chaff and will fall to the bottom of the bowl. In occasional instances they aren't, in which case cleaning the seeds is a lot trickier!

CLEANING SEEDS WITH A HAMMER!

1. Globe artichoke and cardoon seeds need a hammer to release them from the flower head.

2. It takes persistent tapping to release the seeds, which are attached to feathery parachutes for wind dispersal.

3. This is what the seeds of globe artichokes and cardoons look like after they have been screened and the dust blown off using the hair dryer set to cold.

4. Light tapping with the hammer is also needed to release Greek cress (*Lepidium sativum*) seeds.

5. The small brown seeds fall to the bottom of the container. They are then screened and the dust is blown off with the dryer.

November

PUTTING THE GARDEN TO BED FOR WINTER

There's a lot of clipping and snipping to be done in November, doing what I refer to as "putting the garden to bed for winter." Apart from grasses with interesting seed heads, plants that are still flowering or that have berries for birds, we go to town cutting back the borders. This opens them up for easier weeding and for feeding the soil. TIP: It's much easier to do this before heavy rains turn vegetation into a wet and slimy mess!

In winter I leave sections of the food garden fallow to give the soil a break, and replenish depleted nutrients with a heavy mulching of organic waste matter. Feeding the soil at The Garden Path consists of adding layers of aged horse manure, compost, leaves and seaweed. I collect seaweed from local beaches, but you can use granular kelp as a substitute if there is no nearby ocean. A dusting of dolomite lime over the garden beds keeps the soil pH neutral in regions that experience heavy winter downpours. These same abundant rains mean you do not have to wash traces of salt off the seaweed before applying it. There's no need to worry about weeding the garden, as weeds are smothered under these layers, which break down over winter to create a loose friable tilth that is teaming with earthworms. I refer to this as an organic weed and feed!

Cutting back the borders is a big job in fall!

Organic weed and feed at the end of the season.

Lots of Lovely Leaves!

Some gardeners love 'em, some curse 'em, but most don't realize what a wonderful resource leaves are. Leaves provide nitrogen and phosphorus as they break down. Piles of wet leaves may damage lawns and smother plants, but when added to compost piles or left to rot into luxurious leaf mulch, they add organic matter and nutrients to soil.

In November I stockpile leaves by stuffing them into wire cages. If you pack leaves tight into the cages, pushing all the air out, they don't break down. This way you can shake a cage of dry leaves into the compost bin or over a lasagna garden whenever you need to.

Leafy Tips

- Large trees such as oaks, maples, sycamores and chestnuts are wonderful sources of nutrient-rich leaves.
- A heap of leaves breaks down into a pile of rich leaf mulch in one year (faster if you turn the pile).

Shallow-rooted plants such as rhododendrons, azaleas, camellias, hydrangeas, pieris, skimmia and heathers just LOVE leaf mulch.

- Don't position leaf piles under trees or hedges where fibrous roots will grow into the pile. TIP: If you must, put landscape fabric down first as a barrier.
- Spread leaves out on the lawn or driveway and run the lawn mower over the pile to reduce it to one tenth of its volume. The shredded leaves can then be sprinkled over garden beds, where they quickly break down into soil.
- Don't save leaves showing signs of disease such as rust, black spot or mildew, since these pathogens may survive without hot composting to destroy them. Dig a hole and bury them in the garden where millions of microbes will destroy them in no time at all.
- Avoid shiny waxy leaves, such as arbutus, that are slow to break down and can clog up your composting plans.

GREEN MANURES

Green manure crops have the ability to improve soil conditions on many fronts. They prevent the erosion of ground left fallow, their roots help to reduce soil compaction and improve drainage, and when turned under, green manures increase organic matter and soil fertility. They are also fast growing and help to suppress weeds. Green manures that are legumes (e.g., field peas and favas) have the additional benefit of bacteria on their roots that fix nitrogen from the air and add it to the soil.

When dug into the soil, green manures feed the soil web of life (worms, micro-organisms and other soil-borne organisms), which in turn breaks down nutrients to make them available to plants. Green manures therefore also improve plant health. It only takes four weeks for the green manure to decompose and the enriched soil to be ready for planting.

Winter Green Manures

- **Fall rye** (*Secale cereale*): Winter-hardy annual. One of the most effective green manures. Sow in November. Grows fast in early spring. TIP: Don't let rye get established as it becomes harder to dig under. Sowing rate 18 oz. (510 g) per 300 sq. ft. (28 sq. m).
- **Fava beans** (*Vicia faba*): These small-seeded broad or bell beans are winter-hardy nitrogen fixers. Sow in November. TIP: If you cut the stalks down to ground level the beans may regrow. Sowing rate 18 oz. (510 g) per 100 sq. ft. (9 sq. m).
- **Field peas** (*Lathyrus hirsutus*): Hardy to 10°F (-12°C). Tolerant of heavier soils, field peas can be sown with fall rye in fall, or planted in early spring. Sowing rate 18 oz. (510 g) per 100 sq. ft. (9 sq. m).
- **Hairy vetch** (*Vicia villosa*): A legume and nitrogen fixer. Slow growing in fall, but bursts into action come spring. Sow in spring to summer, then dig in after three months or leave to overwinter. Dig in before flowering and don't let it go to seed. Sowing rate 18 oz. (510 g) per 100 sq. ft. (9 sq. m).

Fall rye in early spring.

Crops such as fall rye, winter wheat, winter barley and field pea germinate well in moist soils that have cooled down after summer's heat. Over winter months the soil will be covered with a low mat of green that grows taller in spring when it warms up. Cut this grass down before using a garden fork to up-end the crop and turn it under. If your soil is hard and compacted, a rototiller makes the job easier, but beware that over-tilling destroys soil structure.

Summer Green Manures

- **Bee's friend** (*Phacelia tanacetifolia*): A fast-growing annual that can be sown March to September. It's hard to dig in the foliage before the blue flowers open once you see how pretty these flowers are! Sowing rate 18 oz. (510 g) per 1,000 sq. ft. (93 sq. m).

Bee's friend, Phacelia tanacetifolia.

- **Buckwheat** (*Fagopyrum esculentum*): A fast-growing annual that is excellent for building soil, loosening clay and adding phosphorous. It tolerates most soil types, and grows fast enough to smother weeds. Sow in late spring/early summer. Can be dug under only six to eight weeks after sowing, and is best done when 40 percent of the flowers have appeared. These white flowers attract bees. For buckwheat grains, harvest when most of the seeds are ripe, but before they shatter. Sowing rate 2.2 lb. (1 kg) per 1,000 sq. ft. (93 sq. m).

- **White clover** (*Trifolium repens*): Low-growing cover crop that serves as a nitrogen fixer. Sow March to August. Prefers sandy soils. Flowers attract and feed beneficials. Sowing rate: 18 oz. (510 g) per 1,000 sq. ft. (93 sq. m).

Using legumes, like fava beans, as a green manure helps to add nitrogen to the soil. Kristin Ross photo

THE BLUE ORCHARD MASON BEE

The blue orchard mason bee (*Osmia lignaria*) is a solitary, indigenous bee that nests in forested areas in North America. These wood-dwelling, non-aggressive bees are effective pollinators that emerge when fruit trees blossom, visiting up to 2,000 blossoms a day. They are shiny and blue-black in colour, and are easily mistaken for bluebottle flies.

Because bees are the principal source of pollination for flowers, fruits and vegetables, it's in the gardener's interest to provide a healthy, pesticide-free habitat for them. Blue orchard mason bees have a limited foraging range of 300 ft. (90 m), so you can count on them pollinating plants close to their nests. Nesting boxes are simple to make or can be purchased at garden centres. Make sure the nesting cavities are in stackable layers so they can be removed and cleaned out to prevent the spread of deadly bee mites.

HOW TO CLEAN A BEE BOX

Left top: The stackable trays holding the cocoons need to be emptied and washed at the end of each year.

Left middle: Cocoons are covered in mites and need to be washed.

Left bottom: The empty cocoons and mites float to the top. Healthy cocoons sink to the bottom.

Right top: Washed cocoons need drying before being left in a sheltered place over winter.

Right bottom: This bee box stores dried cocoons until spring, when juvenile bees hatch and fly out of the hole.

242

FALL CLEANUP CHECKLIST

- Keep tools sharp, well lubricated and sterilized using a 10-percent solution of hydrogen peroxide or rubbing alcohol in a spray bottle, to prevent spreading disease between plants.
- Cut back herbaceous perennials, leaving seed heads and berries for the birds, and any grasses and plants with winter interest. TIP: Chop up tough stalks into smaller pieces before composting and they will break down faster.
- Rake beds to remove diseased leaves, e.g., black spot on roses, scab on fruit-tree leaves, rust on hollyhocks. Do not compost these, but dig a trench and bury them.
- Remove stakes, tomato cages and plant supports and store in a protected place for winter.
- Lift boards and debris and tidy up old plant pots and areas where slugs and caterpillar cocoons may overwinter.

COMPOST

- Empty bins of ready compost, and mulch the garden with it. Top-dress planter boxes with it too.
- Turn full bins or large piles of garden waste to mix and aerate them and moisten as you are turning. Protect compost against leaching from winter rains with a large sheet of plywood.

VEGETABLE GARDEN

- Remove all spent annual vegetables, e.g., squash, tomatoes, beans.
- Now's the time to feed your soil by adding leaves, compost, manure or seaweed.
- Sprinkle beds with dolomite lime to add calcium and magnesium.
- Sow fall cover crops such as fall rye, winter wheat, barley or field pea to be dug under as a green manure in the spring.
- Mulch frost-sensitive plants (e.g., artichokes, beets, carrots) for an extra layer of protection.

GREENHOUSE

- In the greenhouse it's time for a big cleanup. Sweep or rake the floor, clean any algae build-up off the glass (inside especially), and scrub shelves and benches to remove insect cocoons and egg masses. Use a 10-percent solution of hydrogen peroxide or rubbing alcohol in a spray bottle to clean surfaces.

WINTER PROTECTION

- Protect container plants from root freeze, either by moving them closer to the house, under the eaves or deck, into a sheltered corner, or into the greenhouse or garage. To give container plants an extra layer of defence, place the container inside a bigger one and insulate the layer between with burlap bags, straw or shredded newspaper.
- Wrap frost-sensitive plants such as banana trees or tropical palm trees.
- Tropical fruits such as Meyer lemons and limes should be protected in a heated greenhouse or brought into the home and placed by a bright window.
- Fasten all climbing plants to their supports to protect against high winds.

SOFT FRUITS

- Prune off any dead or diseased branches. Thin canes of soft fruits, blackcurrants, gooseberries and raspberries to strengthen the plants.

FRUIT TREES

- To protect against fungal diseases, dormant spray all surfaces of fruit trees with fixed copper, 2 Tbsp. (30 mL) per 1 gal. (4.5 L) of water.
- Wrap fruit trees with bands of Tanglefoot™ to protect against winter moth.

PRUNING

- Prune back rose canes subject to wind damage by about one third.
- Prune off any dead or diseased branches of plants.
- Prune off all thin and spindly canes from blackcurrants, gooseberries and raspberries to strengthen the bushes.

REDESIGNING

- Fall is the best time to redesign the garden or add a few finishing touches.

December

GROW YOUR OWN LIVING POWER FOOD

Winter often means having to depend on more expensive but less nutritious produce that has been transported from far away. There's a simple solution to boosting the nutritional value of your diet in winter—sprouting seeds. I regard sprouts as precious winter food. They strengthen the immune system by providing the greatest amounts of vitamins, minerals, proteins and enzymes of any food per unit of calorie, and in a form that is easy to digest.

Spouts are little powerhouses of nutrition. Alfalfa sprouts, soybeans, clover and oilseeds (e.g., flax) are the most significant dietary sources of isoflavones, coumestans and lignans; broccoli sprouts are known to contain high concentrations of a cancer-fighting compound called sulforaphane.

These dietary phytoestrogens play an important role in the prevention of menopausal symptoms, osteoporosis, cancer and heart disease. Research shows that eating 4 oz. (113 g) of mixed broccoli, radish, alfalfa or clover sprouts every day protects against cancer.

Best of all, this wonder food is inexpensive to make and does not require any special equipment. Organic seeds for sprouting are inexpensive to buy in bulk from any health food store. Packaged blends of seeds are also available for less than five dollars. I save my own seeds from the garden for sprouting. Almost any whole natural seed, bean or grain will sprout, but pea, sunflower, radish, broccoli, mustard and cress seeds make great eating sprouts when germinated.

How to Eat Sprouts

- Use them in sandwiches and salads—anywhere you would use lettuce.
- Bean sprouts are perfect for stir-fries.
- Sprouts can be folded into omelettes just before serving.
- They make great garnishes for winter soups or casseroles—add just before serving.
- Add ½ cup (125 mL) of sprouted wheat to a loaf of homemade bread for extra nutrition.

Mild Sprouts

- Alfalfa
- Flax
- Red clover
- Black sunflower
- Broccoli
- Quinoa
- Cress

Seed Sprouting

For 1-qt. (1-L) jar

SEEDS	QUANTITY	TIME	LENGTH OF SPROUT
Adzuki bean	¾ cup (180 mL)	4 days	½ in. (1 cm)
Alfalfa	1½ Tbsp. (22 mL)	4-5 days	1½ in. (4 cm)
Broccoli	1½ Tbsp. (22 mL)	4-5 days	1½ in. (4 cm)
Buckwheat	1½ Tbsp. (22 mL)	4-5 days	1½ in. (4 cm)
Clover (red)	1½ Tbsp. (22 mL)	4-5 days	1½ in. (4 cm)
Garbanzo	1 cup (250 mL)	4 days	½ in. (1 cm)
Green lentil	¾ cup (180 mL)	4 days	½ in. (1 cm)
Mustard	1½ Tbsp. (22 mL)	4-5 days	1½ in. (4 cm)
Mung bean*	¾ cup (180 mL)	3-4 days	3 in. (8 cm)
Radish	1½ Tbsp. (22 mL)	4-5 days	1½ in. (4 cm)
Soybean**	1 cup (250 mL)	4 days	½ in. (1 cm)
Yellow pea	½ cup (125 mL)	4-5 days	½ in. (1 cm)
Wheat kernels	1 cup (250 mL)	5-8 days	2 in. (5 cm)

Grow in a tray in complete darkness

**Should not be eaten raw—steam or sauté before eating

Spicy Sprouts

- Fenugreek
- Mustard
- Radish
- Onion

Crunchy and Sweet Sprouts

- Green lentil
- Mung bean
- Adzuki bean
- Soybean
- Pea
- Garbanzo bean

Chewy Sprouts

- Wheat
- Buckwheat

Bags of organic seeds for sprouting are very inexpensive to purchase in bulk from a local health food store.

HOW TO SPROUT SEEDS IN FIVE DAYS

Sprouting seeds in a wide-mouth, quart-sized Mason jar works very well. (Use the chart as a guide to the quantities.) For larger amounts you can use a gallon glass jar. Cover the seeds with water and leave to soak for eight hours or overnight.

Place a fine mesh screen (available from any hardware store) over the mouth of the jar, using an elastic band or metal ring. TIP: Make sure the screen is firmly in place so you do not inadvertently wash your seeds down the drain when rinsing! Invert the jar at a 30-degree angle to allow excess water to run off. Place in bright light, but not direct sunlight. Rinse the sprouts twice daily. Simply fill the jar with water, swish and drain.

Continue until the sprouts are ready to eat (indicated by the length on the chart or by your personal preference).

To remove the hulls from sprouts of smaller seeds, such as alfalfa, place the finished sprouts in a large stainless-steel bowl and fill with water. The hulls will float to the surface and the sprouts will sink to the bottom. Pour or scoop off the floating hulls. (I use a tea strainer.) Replace the cleaned sprouts in their jar (or two, if necessary) and invert to drain.

To store, replace the mesh screen with a metal lid and keep in the fridge. Sprouts will keep for up to two weeks refrigerated in a sealed jar. You can also purchase stackable trays that make sprouting convenient.

Top to bottom:

Use wide-mouth Mason jars.

Place fine mesh screen over mouth of jar, rinse seeds and then drain.

Sprout seeds until they are ready to eat.

Stackable sprouting trays save space.

Sprouting Seeds in Soil

Use this method for buckwheat, peas, unhulled sunflower, wheat or barley seeds.

- Soak wheat, peas and barley for 8 hours, buckwheat or sunflowers for 12 hours.
- Fill a shallow tray/box two-thirds full of a lightweight, soil-less growing medium. Make sure you provide drainage before watering.
- Spread soaked seeds on the growing medium so they are just touching.
- Put the tray in bright light for 5 to 8 days—a windowsill or on top of the fridge works well.
- Keep the growing medium moist. TIP: Adding a few drops of liquid kelp to the water increases the nutritional clout of the sprouts.
- When the seedlings are 4 in. (10 cm) tall they are ready for harvest. Cut with scissors as needed.

Sunflower seeds are best sprouted in trays of sterilized growing mix.

PHYTONUTRIENTS—ANOTHER REASON TO GROW YOUR OWN FOOD

"Once our personal connection to what is wrong becomes clear, we have to choose. We can go on as before, recognizing our dishonesty and living with it the best we can, or we can begin the effort to change the way we think and live."
Wendell Berry

As a species we have developed over the past ten thousand years of agriculture eating plants grown in healthy soils and ripened under the sun. In comparison to what we were eating as we evolved let's consider the fruits and vegetables we are consuming today, grown under an industrialized agribusiness model. On the surface, produce looks healthy, but it shows high levels of pesticides and is grown either in depleted soils (or hydroponically with no soil at all!). Fruits and vegetables are harvested under-ripe, transported vast distances, stored in warehouses and, hardly surprisingly, are found to be low in phytonutrients.

Soil degradation, industrial food production, poor dietary habits, processed food and pesticide residues on food mean that for many, today's diet is deficient in the essential nutrients needed for good health.

Recent trials revealed low levels of phytonutrients in salad greens grown under glass, and it has now been discovered that glass obstructs a particular UVB band of sunlight that stimulates the production of phytonutrients.

For many years researchers recognized that diets high in fruits, vegetables, herbs, grains, seeds, nuts and legumes prevented diseases such as heart disease, diabetes, cancer and high blood pressure. Scientists once believed that it was the vitamin, mineral, fibre and enzymes of plant foods that prevented malnutrition and disease.

In the 1990s it was discovered that plants manufacture elements for defence against attack from harsh sunlight, oxidation, viruses and bacteria, insects, disease and background radiation. These elements, called "phytonutrients" are neither vitamin nor mineral, but part of the plant's defence system as it ripens and sets seed.

247

Phytonutrients have now been found to protect many immune functions in the body (blood, skin and organs) from the daily onslaught of toxic chemicals and carcinogenic compounds prevalent in our modern world. Researchers presently estimate there are between thirty to fifty thousand phytonutrients, although only one thousand have been isolated to date, and of these a mere hundred analyzed and tested. In the future, plant-related disease prevention will be at the forefront of nutritional research worldwide.

Important Sources of Phytonutrients

- Garlic, onions, scallions, shallots and chives (potent sulphur compounds)
- Extracts of bilberry, ginkgo biloba, milk thistle and grapes (seed and skin)
- Siberian ginseng
- Green tea
- Flax seeds, hemp seeds and evening primrose oil
- Broccoli, Swiss chard and spinach
- Dandelions
- Globe artichokes
- Extra-virgin cold-pressed olive oil and borage oil
- Peppers and red beets
- Apples, grapes and fresh melons

Fresh salads from the garden burst with vitality.

- Strawberries and blueberries
- Pink grapefruit, lemons, oranges, tangerines and limes (pulp and rind)
- Sea vegetables (dulse, wakame, kombu, nori)
- Fermented soybeans

Until the last few decades, grains were eaten whole and regarded as "the staff of life." When wheat germ and bran are discarded during processing, only a fraction of the original health value remains. (Whole wheat flour contains 96 percent more vitamin E than white flour.)

TOP FOODS	PHYTOCHEMICAL	REQUIRED INTAKE
Broccoli, spinach	Isothiocyanates	2 cups (475 mL) per week
Carrot, cantaloupe	Phthalides	1 cup (250 mL) per week
Flax seed, olive, avocado	Lignans	1 tsp. (5 mL) oil per day
Garlic, onion	Allicin	1 clove per day
Green tea, wine	Catechins	1 cup (250 mL) per day
Soy, green peas	Isoflavones	1 cup (250 mL) soymilk or ½ cup (125 mL) per day
Strawberry, grape	Ellagic acid	1 cup (250 mL) per week
Tangerine, orange	Liminoids	1 whole per day
Tomato, red pepper	Lycopenes	1 whole or ½ cup (125 mL) per day
Whole grains, wheat germ	Phytates	¼ cup (60 mL) per day

FOOD FOR THOUGHT

Essential fatty acids are important for everyone throughout their life, but are especially important for normal brain development in children. Much of the grey matter of the brain is made up of fat, specifically omega-3 fatty acid (docosahexaenoic acid or DHA). DHA plays an important role in the composition of the myelin sheath, the protective wrapping around the nerve cells that signal chemical messages in the brain.

It's important to maintain an appropriate balance of omega-3 and omega-6 essential fatty acids in the diet, as they work together to promote health. Omega-3 fatty acids generally reduce inflammation; while omega-6 fatty acids tend to promote inflammation. The typical American diet contains 14 to 25 times more omega-6 fatty acids than omega-3 fatty acids, and many researchers believe this could be a significant factor in the rising rate of inflammatory disorders in the United States.

In contrast, the Mediterranean diet consists of a healthier balance between omega-3 and omega-6 fatty acids. Mediterranean fare is typically low in meat (high in omega-6 fatty acids) and emphasizes foods rich in omega-3 fatty acids—whole grains, fresh fruits and vegetables, fish and olive oil, along with moderate wine consumption. Repeated studies have shown that people who follow this diet are less likely to develop heart disease.

SOURCES OF OMEGA-3 FATTY ACIDS

Increase your intake of omega-3 fatty acids by eating flax seeds/oil, hemp seeds/oil, pumpkin seeds/oil, purslane, walnuts and walnut oil. TIP: Whole seeds should be ground and consumed within 24 hours or refrigerated.

Food Combining

Protein molecules are composed of building blocks called amino acids. There are 22 known amino acids, most of which are synthesized in the body—but there are 8 that cannot be synthesized, and these are referred to as essential amino acids. All of these need to be present at the same time, and in the right proportions, for protein synthesis to occur. Our bodies are composed of 20 percent protein by weight; adequate protein is important for tissue growth and repair, metabolic functioning and the formation of disease-fighting antibodies.

Grains, beans, nuts, seeds and dairy are all valuable sources of these essential amino acids, and in combination assure an adequate intake of amino acids for complete protein synthesis.

Try one of these three combinations with fresh vegetables from the garden, and quit worrying about getting enough protein in your diet:

1. Grains combined with beans
2. Grains combined with dairy products
3. Beans combined with seeds

Increase your intake of omega-3 fatty acids by topping fresh garden greens with crunchy pumpkin seeds.

SECRETS OF SUCCESS

As December draws to a close, it's time to review the gardening year just passed. It's really not that complicated to grow an abundant food garden when you follow these few secrets to success. Happy Gardening!

Feeding the Soil

In early spring, when the garden breaks dormancy, it signals that the soil food web is slowly coming back to life. When the weather warms up, renewed microbial action enables plants to access nutrients from organic matter in the soil. It's all about the microbes when it comes to growing healthier plants that attract fewer problems from pests and diseases. Keep the "Four Secrets" in mind and you can't go wrong—compost, manure, leaves and seaweed!

Organic Weed and Feed

Each time the soil is disturbed by tilling or digging, dormant weed seeds come up to the surface. Out-of-control weeds compete for moisture and nutrients with crop plants. The secret is to prevent unwanted plants from getting out of control in the first place. Thick mulches of compost, leaves, straw or hay smother dormant weed seeds and suppress weeds by depriving them of light and air.

A weed-infested strawberry bed.

Weeds and seeds are smothered under layers of thick mulch.

250

Black cherry tomatoes in 5-gal. (23-L) pots.

You Don't Need a Garden to Grow Food!

Try growing salad greens, kale, chard, zucchini, tomatoes, peppers, cucumbers or beans in funky pots or planters. Herbs, being Mediterranean plants, thrive in hot and dry conditions, so are perfect for planters situated in full sun. In summer, pick fresh sprigs of mint, parsley, chives, oregano or basil from pots outside the kitchen door. Heat-loving plants such as tomatoes, peppers, cucumbers, eggplant and basil also thrive in planters in full sun.

The quality of the growing medium will determine the health and productivity of plants. Don't use 100 percent garden soil, which sets to concrete when it dries out. Free-draining fertile growing mediums are best, with added granular fertilizers that release nutrients slowly as the plants grow.

When roots fill pots, it's harder for them to absorb nutrients from the medium. To promote longer fruiting, feed plants (tomatoes, eggplants and peppers) with compost teas or liquid seaweed (high in potash).

Thornless blackberries intertwined with clematis.

Vertical Planting

Vertical gardening is the answer! Teepees made from alder poles, bamboo or willow, with strings of garden twine for extra support, work perfectly for pole beans, vining tomatoes, cucumbers and trailing vines. Trailing berries look great twined around arbours with a clematis or climbing rose.

Above: Mixed borders and hedgerows provide for wildlife.

Left: Grow winter vegetables off the ground, away from bugs.

Winter Vegetables in a Snap!

You don't need a greenhouse (or any structure) to grow winter food. Flats of winter veggies can be seeded outdoors in June/July for transplanting in August. These will provide nutritious greens and vegetables from fall until the following spring. The secret to success is keeping the seedlings off the ground, away from all the earwigs, slugs and sow bugs that love to eat them, plus knowing how to spot signs of green cabbage worms!

Gardening with Wildlife

Gardening with wildlife opened my eyes to new ways of enhancing the health of my garden. Broad-spectrum insecticides can be fatal to wildlife, but by encouraging healthy populations of beneficial insects into the garden it's unnecessary to use such products.

When food grows alongside hedgerows of shrubs, flowers, grasses, herbs and berries, it attracts a diversity of wildlife and many beneficial creatures into the

Pacific tree frog in a 'Peace' rose.

garden. By growing plants that feed wildlife and providing habitat (nesting boxes, bee boxes, log piles) and cool water in hot summers, the balance of good health can be restored and maintained in our gardens.